RURAL
Radicals

RURAL RADICALS

Righteous Rage in the American Grain

Catherine McNicol Stock

CORNELL UNIVERSITY PRESS

ITHACA AND LONDON

First published 1996 by Cornell University Press.

Library of Congress Cataloging-in-Publication Data
Stock, Catherine McNicol.
   Rural radicals : righteous rage in the American grain / by Catherine McNicol Stock.
      p.   cm.
   Includes bibliographical references and index.
   ISBN 0-8014-3294-4 (alk. paper).
   1. Radicalism—United States—History.   2. Political violence—United States—History.   3. Farmers—United States—Political activity—History.   4. United States—Rural conditions.   I. Title.
HN90.R3S67   1996
303.48'4—dc20   96-3023

This book is printed on Lyons Falls Turin Book,
a paper that is totally chlorine-free and acid-free.

FOR MY MOTHER AND FATHER

Contents

Courtesy of Don Wright, *The Palm Beach Post.*

PREFACE

THIS BOOK began when I saw a cartoon reprinted in the Sunday *New York Times* on May 7, 1995, just weeks after the devastating bombing in Oklahoma City. In the cartoon, a group of people in a farmhouse discuss how they will pay for the materials they need to build "a bigger bomb" to "wipe out the federal government." One of them suggests that they simply wait until they receive their federal farm-subsidy check before going shopping. At first I laughed at the cruel irony of farmers' planning to blow up the hand that fed them. Then I realized what an important insight into radicalism in rural America the cartoon displayed. Hatred of and dependence on the federal government have long been a part of rural politics. Likewise the support of causes and ideologies on both the right and the left—and the violent assertion of them—is a unique heritage of the rural experience in the United States.

What follows is not intended as an intensive investigation into primary materials, a detailed study of any one radical movement in any one location, or a prolonged debate about the historiography of American radicalism as a whole. Instead, it is an extended interpretive essay that draws together two themes that are generally presented separately in treatments of rural radicalism: the politics of rural producer radicalism and the culture of vigilante violence. This approach makes it substantially different from the kind of work most historians do: the book no doubt omits important aspects of individual accounts and overlooks critical nuances that have made the experiences of different people in different places unique. It makes no pretence, for example, of exploring many of the autonomous rural political movements of people of color in the United States. (I explain this choice and others in "A Note on Method.") I mean no disrespect by doing so. My goal is to understand more completely the rural radical movements of our time—most of which are led by whites—by presenting a new framework through which to examine rural radicalism in the past. I am suggesting neither that American history is monochromatic, nor that it can be neatly packaged or easily understood. But it is worth knowing as fully as we possibly can.

I would not have been able even to begin this book without the ongoing encouragement of Peter Agree at Cornell University Press. Peter convinced me that there "was such a thing" as a general-interest book like this written by an academically trained historian like me. David Danbom and Nancy Grey Osterud read the manuscript in its entirety for the Press. It is an altogether different book than it would have been without their careful comments. It is an altogether better book due to Marilyn Sale's copyediting. I have also benefited from the advice offered by several of my colleagues at Connecticut College, including Michael Burlingame, Marc Forster, William Frasure, Jeffrey Lesser, and especially MaryAnne Borrelli and Lisa Wilson. Outside the college, Jean-Christophe Agnew, Patrick Nicholas Allitt, Patricia Donovan Baker, Melanie Cameron, Christopher Clark, Ann Fabian, Claudia and Christoph Gradel, Pamela Haag, Robert Johnston, Sarah Finney Johnston, Glenn Wallach, and Robert Westbrook gave good suggestions, as well as an occasional dose of reality.

I worked with a research team whose patience and dedication knew no bounds. The book would have no illustrations were it not for the skill and generosity of Suzanne Cleworth-Jones. Tina Falck likewise provided critical assistance when I needed it most. Connecticut College students Elizabeth Duclos '95, Keith Golembiewski '98, Edward Hart '95, Kerry Newhall '98, Sara Schaefer '96, and Michael Sneideman '94 now know more about rural political movements than they ever wanted to, I'm sure. My appreciation is little compensation for their hard work.

Funding for the project came from grants from the R. F. Johnson Faculty Development Fund at Connecticut College as well as from the office of the Provost and Dean of the Faculty. But it has taken much more than money to allow my career to reach this point. For exceptional support of a junior faculty member, I give special thanks to the administration of Connecticut College, the American Studies Faculty Group, the History Department, and its long-time chair, Edward Brodkin.

Of course, the main burden of meeting deadlines fell on my family: my husband, Peter J. Lefeber; my parents-in-law, Lois M. and Peter E. Lefeber; and my children, Nick, Sarah, and John. I owe them all more than I can say. Bogumila Zielinska and the teachers and staff of the Wightwood School in Branford, Connecticut, added the daily love and care for all of us that have made our household flourish over the past several years.

But last, I thank my parents, Arthur J. and Barbara Finch Stock. Many times in my life I have hesitated to take on tasks that seemed insurmountable. Each time they have encouraged me to try. Twenty years ago this fall, I left my parents' house in Minneapolis and took an airplane east, heading for Yale College. I have traveled a long way since then and have encountered occasional turbulence. But I have never felt that I have gone very far away from home. No greater gift can parents give a child.

CATHERINE McNICOL STOCK

New London, Connecticut

RURAL
Radicals

INTRODUCTION

AMERICAN RADICALISM –
LEFT, RIGHT, AND RURAL

SO MANY shocking images were transmitted in the first hours after the April 19, 1995, bombing of the Alfred P. Murrah Federal Building in Oklahoma City that it was difficult for Americans to sort them out. Dead and dying children, desperate parents, rescue workers overcome by grief and horror—these scenes seared the minds of everyone who had thought of the American heartland as a safe place. How simple it was in those first hours to presume that such an unthinkable atrocity was created by people from outside the United States, people who do not look, act, or understand the world as we do. But then came the reports that the alleged perpetrator of the bombing seemed to be as much a representative of America's heartland as the victims were. A small-town boy, a Gulf War veteran—white-skinned, blue-eyed, cleancut, and well-shaven even as he marched under heavy guard in orange prison clothes—he seemed as an old army buddy described him, "so gullible, so vulnerable, just kind of a nerd."[1]

But if these words describe Timothy McVeigh, he was also, along with his alleged accomplices, associated with a large network of militia men, conspiracists, survivalists, Identity Christians, white supremacists, and other "hate radicals" based in remote rural areas of the United States from Montana and Idaho to Michigan, Missouri, and Maine. According to the federal indictment, in the year before the bombing McVeigh wandered the rural Midwest and South, attending gun shows and conspiring with sympathizers in such towns as Alliance, Nebraska, McPherson, Kansas, and Royal, Arkansas. He had placed a phone call to Elohim City, Oklahoma, the headquarters of a sect of Identity Christians similar to the violent group called the Covenant, the Sword, and the Arm of the Lord. He had told them, and many others, that he especially hated the federal government because it was responsible for the FBI attack in Waco, Texas, on April 19, 1993, which resulted in the deaths of more than seventy Branch Davidians, including many women and children. He had read, sold, and given away copies of *The Turner Diaries*, a 1979 novel that celebrated an armed uprising by whites against the nation's African Americans, Hispanics, and Jews. He had hidden guns in every nook and cranny of his home and car. When a friend was asked whether McVeigh liked to talk about anything other than guns, he thought for a while and then said, "Not really. Just guns."[2] Finally, McVeigh and at least two other men who shared his convictions had allegedly chosen the Murrah Federal Building as their target and gathered the materials they needed to destroy it, including fertilizer for a bomb.

The leaders of the right-wing militias, survivalist groups, and Identity Christian sects with whom McVeigh, Terry Nichols, and Michael Fortier were said to be associated quickly denounced the bombing and denied any connection with it. They did not, however, condemn the political, racial, and religious beliefs that implicitly bound them to it. As an editor of the *New Republic* wrote, "The bombing of the federal building was an act of terror, that is, a political act [presented in] the language of right-wing anarchy . . . the idolatry of guns, the rage at authority, the paranoid picture of American culture, the extreme patriotism expressed as extreme intolerance."[3] Most of all, *Harper's Magazine* reported, these "politics of horror" were the politics of hatred: hatred of the increasing power of the federal government, financial institutions, multinational corporations, liberal politicians, Jews, and members of the news media who, the radicals believed, had "sold the nation's soul into bondage."[4]

Timothy McVeigh and his confederates were not the sweet and simple country folks that most Americans thought they knew. For centuries Americans have thought of rural people, farm families like the Nicholses in particular, as the moral backbone of the nation and have believed that they represented freedom, morality, hard work, dedication to family, and community solidarity. While rural Americans have declined in number—going "from majority, to minority, to curiosity," as David Danbom notes—they have risen in popular esteem.[5] Politicians, journalists, novelists, historians, and philosophers continue to remind Americans of the importance of rural people, rural places, and rural ways of life to the economic and moral health of the nation. Many forms of popular culture, too, including country music and films about saving the family farm and fishing the family river, reinforce these stereotypes. At the same time, however, most Americans have only the remotest connections with the day-to-day realities of rural America and most frequently idealize its value while passing through on summer vacation or flying over in a transcontinental jet. So it is difficult for us to know what rural people are thinking or experiencing.

Similarly, McVeigh's purported political ideology does not conform to standard conceptions of rural politics in the modern liberal state. Just as most Americans presume that fertilizer is used to help plants grow and not as a bomb ingredient, most presume that farmers and other rural people want more from the federal government—more farm aid, more price supports, more import quotas, more regulation of large corporations and agribusiness—rather than less. But most Americans are wrong if they think that the new rural radicals support these ideas. Not a friend or an advocate anymore, government—even the Department of Agriculture—is now a target, the centerpiece of an international Zionist conspiracy to destroy the liberty of white Christian Americans. Likewise, although some rural radicals practice maneuvers, hunt, camp, and live in wilderness areas, they condemn other Americans who work to protect natural resources, such as the officials of Fish and Wildlife Service. Despite their purported love of country, the heroes and martyrs of the new rural radicals are not members of their local chapters of the Veterans of Foreign Wars but extremists who have chosen to quit living in America as we know it, who have moved to such places as Hayden Lake and Ruby Ridge, Idaho, and who have disavowed the American government's authority over them.[6]

The new rural radicalism, when examined in detail, proves difficult to place in the conventional political spectrum. In its members' contempt for the federal government, profound antiauthoritarianism, mockery of big business and finance, dedication to complete local control of the community, and desire to establish wilderness compounds, the new rural radicalism of the 1990s sounds surprisingly similar to the counterculture rhetoric of the far left in the 1960s. In fact, in northern California, the Pacific Northwest, and the rural Northeast it is not unusual for gun-toting paramilitary leaders to live next door to latter-day hippies and marijuana growers. The 1995 bombing of the Murrah Federal Building reminded some observers of the 1970 bombing of the University of Wisconsin's Army-Math Research Center by a member of the local Students for a Democratic Society.[7] Nevertheless it is nearly impossible to think of people who spend weekends at gun shows or in preparation for a siege by the FBI, who believe that McCarthyism did not go far enough or that African Americans are a species different (and lower) than that of whites, who teach their children to carry guns, or who collect Nazi paraphernalia as anything but the most extreme conservatives. Such similarities may leave us confused, wondering at the efficacy of conventional political categories, when both the left and right shoes seem to rub these people the wrong way.

However shocking, confusing, or contradictory it seems, the recent rise of rural radicalism should not have surprised Americans so much. For the past fifty years, we have blamed most domestic discord on problems associated with urban life, but for hundreds of years—and even in this century—the concerns of rural men and women have also often heated to the boiling point. Rural radicalism is in fact older than the nation itself. When white men and women traveled to British North America, they carried with them memories of extralegal crowd actions and peasant uprisings from early modern Europe. It was not long until they made use of these folkways, with regional twists and variations, in their new homes. As early as 1676 and increasingly in the mid-1700s, settlers who were ardently committed to their dreams of representative government and economic independence rose up to protest unfair land laws, unresponsive provincial assemblies, and the imposition of new taxes. Not surprisingly, these grievances presaged those that bound all colonists together in the struggle against the British crown. What is surprising is that when the Revolutionary War ended and the settlers became citizens of the new Republic, radicalism in rural America did not abate; to the contrary, it intensified because many citizens believed that the political and economic freedoms they had sought were still not distributed equally. Between 1776 and 1800, federal and state authorities in every region were called to put down uprisings in the countryside, led by men who had fought in the Revolution, but who now took on names like the Liberty Men, White Indians, Shaysites, and Whisky Rebels—and who fought against their former officers in that war. After a period of relative calm in the age of

Jefferson and Jackson, increased urbanization and industrialization in the late nineteenth century renewed tensions between rural Americans and their political and economic leaders. Between 1865 and 1940, millions of farmers, workers, and small-townspeople joined together to fight the power of monopolies and large corporations, government bureaucracies, and agribusiness and to protect the control of their communities. Modern rural radicalism is thus hardly a new-fangled idea or a fly-by-night phenomenon. Instead, it follows an abundant, meaningful, and "all-American" heritage.

An awareness of the history of radicalism in the rural United States is crucial to understanding that radicalism today. But simply telling the story of rural protest movements does not clear up the confusion we feel about their contradictory politics. In fact, were we to travel back in time to determine once and for all whether rural radicalism has been progressive or regressive, liberal or conservative, a force from the left or the right in American society, we would return as confused as ever. The first important rural rebellion in British North America, for example, was Bacon's Rebellion, named after the Englishman Nathaniel Bacon who in 1676 organized five hundred newly freed indentured servants in an armed uprising against neighboring Native Americans, an attack that led to the ransacking of the colonial capital at Jamestown, Virginia. Because these frontiersmen sought access to land and freedom from an aristocratic authority, they have often been seen as the progenitors of the colonial struggle against the British. At the same time, however, Bacon's Rebellion was a socially conservative movement with profoundly undemocratic results. Among the primary goals of the rebels, for example, was the annihilation of all those Native Americans who legally occupied the land the rebels desired. In fact, they killed Native Americans in direct defiance of government orders to desist. Most important, however, the intense racial hatred that frontiersmen in Virginia felt for Native Americans laid the cultural and ideological groundwork for the successful introduction of slave labor there in the subsequent quarter-century, when elite planters realized how powerful a social glue such hatred could be.[8]

Another example of radicalism in rural America—the Populist movement of the late nineteenth century—has provoked heated debate for more than three generations. Farmers and small-townspeople in the Midwest and South in the 1870s and 1880s struggled against soaring prices for consumer goods, rising interest rates, and falling income from crops. Living in an era of corporate consolidation, they blamed their troubles on the strangleholds of middlemen and railroads, the power of eastern bankers and financiers, the gold standard, and the exclusive and undemocratic nature of national party politics. Organizing first on a grass-roots, picnic-by-picnic basis, the Populists aimed to create an alternative political economy they called the cooperative commonwealth. In 1892 the People's Party congregated in Omaha, Nebraska, and nominated their first candidate for president, James Baird Weaver. Weaver won more than one million votes and carried with him scores of local officials in western and southern states. In 1896 the People's Party reluctantly merged with the Democrats and nominated William Jennings Bryan for president. After a barnstorming tour of small towns where he told of the eternal importance of the farmer in the famous "Cross of Gold" speech, Bryan lost to William McKinley. Nevertheless, his impassioned defense of agrarianism echoed in American politics for another thirty years.

As any teacher who has ever tried to present balanced material on the Populist movement knows, it is extremely difficult to assess either the movement's fundamental values or its political legacy. The Populists advocated radical reforms of corporate capitalism as well as significant alterations to the political process. At least some of their reforms, such as the direct election of senators, the graduated income tax, and workers' rights to collective bargaining, were adopted by the politicians of the Progressive and New Deal eras and are taken for granted by many Americans today. Likewise, Populist men not only allowed but encouraged women and African Americans to participate—even to lead; they also supported increased civil and political rights for both groups. On the other hand, Populists could be, as Richard Hofstadter puts it, "illiberai" and "ill-tempered."[9] Some leaders in the North were blatantly and unabashedly anti-Semitic. Populist legislators in the South participated in the creation of Jim Crow legislation in the 1890s. Tom Watson, the Georgian who ran with Bryan as the vice-presidential candidate, was crucial to the reorganization of the Ku Klux Klan in the late 1910s. It is no surprise then that some historians have compared the Populists with the conservative champions of Senator Joseph McCarthy in the 1950s and even to the petit-bourgeois supporters of Adolf Hitler in 1930s Germany.[10]

But how could Bacon's Virginia frontiersmen have been both fundamentally egalitarian and genocidally racist? How could nineteenth-century midwestern and southern farmers have been both intrepid democrats and protofascist conservatives? How could today's rural militia men call themselves patriots and target the government for destruction? The answers lie in the material, economic, political, and cultural circumstances that the members of these groups have shared because they have lived in rural America. Far from centers of political and economic power, engaged in the difficult labors of agriculture and extractive industry, increasingly unable to participate in aspects of American culture available to city dwellers, rural Americans have often turned to collective protest to make themselves heard. And because they have also shared a culture of hardship, self-defense, and intolerance, that protest has more often than not manifested itself through acts or threats of violence.

Five contexts of rural life help to explain the nature of rural radicalism and, in particular, its contradictory position in conventional American politics. These are: frontier life, class, race, gender, and evangelism. Some of these contexts are shared by rural and urban Americans alike. As a consequence, some grievances expressed by rural people are shared by their city cousins. Only in the countryside, however, do all five factors appear together, reflecting, reinforcing, and transforming one another over time. There they create a special mix of contradictory experiences, impulses, ideologies, and actions ready to boil over into radical protest and collective violence in moments of economic, political, or cultural strain.

The first of these potentially contradictory contexts is the frontier experience. Today historians are reluctant to use the word "frontier" because others have so often associated it with a grand narrative of white civilization and imperialism. They remind us that many peoples inhabited the American landscape and that no single word or narrative scheme can adequately tell all their stories.[11] Nevertheless I find that the word "frontier" can still describe two important, if limited, concepts: first, it depicts the place (even if not exactly a line, it was a crossroad) where Euro-American and Native American, Hispanic and Asian cultures met in the seventeenth, eighteenth, and nineteenth centuries. Second, the term "frontier" and more precisely "frontiersman" describes a self-conscious and often politicized frame of mind embraced by Euro-Americans. Indeed, without using the term in both these ways, we would be hard put to discuss rural radicalism at all, especially in the colonial and early national periods. In those years, nearly every American lived in a place that would seem rural to us today, but those who rose up in protest lived in even more rural places than their compatriots did; they lived on the western edge of white settlement. Moreover, they believed that their economic and political problems were problems of the frontier. In Virginia, North and South Carolina, Massachusetts, Pennsylvania, and later in Nebraska, Texas, Washington, and a dozen other states, self-proclaimed frontiersmen—and women—rose up against their more powerful and comfortable brethren in the East.

What did people on the frontier find to be so unhappy about? One thing is certain: no matter the century or the region, life on the frontier was anything but luxurious, anything but the easy fortune it was frequently promised to be. It was dangerous, harsh, exhausting, and sometimes utterly unrewarding. And along with physical hardship, settlers also experienced significant political isolation. If colonists in Boston, Philadelphia, and Charleston felt cut off from sources of power and authority in London, those on the frontier felt cut off from sources of power and authority in Boston, Philadelphia, and Charleston. Moreover, they came first to understand and then to condemn the fact that political power often translated into economic power. Thus they complained that they were underrepresented in the provincial and early national assemblies and that legislators cared more about the needs of the eastern rich than the western poor. Likewise, they complained that easterners did not want to create such basic infrastructures of government as courthouses and jails and schools which westerners required to improve their lives. For a time, during the Jefferson and Jackson administrations, these frontier people believed that the government and the small farmer were finally seeing eye to eye. With the coming of Reconstruction in the South and industrialization in the North, however, they quickly reversed themselves. After the Civil War, they attacked both the Democratic and Republican parties for attending to the needs of large corporations and ignoring ordinary Americans, while their lives became more difficult and humbling with every passing year.

Perhaps to counter this physical hardship and political isolation, settlers developed strong and self-defensive communities. When we think of a frontiersman we think of an ardent individualist like Daniel Boone who moved each time he could see the smoke from his neighbor's cabin. And although there certainly were men on the move in the West (even Laura Ingalls Wilder's "Pa" could never settle down for long), and perhaps some men who purposefully moved to get away from "civilization," more commonly people gathered together and created rich community lives, filled with social, religious, and political institutions. Women on the frontier were especially important to the task of creating and re-creating what John Mack Faragher has called "habits of mutuality" in their new homes.[12] Barn-raisings, for example, where families got together and built a new barn in a day or two were planned and facilitated by women who cooked for days beforehand, cared for one another's children, served food and drink, and cleaned up while men were pounding nails. At such occasions, and many others besides, women also quilted, exchanged child-rearing advice, and generally extended kinship ties in cooperative labor. Families moved in and out of town in the American West, especially in mining and lumbering regions. As long as they remained in one place, however, they formed strong collective relationships and systems of mutual reciprocity with their neighbors.[13]

Such places and such relationships, we know, could foment democratic and egalitarian impulses. Settlers who worked alongside one another under difficult and isolated circumstances sometimes became willing to extend the rights of citizenship and economic opportunity throughout their community, but they could act and feel in opposite ways as well. Anyone who has had the unfortunate experience of not fitting into a small community knows that small differences can loom surprisingly large there, and large differences can be insurmountable. Moreover, frontiersmen did not take up the role of dispassionate mediators or negotiators when they felt the safety of their community was at stake. At the very least they ostracized those people they found intolerable. And they could do even more. Away from many of the structures of government, frontiersmen learned to take the law into their own hands and to be proud of it. More often than not, they defended their communities by force.[14]

Yet not all rural radicals lived or live on the eighteenth- and nineteenth-century frontiers or even on the imagined frontier of the twentieth century. Thus all of the contradictions of rural radicalism cannot be explained through that single context. Several other factors must be added to the mix that helps explain the new rural radicalism of our time. One of these is class. In other writings, I have explained the divergent political positions that developed in the 1930s from the "contradictory class location" of some farmers, shopkeepers, and professionals in small communities, that is, members of the old middle class.[15] Because they were at once employers and laborers, independent small producers found themselves able to take on the political positions of either rich or poor in America. In rural America there were divisions between farm and town, and between large landholders and small landholders, tenant farmers, and agricultural workers. In good times, it was easy for members of the old middle class—and people who desired such independence but had not yet achieved it—to associate with rich and powerful Americans in their communities and in faraway centers of economic influence. But in hard times, they often saw how fine a line separated their prosperity from desperate poverty. In postindustrial America especially, when only cash cropping is practiced on most farms and little "safety first" subsistence growing remains, it is possible for the farmer who grows food one year to be unable to afford to buy it the next.

Of course, the full complement of class positions and associated ideologies available in the 1930s was nowhere in sight in colonial or early national America. Neither "capitalism" nor "class" appeared in the American lexicon until the nineteenth century.[16] Still, the backcountry farmer and settler aspired to and sometimes demanded things that a beleaguered resident of the Dust Bowl would have also affirmed: access to land, access to markets, and an ability to support oneself and one's family from the fruits of one's own labor. As we will see, at first this ideology led the settler to resist landlords and wealthy speculators in the hope of avoiding becoming a permanent tenant. Increasingly in the nineteenth century, it also led the farmer to avoid the possibility of having to leave the farm for a dependent position as a wage laborer, even if temporary stints at wage labor might protect independence on the land. In the early twentieth century it would mean maintaining control over decisions about land and production free from the interference of a corporate-friendly federal bureaucracy. Thus while many rural rebels have seemed to be struggling against capitalism itself, more often than not they have struggled against what antimonopolists in the New Deal would call "bigness"—big landowners, big speculators, big business, big government, even big farm organizations—as well as its inverse, the insignificant "smallness" of wage work or tenancy.

Closely related to the politics of class are the politics of race. The so-called independence of "middling" Americans was founded, first, on the dispossession of Native Americans and Hispanics from their land and, second, on the institutionalization of African slavery. Many more

white farmers of course would have lost their independence and become tenants or wage workers if it were not for the continent of land
available to them after it had been stolen or pried away from its first inhabitants. Likewise, the egalitarian society of the white South was
based on the "unfreedom" of an enormous enslaved work force. In
those times, racial entitlement was borne of ethnocentrism and of close
and often sexually violent encounters with people of color.[17] Whites
greatly feared the just retribution of Native Americans on the frontier,
the uprisings of slaves, and worse, the possibility that they might become "uncivilized" by their encounters rather than the other way
around. Given how many whites did not return from captivity among
the Native Americans and how often white men raped African American women, perhaps they had reason to worry. By the twentieth century, however, many rural places were the "whitest" of all places in
America, and whatever collective memories of multiracial encounters
persisted, they had no basis in immediate experience. Nevertheless, in
the 1920s and in our own time as well, some rural Americans sought
out people of color to blame for the troubles of modern society.

Rural people had similarly contradictory experiences relating to
gender. Much of the economic independence and "republican manhood" so ardently sought by rural men was made possible by their dependence on women. In fact, no Americans have ever depended so
thoroughly on the productive labor of women as have American farmers. Raising poultry, eggs, vegetables, spinning cloth, making clothes,
canning food, smoking meat, and promoting and establishing community networks of reciprocity—not to mention reproducing the
workforce—all were the unpaid but economically invaluable labors of
American farm women. For centuries, farm women were not legally en-
titled to any of the value—cash or kind—of what they raised. Rarely if
ever were they considered to be full and equal partners in the farming
enterprise. And although today's farm women have many more legal
rights, their domestic circumstances are similar, for although their domestic production is less prevalent, they take off-farm jobs to supple-
ment farm income. Sometimes their off-farm income allows the
farming enterprise to survive. Nevertheless, women rarely make major
decisions about farm management.[18]

The potential contradictions here are myriad. Under some circumstances—wartime, illness, or other emergency—rural men and women
on farms recognized women's own productive and managerial skills,

and by extension considered their potential legal rights. It was while she was managing the farm when her husband was away that Abigail Adams urged John to "remember the ladies" in the Constitution. He did not, of course, but in the industrial era other men would reach the conclusion that women who could work, and think, and pray, and raise a family should also be able to vote and, more important, that time-worn ways of creating community networks and systems of reciprocity were politically valuable. Populist men encouraged female membership and leadership and made great use of women's cooperative skills in imagining a new commonwealth. Some twentieth-century rural cooperatives were owned and managed by women. By the 1980s, women participated widely in the coalitions dedicated to saving the family farm.[19]

But some rural men (and women) have also held fast to traditional patriarchal relationships and have taken up arms to protect them. Threats to American "womanhood"—whether made by Native Americans, African Americans, Mormons, or Jews—were met with deadly force. So were women who did not behave in a manner becoming to virtue in a rural community. Today's rural "warriors" have taken hypermasculinity to its extreme. Along with their guns, ammunition, and camouflage gear, some militia men and survivalists have procured mail-order brides from Asia, engaged in polygamous marriages for quick and efficient spreading of their Aryan seed, and even taken female captives.[20] It is hard to imagine why women—except for protection from a perceived threat of violence—would today choose to become a "warrior wife." But Randy Weaver's wife Vicki did not think that role so strange. As an Iowa farm girl she had learned all she needed to know to survive a government siege on Ruby Ridge, Idaho, for more than a year and a half.

The final context in which the contradictions of rural radicalism developed was fundamentalist and evangelical Christianity—especially Protestantism. Again, rural Americans were not the only Americans who experienced the multiple revivals in the American past. Nevertheless, statistics show that the largest concentrations of fundamentalist and evangelical sects are in the South, Rocky Mountain West, and Midwest.[21] Today we tend to associate these faiths with social conservatism. But these links have not always existed. The first Great Awakening of 1730, some historians argue, reinforced the break from hierarchical authority as represented by the elite leaders of Congregational and Anglican churches. Revivalist preachers in the Second Great Awakening of the 1820s told American men and women that they did not have to look to elites to determine their spiritual paths but needed only to examine their own free souls. So threatening was this message in the "burned-over district" of New York, in fact, that Joseph Smith, the prophet of one new sect, was chased from town to town by faithful Protestants and eventually murdered. Few would recognize the religion Joseph Smith founded in today's conservative Mormon Church.[22]

This book charts the course of rural radicalism in the United States in an attempt not to justify but to understand more fully the tragedies lately witnessed upon our land. It asks three questions: First, where did these angry white rural men come from? Second, what explains their contradictory politics? And finally, why in our time does the strand of vigilantism and intolerance in rural America seem to have overwhelmed the strand of democratic reform? The three parts of this book address these questions. The first explores traditions of rural radicalism usually associated with the left, a tradition I have called rural producer radicalism. The stories illustrating these traditions are presented in chronological order, because in general they were discrete political movements in discrete moments of historical time. The second chapter, on the so-called far right, charts the sourer side of rural radicalism, which I call the culture of vigilantism. Because hatreds and intolerances are sustained over longer periods of time and manifested less often in specific political acts, this chapter is arranged by theme rather than by chronology. In the third chapter, politics and culture, hope and hate, the left and right are drawn back together, a confluence, I hope to show, which has always existed. The unique heritage of rural America sets the stage for a radical politics that, as Michael Kazin has said of our populist tradition more generally, doesn't "fit into neat categories of right or left."[23] Perhaps the neat categories were meant for somebody else.

When I began this project, I was determined not to make a personal judgment about which of the two strands of rural radicalism was "better" for America. After all, nearly every so-called progressive rural movement I describe contains elements of vigilantism and intolerance. Few white leaders preached doctines of nonviolence in rural America. Many organizations springing from rural producer radicalism also are related by leadership, membership, or ideology to heinous acts of repression. On the other hand, some of the most intolerant groups—the

Klan, for example—could be construed as populist or democratic because they make manifest the will of the people over a repressive or unresponsive authority. Despite these very important similarities, which
form the core of this essay, I still will not conclude that all rural movements on the left and all rural movements on the right are exactly the
same. Two strands in exquisite relation to each other, the left and the
right in rural America are closely related—and much more closely related than recent historians have been willing to admit—but they are
not identical. I must still choose Iowa over Idaho and pray that the best
hope for America will someday shake loose its angry demons.

1

THE POLITICS OF PRODUCERISM

IN JULY 1994, the *New York Times* began reporting a new "insurrection in, of all places, Iowa." With shock and wonder, it told of a coalition of farm groups that was proposing the elimination of most of the farm-subsidy programs administered by the Department of Agriculture. In their place, it recommended a simple "revenue assurance plan"—cash payments to farmers ruined by unforeseeable disasters like hail storms, drought, or international conflict. To most Americans, this was the strangest and most baffling response to the Republican Congress's proposed budget cuts that they could possibly imagine. Why would farmers seek to cut themselves loose from the liberal state when for sixty years "few people [had gotten] a better deal from the Government" than they had? Were they motivated by resurgent antifederalism, like the many members of the New Right who had taken to calling themselves populists? Were they the veiled representatives of agribusiness, gleefully hoping to put more family farmers out of business and replace them with super farms? Or were they simply foolish and naive country folks, looking to do their part to balance the federal budget and get their names in the newspaper and on television?[1]

As it turned out, they were none of these. The Iowa Farm Bill Study Team's proposal to curtail "agricultural welfare" was neither as conservative nor as new as these reports made it sound. The group's members believed that government programs designed to help farmers had actually nearly destroyed them. While paying lip service to the family farm, government agencies had encouraged expansion and indebtedness and had affirmed the ambitions of large landholders and multinational agribusiness corporations. Moreover, for more than fifty years, farmers had spent as much time learning about government regulations and programs—as well as about how to sidestep or swindle them—as they had managing their own affairs. If this was getting the best deal from the government, Iowa farmers decided that they had had enough.

Nor was the farmers' proposal particularly new. To the contrary, the desire to own small property, to produce crops and foodstuffs, to control local affairs, to be served but never coerced by a representative government, and to have traditional ways of life and labor respected— what I call the ideology of rural producer radicalism—is the stuff of one of the oldest dreams in the United States. It is one of the dreams that became the United States. When the Iowa Farm Bill Study Team asked that farmers be set loose from federal supervision, it borrowed a page from the Farmers' Holiday Association, which had actively resisted the imposition of Franklin Roosevelt's domestic allotment plan in the 1930s because its members feared the encroachment of hundreds of thousands of federal bureaucrats. But the Farmers' Holiday Association owed a debt to the Populist movement of the late nineteenth century whose millions of supporters had dreamed of remaking industrial capitalism into a cooperative, egalitarian, producerist democracy. And in the rhetoric of Populism could be heard the distant echoes of eighteenth-century frontiersmen in New Jersey, New York, Vermont, North Carolina, Massachusetts, Pennsylvania, and Maine who took to the fields and roads with guns, clubs, and burning torches to ensure equal access to land and equal treatment from provincial and early American governments. Across three centuries and a continent of land, the Iowa insurgents could have found like-minded souls in the American past.

Like-minded souls still live different lives in different times, however. The particular economic, political, and social circumstances that gave rise to producer radicalism in rural America varied substantially over three centuries. So did the strategies the insurgents chose and the race, class, and gender of those rural producer radicalism called. As we shall see, in the colonial and early national eras, rural rebels, nearly all white men whose wives and daughters may have supported but nonetheless stayed behind the scenes of public debate, lived in isolated frontier communities far from sources of power in the East. They mobilized around the desire for access to freehold land and fair representation in provincial assemblies. To do so, they relied on the time-worn habit of crowd action in early modern Europe. By the mid-nineteenth century, however, frontiersmen were more centrally located on the American continent and in the American cultural imagination. They were no less aggrieved, however, when the rise of industrial capitalism threatened small production and corrupted democratic processes. They turned to creating huge networks of cooperatives and independent political parties, which both included and reflected the experiences of women, African Americans, and wage workers. In the early twentieth century, such alliances became more complicated as class interests divided rural politics. In general, wealthier white farmers and businessmen continued to work within major political parties. Small farmers, tenants, sharecroppers, and workers in extractive industries followed the Populist heritage toward socialism.

When Franklin Delano Roosevelt instituted the New Deal programs for agriculture in the 1930s, he initiated a major rapprochement between rural people and the state. It was, in fact, an alliance that would continue without serious or sustained challenge until the 1990s. Nevertheless, as the actions of the Farmers' Holiday Association and the Southern Tenant Farmers' Union and the presidential aspirations of Huey Long in 1935 demonstrated, the alliance was built on shaky ground indeed. For many years, men and women would remember that rural producer radicalism had meant more than just the promise of a single seat at a stranger's dinner party. It meant being able to host the dinner and choose the menu themselves. Many who came to this important realization and acted upon it did so in, "of all places," Iowa.

"Almost a habit of the country":

RURAL PRODUCER RADICALISM ON THE
BRITISH NORTH AMERICAN FRONTIER

Most Americans today do not know a farmer by name and have probably never visited a working farm. And if it were not for the disturbing images of farmers and ranchers storing caches of arms on their property and joining militias, we would still think of rural people in much the same spirit as Thomas Jefferson did when he summarized the significance of producerism in *Notes on the State of Virginia* nearly three hundred years ago: "Those who labor in the earth are the chosen people of God, if ever he had a chosen people, whose breasts he has made his peculiar deposit for substantial and genuine virtue."[2] As producers of real things that all humans require, as owners of property, and as handlers of nature, Jefferson argued, cultivators of the earth were America's most valuable citizens: "They are the most vigorous, the most independent, the most virtuous, and they are tied to their country, and wedded to its liberty and interests, by the most lasting bonds."[3] Furthermore, Jefferson believed that rural people were the moral backbone of the new republic. Far from cities and the corrupting influences of urban life, farmers and other rural people ensured the safety of America's most cherished ideals: equality, independence, and liberty. Most important, Jefferson believed that a large number of small property holders was better for American society than a small number of large ones to whom the rest were indebted. Without independent yeomen, and without land onto which future yeomen could move, the dream of the virtuous republic was doomed.

Jefferson's praise for rural life and agrarian producerism in the early nineteenth century, however, was a far cry from what some of the older revolutionary leaders, Whigs, and Federalists had thought about their country cousins in the middle and late eighteenth century. Not only did Samuel Adams and others think that farmers were crude and uncultured, they also wondered whether some of them, frontiersmen especially, were really loyal to the American cause. And it is not altogether surprising that they wondered. Between 1650 and 1750, colonists on the Euro-American frontier rose up against eastern centers of power more than forty times.[4] Between 1750 and 1850, they would rebel twenty more times.[5] Sometimes the protesters rebeled against unfair land laws, formed their own militias, and destroyed the homes of local landlords, proprietors, merchants, and lawyers. In other instances, they protested unresponsive, corrupt, or unrepresentative governments. They emptied jails, burned public buildings, closed court systems, and organized their own governmental institutions. In the years just before and after the Revolution, at least one frontier insurgent—Ethan Allen of Vermont—became so thoroughly disgusted with American political and economic leaders that he asked Great Britain to recognize the Republic of New Connecticut as an independent nation.[6]

How did rural people, these angry and disaffected prerevolutionary settlers, become glorified by Jefferson and many others since as the quintessential Americans? The answer is based in the transformation of the United States from a premodern patriarchal society to a modern liberal one, and in the role that people on the frontier and their political movements played in that transformation. Settlers had struggled to protect their property and be free from corrupt and authoritarian government for a century before the Revolutionary War was fought over the very same issues. The ideology of the Revolution thus was intimately familiar to them. What troubled them, however (and would frighten American leaders) was that, in their early struggles, settlers had fought not against the British but against elite Americans in the East—many of whom subsequently called themselves Patriots and came back to their country cousins for their support, their money, and their lives. As historian Carl Becker put it in 1909, for frontier Americans the object of both the prerevolutionary struggles and the Revolution itself was not simply home rule but also "who should rule at home."[7] The Revolution alone did not answer this second question. It was not until the presidential election of 1800 that many setters believed—perhaps rightly and perhaps not—that those who ruled "at home" were acting in the best interest of all, no matter where they lived or how rich or poor they were.

In one sense, rural Americans had been radical—or at least potentially radical—from the very beginning of settlement. New England Puritans, of course, were religious extremists. They had crossed the Atlantic with their families to live in an utterly unknown wilderness. They had risked their lives to worship in the way they believed was true to God's word. Just as they had no intention of recreating the Church of England in America, so they also refused to re-create fully the hierarchical political structure they had left behind. In its place they developed tiny utopian communities whose political decisions were debated, if within limits imposed by the church, in town meetings and other open forums. In Pennsylvania, Quakers tried to match religious with political innovation. To the south, Virginia colonists may have been somewhat less zealous, but they were no less unorthodox. Poor, young, indentured, imprisoned, the early Virginians were survivors of the highest order. Men who conquered "seasoning" in the malarial environment still faced seven years of hard labor for their masters. Women who survived childbirth sometimes outlived a handful of husbands. None of them had come so far or endured so much simply to be returned to a position of social, economic, or political dependence.

Colonists were also well prepared for radicalism because they carried with them collective memories of crowd action and agrarian insurgency from their homes in premodern Europe. Several historians have shown how frequently European men and women organized themselves "out-of-doors." One account by an amused aristocrat suggests that common people in Europe lived by "remembering the last [festival] and expecting the future [one]."[8] Although this description may be an exaggeration, festivals, carnivals, and holidays were enormously important parts of the cycle of seasons. Even in England, where celebrations were minimized by months of difficult weather and increasingly Protestant sensibilities, families could still count on celebrating several feast days, Plough Day, May Day, and St. John's Eve. What interests historians most about such celebrations are the distinctly antiauthoritarian activities in which local people participated. By their very existence, Peter Burke notes, festivals were "opposed to the everyday, a time of waste precisely because the everyday was a time of careful saving." Many pastimes and rituals on carnival days also reinforced the concept of a "topsy-turvy" world by upsetting the carefully maintained hierarchy of authority in that era. In one parade, for example, "the son is shown beating his father, the pupil beating his teacher . . . the king going on foot while the peasant rides."[9] The authority of gender roles was also reversed at carnivals and festivals. On Hock Tuesday in England, for example, women captured men and made them pay a ransom for release.

But most of the time these topsy-turvy rituals were not as seditious as they seemed; in fact, they may have been exactly the opposite. By institutionalizing disorder—in essence by authorizing disorder on particular days and not on all the rest—European elites were able to control it. Likewise by reinforcing the comedic or absurd elements of disrupted social relations (the thought of a woman capturing a man, after all!), the proper kinds of social relations were actually fortified. For example, some of the most notorious crowds were those that gathered around the gallows to witness an execution. Much has been made of the festive atmosphere on hanging days. Entire families attended, taking a day off from work at home, in the fields, or in the shops to eat, drink, see friends, and watch the proceedings. But hanging days were certainly much more than opportunities for altered behaviors. Every time an execution went off according to plan and a murderer, pctty thief, pickpocket, or beggar woman was killed, ordinary people were acutely reminded of the power of the state in their lives.[10]

Still there were times when festival days, carnivals, and crowd gatherings were transformed into something polite society was not expecting. At hangings, for example, the crowd sometimes rescued the condemned in the belief that he or she was unjustly accused. Similarly, if the execution was botched— if, for example, the hangman's noose did not quickly snap a victim's neck and he or she was swinging and suffocating in agony—the crowd might free the prisoner. Nor were feast days and carnivals reliably festive. "Riots and rebellions frequently took place on the occasions of major festivals," writes Burke. "It is hardly surprising to find that members of the upper class often suggested that particular festivals ought to be abolished."[11]

Along with festivals and carnivals, then, the colonists brought with them memories of direct crowd action that had the potential of taking specifically political forms because the local community acted collectively against the power of an elite authority. The most common kind of riot in England was a food or bread riot, an extralegal mechanism by which ordinary people could correct a perceived injustice in the "moral economy." The earliest recorded instance of a bread riot was in 1520, and more than forty occurred between 1585 and 1660. By the 1700s, two of every three public disturbances were food riots. George Rudé tells us that when food prices climbed too high or the supply fell too low, crowds—sometimes full of women with their children—dispensed a "rough-and-ready kind of 'natural justice' by breaking windows . . . storming markets . . . and 'pulling down' their [enemies'] houses, farms, fences, mules, or pubs."[12] However ardent they were, crowds rarely sought to take the lives of their oppressors, but only tried to improve their own conditions when the government proved unable or unwilling to do so. Nevertheless, they showed the power that community members held when acting collectively.

In rural England at the beginning of the eighteenth century, however, riots began to take even more distinctly political forms. By then two important agricultural transformations had taken place in the English countryside. The introduction of improved farm technology had increased farm production and doubled the incomes of large property owners.[13] The second revolution had begun centuries before but culminated in the eighteenth century when both the enclosure of land previously used in common by rural villagers and the consolidation of small farms by large landowners was complete. Both transformations helped to create a large new group of laboring poor, who had no political rights and resorted to the traditional riot. When threshing machines were introduced by large landowners, for example, or when Parliament authorized the construction of a tollgate or turnpike on a road that had been freely traveled, rural people organized to undo the damage. And they did not always just break into shops or destroy small amounts of property; they sometimes threatened the very lives of elite men in their communities whom they held responsible.[14]

Celebrating out-of-doors, acting outside the law to enforce just laws or to bring balance to the moral economy, organizing the community to maintain local control, and using mob violence to change political policies were customary practices of all those who traveled from England to America in the colonial period. As in England, crowd behavior in America took a remarkable number of forms including urban brawls and vandalism, tar-and-featherings, mob violence and personal assaults, and not all of them were meant to upset the status quo. One historian who has enumerated the riots in colonial America between 1645 and 1760 suggests that the total lies between seventy-five and one hundred.[15] Of these, he suggests that only between eighteen and forty were actual attempts by colonists to overthrow provincial governments. Altogether these multifaceted incidents made British North America a place of considerable social turmoil. According to one contemporary North Carolinian, the "resort to force and violence was . . . a common occurrence, almost a habit of the country."[16]

Some of the most important riots in colonial America concerned access to and control of a limited amount of land. As Edward Countryman notes, "In the northern American countryside, the problem behind crowd action was not provisions, or whorehouses, or press gangs [as it was in urban areas]; it was how and under what conditions and by whom a limited amount of land would be owned and occupied."[17] Rural Americans rose up to protest land laws or lease practices throughout British North America and the fledgling United States.[18] In New Jersey and New York in particular, farmers let it be known that a society of hierarchy, dependence, and permanent tenancy was not the one they had moved halfway around the world to create.

Was there really a limited amount of land in British North America? From our vantage point in the crowded and resource-scarce twentieth century, this is difficult to imagine. As late as 1760, the total white population of British North America was only two million people, or less than the present-day population of most of the boroughs of New York City. Wasn't there enough land for everyone? Wasn't the eighteenth century in fact the time when every free man who came to American shores had a clear chance of improving himself? Well, as it turns out, this is not exactly the way it was. Our sense of the enormity of the nation's land and the government's devotion to its equal distribution among ordinary people derives from shared cultural memories of the late nineteenth, not the early eighteenth, century. After the Civil War, Americans were empowered by ideas about free land and free labor and propelled by the provisions of the Homestead Act and improved transportation and communication networks. Americans on the colonial and early national frontiers could only dream that someday such an agrarian utopia would be possible—and fight to make it so.

Hardly an empty continent, in the 1700s British North America was a narrow strip of land with a vast ocean to the east, hostile European and Native American nations to the north, west, and south, and a burgeoning population within. Once settled, British North America and New England especially became extraordinarily healthy places to live, raise a family, and grow old—sometimes very old. One historian tells of a Massachusetts man who, having waited for decades to inherit property from his parents, lived only two years after their deaths. "For some," he concludes, "childhood in New England must have seemed much too long."[19] Around mid-century, when increased immigration, large family size, and relatively low infant mortality were added to improved life expectancy, the land crunch was on. Between 1750 and 1770, the population of British North America doubled. Because the high cost of the French and Indian War had convinced British officials to cut off new settlement in the trans-Appalachian West, however, new areas of unsettled territory were nearly nonexistent.

Demographic pressures like these would have created competition for land in British North America even if all land areas were available for purchase. But, to the contrary, by the mid-1700s freehold property in the colonies was becoming significantly less available to small producers, and in some places a revival of feudalism was occurring. Not that feudalism had ever been far from the minds of the founders of southern and mid-Atlantic colonies in the first place. In fact, Countryman says, "There was more than a hint of feudal ways in the founding of much of North America."[20] The Carolinas, Maryland, New Jersey, and New York were all founded on a proprietary model, wherein large grants of property were given as gifts to elites from the king or were purchased by British aristocrats. Rather than put the lands up for sale, proprietors, patroons, and manor lords only offered them for lease. In the late seventeenth century many of these estates broke up or were given back to the king when they proved to be unprofitable because of low population density.[21] For the few proprietors who held onto their estates until the mid-1700s, however, an altogether different demographic picture emerged. With a burgeoning and youthful population seeking somewhere—anywhere—to lay down roots, proprietors of some of the great estates began to grow rather rich indeed by leasing their land. By the 1760s the largest proprietors earned as much as English noblemen. By one estimate, for example, Lord Baltimore's income from Maryland was more than thirty-thousand pounds a year.[22]

Of course, a feudal revival in the 1740s would ruffle far fewer feathers than it would in the 1990s. As radical—or potentially radical—as colonists were, they had also reproduced in British North America a vastly hierarchical and unequal society, not so very different from the one they left behind. Gordon S. Wood surmises that British subjects "still took for granted that society was and ought to be a hierarchy of ranks and degrees of dependency and that most people were bound together by personal ties of one sort or another."[23] In all aspects of daily life, relationships of dependency ordered the world. Most dependent of all, of course, were women, children, servants, and African slaves whose labor value did not belong to them and who had few or no legal rights. But even white men were dependent on others, especially those who held positions of economic and/or political power in their communities. In such a world, then, the relationship between a tenant and his landlord was but one of the many unequal ties that white men either endured or enforced every day.

Yet the mortar that held conventions, obligations, and unfreedoms together in the New World was slowly cracking under the weight of intellectual, social, and material change in the eighteenth century. As Wood writes, "republicanism"—ideas about the equality of men and the ability of citizens to form governments by consent—"seeped everywhere in the eighteenth-century Atlantic world, eroding monarchical society from within, wearing away all the traditional supports of kingship."[24] Soon dependencies of all kinds would come into question—in the church pew, in the provincial assembly, in the workplace, even sometimes in the home. In the mid-1700s fathers noted with pride the increasing independence of their sons, with some alarm the increasing independence of their servants, wives, and daughters. In the North some even came to see slavery as an unjust and immoral institution. More often, however, white men established and reinforced the significance of their own republican independence on the "natural" dependencies of women and Africans.

Republican ideas were underscored by lived experience. In the middle of the eighteenth century, more people living in British North America could read, write, travel, and purchase a variety of consumer goods than ever before. They had greater mobility and thus were able to increase the distance between themselves and the customs of dependence and deference in their home communities. Seeing more of the world also helped them to imagine a broader vision of politics and society. Many came into contact with the Enlightenment views of science, medicine, and religion for the first time and began to question the premodern rituals and folk beliefs of previous generations. Such real material changes upended convention and reinforced the persistent desires of colonists, particularly those on the frontier, to take charge of their own destinies.

Most important, republican ideals and experiences strengthened American tenants' long-standing resolve not to become a permanent peasantry. According to Cadwallader Colden, an influential contemporary critic of feudal landholding practices in New York, "The hope of having land of their own and becoming independent of Landlords is what chiefly induces people into America."[25] If that was true, we can easily imagine how discouraging the prospects of long-term tenancy and how appealing the notions of republicanism must have been. New Englanders, in particular, Countryman notes, wanted "no lords among them." Having established communities in the wilderness where in theory no man was more important than another and each participated equally in community life, but where in reality many significant hierarchies persisted, "their greatest single fear continued to be that they would lose their farms and descend to the status of tenant under the dominion of a great landlord."[26]

Thus a combination of factors—population growth, land scarcity, republican musings within a hierarchical society, improved material circumstances, the relative strengths and weaknesses of landlords and tenants, and the personal stake that many began to put in their independence—provoked rebellions against manor lords, proprietors, and their allies. Although the elite forces usually quashed these insurrections before much damage had been done and little power had changed hands, in some places riots brought about new laws and new freedoms. And all the riots for land combined to destabilize American society in the pre-revolutionary era. It didn't take much to see that all was not well with the regular order of things in these irregular times—and people on the American frontier had a great deal to do with those times.

The mid-eighteenth-century New Jersey and New York land riots, which were similar enough for us to examine together here, began as disputes over land between large numbers of small farmers and small numbers of politically powerful aristocrats. Access to freehold property was fundamental to republicanism and producerism and, as we have seen, was significantly curtailed by the middle of the eighteenth century. New Jersey, for example, had its roots in a neofeudal land system that had been abandoned and subsequently revived. But from 1700 on, settlers disputed the claims of the proprietors to these lands and particularly to the rich farmlands around Newark. Calling themselves the Elizabethtown Associates, insurgent farmers claimed to have title to the land themselves through Native American treaties. They formed a land company and sold real estate as far away as Somerset County. Farmers then began to pour onto lands claimed by both parties and to cut timber on the land for sale across the border in New York.

Access to freehold land was even more difficult in parts of New York than it was in New Jersey. In the early 1600s the Dutch West India Company had granted patroonships in the colony to wealthy men who could bring fifty settlers with them. The grantors hoped thus to accelerate the previously slow pace of settlement in the New World. After the English takeover of New Amsterdam in 1667, the new governors continued to give large grants to wealthy supporters. But the manors were still barely profitable. Population did not grow as quickly in New York as it did in New England, and manor lords felt pressure from the British government to sell some of their properties. Thus between 1650 and 1740 landlords offered prospective tenants attractive lease terms, just to keep them on their lands. For example, tenants were frequently given lifetime leases at reasonable rates, as well as the right to sell any improvements (such as a house, or a plowed field, or an orchard) to a new tenant.

The same demographic shifts that enriched New Jersey proprietors in the eighteenth century created fortunes and new relationships of power for the manor lords of New York. Increased European migration brought scores of Dutch, German, and Scots-Irish peasants to America. Many did not have the capital available to purchase farms and wanted instead to lease land until they had saved enough money to buy some. At the same time, the population of New England soared and spilled into neighboring counties of New York. Thus "Yankee" squatters joined the "Yorker" tenants on the great estates. Between 1737 and 1746 the population of Dutchess County, New York, grew 11.1 percent per year. By the time of the Revolution two of the largest manors—Renssalaerwyck and Livingston—had more than 250 tenants or somewhere between 800 and 1,500 residents. With leases that ranged between three and twenty pounds per year, the income added up quickly. Berthoff and Murrin estimate that Scarsdale, Philipsborough, and Livingston likely "returned between 1,000 and 2,000 pounds a year, Rensselaerwyck probably more, and Cortlandt Manor less."[27] When he considered his annual income from leases and the rising value of land, Philip Livingston reflected that "Selling I am not fond off att all."[28]

Tensions between proprietors and squatters and landlords and tenants grew in the mid-Atlantic colonies until one side—usually the lords—acted to protect its interests. The New Jersey proprietors, increasingly irked by the audacity of the Elizabethtown Associates, decided they could not just sit back and watch the "clinkers" take over their land and cut down their valuable forests.[29] Soon they announced that they were going to collect back payment on quitrents—vestiges of feudal times when every tenant paid an annual fee in lieu of other services the manor lord might require. So few New Jersey farmers had taken the lords or their quitrents seriously that the total neared fifteen thousand pounds. The proprietors also went to court and filed suit against the Associates. Last, they ordered mass ejections of squatters and, beginning with the arrest of Samuel Baldwin in 1746, hauled off to jail anyone found cutting timber on their lands.

The actions of the manor lords in New York varied with their personalities, the size of their estates, and the relative hostility and influence of the recent arrivals from New England. As in New Jersey, some landlords exercised their new-found power by reviving the remnants of feudalism. Quitrents returned to New York in the middle 1700s. Likewise, landlords began to insist on a multiplicity of services from tenants. Joseph Simson, for example, signed a lease for 160 acres in 1750 from the daughter of Henry Beekman and, in so doing, agreed to build a house, grind his grain at the landlady's mill, obey "all reasonable orders," and plant fruit trees.[30] Other lords built new mansions and increased the size of their personal staffs. At one manor hall, the lord's daughter was wed under a golden canopy, while all the tenants looked on from a respectful distance.

Some New York landlords chose a more severe path in the 1700s, rejecting the role of the manorial baron for an early version of the robber baron. These men transformed the relationship between landlord and tenant to nothing more than a monetary transaction, seeking every opportunity to increase profits. They issued many fewer lifetime leases and they raised rents by as much as 100 percent in ten years. They no longer allowed tenants to sell improvements, and they even evicted long-time residents so that they could offer leases to new men who had agreed to pay more. For these tenants, whatever protection or reciprocal familiarity they had hoped to acquire in return for years of loyalty evaporated like their valleys' early morning fog.

When tenants and squatters had had enough of such humiliations, they responded with the tried-and-true techniques of Euro-American, community-based, collective insurgency. In New Jersey in the late 1740s, rebels pulled down the houses of tenants who cooperated with the proprietors and set barns and fields ablaze in midnight raids of terror. On the Beekman Patent in Dutchess County, New York, squatters also tried to drive long-time tenants off their parcels.[31] Similar troubles came in 1766 to the estates of the Livingstons and Van Rensselaers in Albany County. There, Massachusetts speculators were actually selling off bits of land in the disputed territory between Massachusetts and New York, and long-time tenants were buying it. In retaliation, landlords ordered the land and crops of tenants who cooperated with the disruptive and audacious New Englanders to be burned. In exchange, the New Englanders kidnaped a tenant and gave his lands to a farmer on their side. Robert Livingston requested a guard of fifty British soldiers to protect his life. Similar violence spread to the nearby Claverack Patent. As Patricia Bonomi puts it, "Houses and fields were burned, contingents of armed men clashed in a number of bloody skirmishes, and the inevitable fatality occurred."[32]

Because the rebels understood the connection between economic and political power, they also evolved specifically political strategies.

When the New Jersey proprietors began arresting squatters, for example, the rebels took the law into their own hands. Samuel Baldwin was rescued by a crowd of 150 men reportedly armed "with clubbs, Axes, and Crow barrs."[33] Each time a leader was jailed, larger and larger mobs gathered to free the man, succeeding even when local militia men were ordered to hold him. In one incident, the rioter was freed and the sheriff put in jail—a topsy-turvy outcome if there ever was one. Similar strategies were pursued in New York. During the Great Uprising of 1766, it was said that there was not a secure jail anywhere east of the Hudson River.

The rebels did not just attack symbols of the proprietors' political power, however; they also organized themselves as political units. Again the New Jersey insurgents led the way. Between 1745 and 1748, the rioters' supporters in the assembly filibustered, allowing no laws to be passed to end the violence, while prominent rebel leaders began organizing as if they were the government of New Jersey. One leader, Amos Roberts, established his own judicial system, army, and system of tax collection. Tenants on the Philipse Highland Patent in New York tried the same approach in November 1765, when they learned of the evictions of several long-time tenants. They vowed to protect their land, to free one another from jail, and to rid the area of tenants loyal to the proprietors. They also conducted their own trials and carried out their own punishments against men who stood in their way. Believing that their cause was similar to the New York City protest against the Stamp Act, they called themselves the rural Sons of Liberty. As the violence spread to the Manor of Cortlandt, the mob grew to over two thousand souls. Mob activity continued through the summer months of 1766 and subsided only after the governor called in regiments of the British army.

In North Carolina and Vermont, mid-eighteenth-century rebellions that began as struggles over land ended as outright struggles for control of the government and thus foreshadowed more completely the conflicts of the revolutionary, early national, and industrial eras. The rebellion in North Carolina in the late 1760s, for example, began in a familiar way when poor settlers and squatters disputed proprietary land claims. The last remaining large proprietors in the colony were Lord Granville, whose district included most of the northern half of North Carolina, and Henry McCulloh, whose grants lay in central sections of the colony. In the 1750s and early 1760s farmers resisted evictions for nonpayment of rent, rioted against corrupt land agents, and forced the closing of Lord Granville's land office. But the rioters did not stop there. They also associated the unfair distribution of land with the unfair distribution of political power. Laws themselves, argued George Sims in 1765, were nothing more than "private acts . . . that favour [the officers] in devilish practices."[34] Acting in concert, unfair land laws, corrupt court officials, and greedy merchants forced hundreds of settlers into poverty. These practices suggested that the government was established simply to tend to the ambitions of the rich and powerful—an idea that, however conventional it may have seemed before ideas of republicanism began to corrode the imperial world, no longer sounded right at all.

Settlers in the western counties of North Carolina took up these grievances in the 1760s and pursued them further. They too were tired of what Marvin L. Michael Kay describes as "burgeoning suits by creditors against indebted farmers, [exorbitant] fees collected by court officers, unfair and corrupt distraining practices, and sales of debtor property at public auction, high taxes, and suspicions about the necessity and lawful application of these taxes."[35] Farmers and their opponents were divided by more than their political views, however. In western counties, 40 percent of the wealth was controlled by 10 percent of the population. And the wealthy 10 percent had ties with the even wealthier elite in eastern North Carolina. Moreover, the farmers saw the power of the wealthy as an assault on small producerism. Thus, Kay reports, they "assailed in particular those they considered nonproductive, especially merchants and lawyers" whom they perceived to be living off the honest labors of poor people like themselves.[36]

The North Carolina Regulation was formed after meetings with local officials failed to redress the frontiersmen's grievances. They chose to call themselves Regulators because they wanted to regulate local affairs. They began by petitioning the provincial assembly for new laws and electing new representatives. When these efforts failed, they turned to direct action—courthouse closures and threats on the lives of local men of power and influence. This soon caught the attention—and the fury—of North Carolina's governor William Tryon. After a disturbance at a courthouse near Hillsborough, Tryon issued the Riot Act and ordered militia men to shoot on sight any Regulator who had not confessed to his crimes. Although leaders of the Regulation tried to work with officials to reach a compromise, Tryon insisted on using military force against the rebels. The two armies met in the Battle of Alamance on May 16, 1771. In a two-hour battle, twenty Regulators were killed and one hundred wounded. A leader of the movement was summarily executed on the battlefield; six more were hanged later. Not surprisingly, the battle ended the direct actions of the North Carolina Regulators, but it did not change their minds about the tyranny of corrupt political authority.

Gaining access to freehold land in what would become Vermont required the most determined and deliberate political effort of all. Remote, mountainous, and treacherous, most of Vermont contained little more than French forts and ice houses until the early 1700s. The first permanent Anglo-European settlement was Fort Dummer, built near Brattleboro in 1724. Within only fifteen years of settlement, however, three provincial governments and scores of farmers were battling over the tiny colony's future. The land had originally been part of the holdings of the Massachusetts Bay Colony. In 1741, however, King George II ruled that all Massachusetts claims in Vermont were invalid, and thus sounded the first shot in a long struggle between landlords, speculators, squatters, and small farmers from the two remaining colonies that claimed land there—New York and New Hampshire. Given how strongly Yankees felt about freehold property and communal village structure and how equally strongly elite Yorkers felt about their right to own large tracts of land and to use that land for their economic self-interest, a serious struggle was inevitable. In the battle for Vermont there would be no middle ground for, as Countryman says, "either the land would be held by or from . . . the New York grantees, or it would not. . . . The insurgents were responding not to sudden crises or short-term irritations but rather to structural conditions basic to their existing societies and to major trends in their development."[37]

King George's decision to uphold the New York and deny the New Hampshire claims to the land west of the Connecticut River pushed rural people to rebel. Settlers could not believe their eyes when they read of such a travesty; they could not believe their ears when they heard tell of it. To live under the system of landlords and manor titles or to be compelled to purchase land they had cultivated for years from New York City speculators was unthinkable. When setting ablaze the house of Charles Hutchesson, an army officer who had tried to build a farm near New Perth, rebel leader Ethan Allen summed up his and many other New Hampshiremen's feelings: "God Damn your Governour, Laws, King, Council, & Assembly."[38]

If he could not live under British rule or within the colony of New York, Allen took the logical next step to organize a government of his own. In 1770 he organized the Green Mountain Boys to resist the order of the king and the power of the New York grantees. Like the Elizabethtown Associates, the Green Mountain Boys was a loosely arranged military organization that maintained its own court and penal system. It attacked small farmers who honored the New York titles, replaced them with its own men, and in at least one case sacked an entire village. Likewise, the Green Mountain Boys emptied jails, closed courts backed by crowds as large as five hundred, and punished local officials who accepted the authority of the New York government. One man received two hundred lashes on his bare back as punishment for the crime of serving as a justice of the peace.

The status of Vermont had not yet been decided when the Revolutionary War began, but because Allen and the Green Mountain Boys blamed the king for giving their land to New York, they fought for the Patriot army. Nevertheless they so dreaded creating an alliance with New York that they did not join the original Confederation of States but declared themselves the independent Republic of New Connecticut. When the Continental Congress refused to recognize New Connecticut, Allen and his brother commenced negotiations with Great Britain. Not until 1791 were the people of Vermont convinced that they could join the United States as an entity utterly separate and protected from New York. Even then they drafted one of the most radical state constitutions of its time. By providing universal manhood suffrage as well as the community-based principle of "one town, one vote," the people of Vermont made other state assemblies look like copies of the British House of Lords.[39] In Vermont, settlers wanted access to freehold property and they wanted a government that would reflect and respect the work of ordinary people in their pursuit of personal liberty, community solidarity, and material prosperity. And for a time, that was exactly what they got.

When the domestic violence of the mid-eighteenth century came to an end, few of the questions it had raised had been completely answered. In Vermont, rebels still wondered whether they should trust the federal government. In New Jersey, New York, and North Carolina, rebels had put down their arms but had not been convinced of the importance of deference to their superiors. Indeed, the use of force by their governments may have made them believe even more acutely in the value of freehold land and republicanism than they had before. In 1770 most insurgents still believed that land should be made available to all in small parcels, and not accumulated, speculated on, or rented out by a few aristocratic men. Moreover, they still believed that political affairs were best managed by local men who were accountable only to others in their communities. On the other hand, while most proprietors gave up the idea of fully restoring feudalism in British North America, they did not question the importance of having a ruling class determine political and economic issues for the "meaner sort." But because most rebels were pardoned and moved on to new frontiers, the underlying tensions between rich and poor, aristocracy and meritocracy, paternalism and liberalism would wait two generations before they were, for a time, resolved. Meanwhile all Americans faced the most significant political crisis in their own lives and in the nation's history thus far.

"Come on, my brave boys . . . knock their grey wigs off":

RURAL PRODUCER RADICALISM IN THE REVOLUTIONARY AND EARLY NATIONAL ERAS

For frontier rebels, the American Revolution raised exciting possibilities and complicated questions. As they listened to Patriot leaders and read their letters and pamphlets, settlers could not help but recognize some of the ideas behind the war. After all, they knew from experience what the consequences of tyrannical ambitions were, and—in the South particularly—what the economic slavery that followed loss of land to excessive taxation was like. They certainly resented more than easterners the king's Proclamation Line of 1763, which forbade settlement west of the Appalachian Mountains. They hated aristocracy and they loathed corruption. They liked what they heard about equality among men and equal representation in political affairs. And most of all, they knew what it meant to organize themselves to resist the forces of injustice.

What many settlers could not decide, however, was whose tyranny, oppression, corruption, and injustice they should resist—the

British monarch's or the local elites'. Some home-grown aristocrats who had fought against rebels on the frontier in the 1760s and early 1770s had been miraculously transformed into republicans and in 1775 and 1776 came to enlist "the good people of the land" for the cause of freedom. In North Carolina, the transformation was so transparent that Presbyterian ministers actually used the same biblical passages to recruit farmers to overthrow the king that they had used to convince them not to overthrow the governor during the Regulation! Because settlers were not the fools that elites sometimes took them for, they saw this sudden conversion for what it was. In backcountry South Carolina, for example, as Ronald Hoffman notes, the "low country's cry of liberty and natural rights [was seen] as hypocrisy."[40] And Richard Bushman points out that, in Massachusetts, farmers' understanding of "the value of freehold land and the necessity of protecting lands against marauders in various guises . . . never . . . subsided entirely."[41] They simply wondered—and would continue to wonder even after the war had been won—who the most dangerous marauders really were.

Settlers in different regions resolved their dilemma in different ways. At one extreme were Massachusetts farmers, including the famous Minutemen of Concord, who paid little attention to the rising Anglo-American tensions until 1773, when they received a letter from Boston's Committee of Correspondence asking them to consider rebellion. Surviving manuscripts show that men in 144 towns organized their own committees to consider the issue and, as a whole, joined the Patriot cause.[42] Almost immediately afterward Massachusetts farmers, including settlers from western counties, found themselves on the Revolution's front lines. Local militias repelled British invaders and local people organized to supply the Continental Army. Their determination to keep the countryside secure played a decisive role in the American victory. Although they came into the struggle late, the people of western Massachusetts took the lessons of the war very much to heart. In fact, a few years later some Bostonians would wonder whether their country cousins hadn't learned the ideology of freedom and equality a little too well.

Other frontier Americans made other choices. For some, it was impossible to be fully loyal to either the British or the Patriot cause. In some New York counties, for example, British army officers told them that their best chance of gaining freehold land was to support the British in overthrowing the landlords—while their landlords told them exactly the reverse. The majority of former North Carolina Regulators probably stayed neutral. In the Lower South, the disaffection of many small landholders with both sides—and particularly with the wealthy slave-holding planters among them—caused nearly total social collapse. Their resentment of authority, built up over decades, was empowered through the Patriots' calls to overthrow the status quo and led, as Hoffman says, to "civil conflict, Loyalist action, murder, plunder, militia insubordination, unrest among blacks, defiance by independent-minded whites, [and] opportunism."[43] There, it was the leaders of the Revolution who were forced to ask the hardest questions. They wondered whether, should they win the war, if a society of order and deference could ever be restored.

Some southern leaders saw in this crisis an opportunity both to save the republic and to save their class. Breaking ranks with fellow leaders, Charles Carroll of Maryland and General Nathanael Greene, who was stationed in the Carolinas, began to suspect that an American victory would be impossible and a republic utterly unworkable unless the people consented to the new government. For Carroll, such acceptance required the elite's advocacy of prodebtor legislation that would cost him and other aristocrats large portions of their fortunes. As he put it, "No great revolution can happen in a state without revolutions or mutations of private property."[44] Greene likewise believed that it was far better to let disaffected citizens come back to the fold than to anger and alienate them further. Despite their support of the people, neither leader could have been accused of wanting to "level" society. Nevertheless, they understood—years ahead of others in their rank who still spoke of ordinary people as "poor reptiles . . . struggling to cast off their winter's slough"—that to whatever degree the elite had led the Revolution, in the end its meaning would be shared by all.[45]

Because Americans on the frontier and most members of the American elite held different ideas about "who should rule at home," contests for land, political power, and personal freedom recurred between the end of the war and the presidential election of 1800, a period sometimes called the "continuing American Revolution." Indeed, these years were so arduous in so many ways that they made the previous era seem tranquil. The particular causes of continued discord varied by region and decade. All, however, were grounded in the conflicting visions of America which various members of society thought they had fought for—a classical republic based on dependence, order, and virtue or a democratic republic based on human equality and personal liberty. The Revolutionary War itself did not immediately change the United States into a society dedicated to principles of equality or in which the aristocracy had been "leveled." But by bringing forth these ideas and empowering ordinary people to believe in and act upon them, the Revolution made that transformation possible and perhaps even inevitable.

Between 1780 and 1800, ordinary settlers and backcountry farmers—those barely removed from the frontier—were an integral part of this transformation. In every state from Maine to Georgia, westerners let easterners know that they had not relinquished their primary prerevolutionary objectives—to be independent producers, to be fairly represented in state governments, to maintain control of local affairs, and to be respected for their ordinary labors. Nor had they forgotten their tradition of organizing themselves "out-of-doors." If anything, prerevolutionary beliefs and behaviors became accentuated when American leaders legitimized and promoted them during the war—but rolled them back immediately afterward. When settlers donned their uniforms and marched again, they demonstrated their belief that the objectives of the war had not yet been fulfilled. They still sought to live in a nation in which property, liberty, and representative government were guaranteed to all citizens—not just the rich and well connected.

Partly in response to these demands and partly as a way to suppress them, a new generation of leaders launched a vastly more democratic republic in 1800. The culture of the new society put farmers and their producerist ideals at its heart, creating a period sometimes called the age of the farmer.[46] At the same time, however, it laid the foundation for an economic system that eventually would render small production nearly obsolete. Between 1800 and 1850 farmers were set loose to conquer new lands free from governmental restrictions on trade and individual liberty. Free, too, were emerging merchant capitalists. As James A. Henretta puts it, "For better or for worse, perhaps a little of each, the United States would confront the nineteenth century as an increasingly capitalist commercial society."[47]

Economic and political chaos paved the way for rural radicalism after the Revolution. During the war, class and regional divisions in several states were exacerbated when eastern property owners and merchants grew rich off a war that western farmers paid for through heavy taxes and with their lives. As the war slowly drew to a close, several other factors combined to plunge the new American economy into depression. British manufacturers flooded the American market with low-priced goods, decreasing demand for American-made products. American manufacturers, however, found few markets abroad open to them even if they had products to sell, which southern merchants did not. British creditors meanwhile were free to collect old debts from American wholesalers and regional distributors. In response, local retailers called in debts held by local farmers, few of whom had any cash.

The structure of political life in the new union exacerbated these problems. When delegates met in 1777 to frame a new national government, most were understandably reluctant to give the new centralized authority any real power. They feared the corruption bred by domination and believed that republican principles of government worked best on a local or state level, where men of property and virtue could guide their less fortunate and less reliable brethren. Thus they did not give the new confederation of states some of the powers that today we might consider basic to running a country. The new "friendly union" could not impose duties on British goods to improve the balance of trade. Likewise, it could not impose a single system of taxation to reduce the national debt. It could not print paper currency to stop inflation. And finally, it had no power to coerce individuals or states to comply with any of the laws that it did impose because it had neither a federal judiciary nor a standing army.

Each state wrote its own constitution and monitored its own economic affairs. Thus each new state responded to the monetary crisis, and the debtor crisis in particular, in its own way. The South Carolina, New York, and Pennsylvania legislatures responded conservatively but effectively by printing small amounts of currency and redistributing some parcels of confiscated Tory property. In Rhode Island, on the other hand, where one writer said that "the people are almost drove to desperation. . . . [they are] 'like fire,'" the legislature eventually acted to support all claims by debtors.[48] The state printed a large amount of paper money and required creditors to accept this currency as payment. It even imposed a fine on creditors who refused to accept it. As the currency plunged in value and creditors fled the state, judges were ordered to accept payment in their place.

In Connecticut, New Hampshire, and, especially, Massachusetts, the legislatures' staunch support of the rights of creditors led to rebellion. The Massachusetts Constitution of 1780 reconciled some of the demands that had traditionally divided farmers and merchants but left in place two essential ingredients from the revised (and much reviled) Massachusetts Charter of 1691: property qualifications for office-holders and voters alike. Because only wealthy men could hold office and men without property could not even vote, the Massachusetts legislature was filled with men who had little sympathy for the problems of small farmers and their debts. Led by wealthy, conservative, and powerful Governor James Bowdoin, the legislature refused petitions for paper money and stay laws. Under these circumstances, a mob rebellion was not surprising. What shocked conservative elites in Massachusetts and around the new nation was the size of the uprising. David P. Szatmary estimates that at its height in the fall of 1786 the insurgency "involved almost 9,000 militants or about one-quarter of the 'fighting men' in rural areas."[49] In western Massachusetts, it was said that there were no small farmers who did not support—or perhaps who dared not support—the uprising.

The issues that provoked Shays's Rebellion were similar to those that had provoked land riots in the mid-1700s, but they were also influenced by the unfulfilled promise of the Revolution. Between the high taxes they were compelled to pay (as much as two hundred dollars per household), the insistence of local merchants that they must pay their debts, and the predominance of eastern merchants in the state government, western farmers believed that they were in danger of losing their property and their personal liberty without the benefit of fair representation. Their land would be taken, of course, but that was not all. In some states it was also possible to keep a debtor in the county jail until he paid his debt. Needless to say, farmers found it difficult to pay from inside a debtors' prison. It was difficult enough to stay alive. Samuel Ely, an itinerant minister and radical farm organizer, was jailed in 1783. After some weeks, he wrote that he was "alive and that is all as I am full of boils and putrified [sic] sores all over my body and they make me stink alive, besides having some of my feet froze which makes it difficult to walk."[50]

For centuries, farmers in Europe and America had feared becoming a permanent class of tenants and being thrown into debtors' prison, and in New England in the 1780s these fears became realities. Throughout the region, creditors initiated thousands of suits against small farmers. In Connecticut in 1786, more than 20 percent of all state taxpayers were taken to court. In Hampshire County, Massachusetts, 58 percent of the suits originated in four market towns. Soon farms were foreclosed upon and sold at auction; men without sufficient property to cover their debts were thrown in prison. In both Hampshire and Worcester counties, the majority of prisoners were yeomen; not a single one was a prominent retailer.[51] The way these farmers saw it, a centralized, faraway, aristocratic government had let them down again. One man declared that he would rather live with no government than with the "antient Mode of Government among us which we so much detest and abhor."[52] Another declared, "The great men are to get all we have; and I think it is time for us to rise and put a stop to it, and have no more courts, nor sheriffs, nor collectors, nor lawyers; I design to pay no more; and I know we have the biggest party, let them say what they will."[53]

A society run by "the great men," a society in which a simple, hard-working farmer could be summarily imprisoned and his family pushed to the brink of starvation—this was not the society of freedom and equality for which Massachusetts frontiersmen had risked their lives. No man deserves "any degree or spark of . . . a right of dominion, government, and jurisdiction over [an]other," professed a Northampton farmer who had learned his revolutionary lessons well.[54] As early as 1782 Samuel Ely called upon Hampshire County farmers to attack local creditors and retailers. Later he led a group against a courthouse in Northampton saying, "Come on, my brave boys, we'll go to the woodpile and get clubs enough and knock their grey wigs off and send them out of this world in an instant."[55] Similar protests erupted later in western parts of Connecticut, New Hampshire, and Vermont, where backcountry farmers were connected more easily with one another through the trade waters of the Connecticut River and the culture of frontier life than they were with their political representatives in the East.

Revolutionary War veteran Daniel Shays led the most serious and sustained insurgency. Using newspapers, tavern meetings, and veterans' associations, Shays organized farmers from all over Massachusetts to stop the loss of property to creditors. At first he called conventions and tried petitioning the legislature to resolve his grievances. Soon, however, Shays and his men set off to resolve them by force. They gathered in large groups and forced local courts to shut down so that foreclosures would not be able to go forward. Over and again in the late

"Shays's Rebellion." Former Continental army Captain Daniel Shays
leads a protest against high taxes and eastern authorities in 1786.
Courtesy of Bettmann Archive.

summer and early fall of 1786 crowds of angry men, some in uniform, gathered, as a contemporary noted, "swords and muskets, and . . . bludgeons" and assembled in military style accompanied by "the shrieking of fifes and the beating of drums."[56] Then they compelled officers of the court to walk between them and close their buildings. Most of the men also wore sprigs of evergreen in their hats, just as they had done during the Revolution. They told the world that, from where they stood, the war was not yet over.

Anarchy, liberty run amok, a conspiracy of antirepublicans or secret British Loyalists—all these explanations for the rebellion occurred to leaders in eastern Massachusetts. Like the proprietors of New Jersey and New York, they could not sit back and watch "knaves," "thieves," "madmen," and "the most idle vicious, and disorderly set of men in the community" dismantle the social system that gave them power.[57] However glad they had been to help organize mobs in Boston before the war, now these same leaders sought to put down domestic discord and to prove that republicanism could be virtuous and orderly. After all, mobs were an expression of popular will, unjustifiable in a republic that was built on careful representation and adjudication, not threats or intimidation. Governor James Bowdoin compelled local militias to protect the courthouses. When some local militia men refused, he recruited his own army and solicited private donations for its support. He chose Benjamin Lincoln, a former general in the Continental army and an influential framer of the 1780 Constitution, to assume command. Meanwhile the legislature passed a riot act that made it illegal for any group of men to assemble without a petition and suspended the right of habeus corpus.

Now accused of treason, Shays and his followers realized that their "little rebellion" had become much more; it was an attempt to overthrow the government of Massachusetts. "I had rather be under the devil than such a government as this," said farmer Isaac Chenery.[58] As several historians have pointed out, the rebels were forced into extralegal opposition because there was not any legitimate way of opposing a standing government in early America. Without political parties or competitive elections, they fell back on the strategies that had worked before and during the Revolution, including conventions, correspondence, petitions, congresses, and, of course, mob violence. The irony of this "second revolution" was not lost on observers outside the state or outside the new nation. "America exhibits a curious scene at this time," one Londoner remarked. "Rebellion growing out of rebellion; particularly in that seedling-bed and hot-bed of discontent, sedition, riot and rebellion Massachusetts Bay."[59]

However radical their schemes, Shays's men were relatively easily subdued. Before long they met up with General William Shepard's troops in Springfield, where the rebels had hoped to commandeer the state arsenal. Two thousand Shaysites marched on only nine hundred government troops. Reluctant to fire on men who still wore their Patriot uniforms, Shepard ordered his musketmen to hold their fire, and then to fire two shots above their heads. When they kept coming, he ordered a third shot into the center of the column. As one historian described it, "With the fourth or fifth [shot] the movement was suddenly away from the arsenal and nothing Shays could do could rally them. 'Murder!' they cried as they ran. 'Murder!'"[60] In early February it was General Lincoln's turn. After an exhausting march through a snowstorm, Lincoln's private army surprised the Shaysites, who quickly surrendered, pledged their allegiance to the Massachusetts government, and went back to their farms. Daniel Shays escaped to the north and eventually lived out his days in central New York. Other leaders of the rebellion moved on to another frontier, the Ohio River valley.

However brief its duration or sparse its bloodshed, Shays's Rebellion was not disregarded by elite Americans in Massachusetts or anywhere else in the country. To the contrary, venerable revolutionary leaders from Samuel Adams to George Washington were shocked and dismayed by what they heard and read. Mob action had been an effective part of the revolutionary effort, but these leaders had never expected it to continue once the oppression of monarchy had been abolished. Most distressing to them was the impotence of the federal government to suppress the rebellion. The framers of the Acts of Confederation had refused to authorize a national military force because they feared it might be used to take freedoms away from local citizens as the British army had in the 1770s. Now some of the same leaders wondered whether men like Shays might deserve to have freedoms taken from them. Moreover, they wondered whether a stronger centralized government might not be able to regulate the economy so effectively that these kinds of domestic problems would not occur in the first place. To these men—first called Nationalists, then Federalists—Shays's Rebellion showed that it was time to make major changes in the structure of the federal government.

The Constitutional Convention of 1787 proposed these changes and many more. Representatives suggested that the new government print currency, impose taxes, pay any outstanding national debts, over-rule laws passed by state governments, and mount an armed force to put down domestic turmoil. The Constitution, supported by a federal court system as outlined in the Judiciary Act of 1789, declared that the federal government, not the state or local governments, would now be the supreme law of the land. Not surprisingly, the proposed constitution angered all those Americans—including former Shaysites, former Regulators, and many other frontiersmen throughout the country—who advocated local control of economic and political affairs. Between 1787 and 1789, the majority of people in nearly every state that had experienced rural discontent in the past two decades—including Massachusetts, New Hampshire, New York, North Carolina, South Carolina, and Virginia—opposed the new constitution. As Richard Brown has said of Massachusetts, "The debate over the federal Constitution was in some ways an extension of the controversies that had racked Massachusetts so recently and went to the heart of republicanism. Centralization was set against government close to the people. The interests of merchants, manufacturers (including artisans), market-oriented farmers, and creditors seemed in conflict with those of the semi-subsistence upland farmers who had supported [Shays's Rebellion]."[61]

Despite this opposition, the Constitution was eventually ratified and joyfully celebrated in parades and processions throughout the nation. Although originally in the minority, Federalists had gained several strategic advantages in the fight for ratification. First and foremost, they had the support of nearly every important leader of the Revolution. These leaders and their friends likewise had control over major newspapers in every state. Staunch Anti-Federalists tended to be men without wealth or prestige from frontier areas of each state. While they remained steadfast, the wealthier, eastern opponents of the Constitution (perhaps as many as fifty-six) were converted. So were all the opponents of the Constitution who had insisted that a Bill of Rights be attached to the original document. Nothing, however, changed the minds of many settlers in the western United States. If anything, the ratification of the Constitution increased anxieties about federal power and heightened sensitivity to regional and class differences. By 1793, when Washington began his second term, much of the enthusiasm for the new Constitution had abated. Indeed, the domestic disputes between the administration and many former Anti-Federalists were so deep that some feared that the union would not survive.[62]

The most substantial and widespread uprising in early America took place in the political context of a new federal government and the social context of a new frontier. During and after the Revolution, poor farmers, war veterans, and German and Scots-Irish immigrants took their devotion to liberty and suspicion of centralized authority to the trans-Appalachian frontier—those very counties that had been put off limits by the Proclamation of 1763. While life had always been difficult in the backcountry, the terrain of western Pennsylvania, Virginia, Maryland, the Carolinas, and Georgia made this country seem even farther back than most. Visitors were astonished at the settlers' living conditions: hard dirt floors and roofs and filthy blankets on lice-infested beds, when there were beds at all. Moral life too seemed to have dropped to new depths: some Presbyterian ministers refused to provide service in western counties because they feared for their safety. Others reported that parishioners seemed more interested in fighting and drinking on Sundays than in meditating on the nature of their spiritual lives.

If men and women on the frontier had lived difficult and rugged lives, if they had felt removed from centers of power, and if the experiences of isolation had led to social conflict before, then certainly they would face similar situations on the trans-Appalachian frontier. In fact, interregional conflict came to this region as soon as the settlers did and well before the Constitution was ratified. As Daniel Shays was fighting for the rights of small farmers in western Massachusetts, farmers along the western frontier from Pennsylvania to Georgia resisted land laws and taxes imposed by their faraway state governments. After the Constitution was ratified and political and judicial power centralized, however, resisting laws would become a great deal more difficult. Still, their aversion to central government never disappeared. As soon as the Washington administration proved itself more interested in the eastern elite than the western poor, they would be ready to fight.

Americans on the trans-Appalachian frontier shared several concerns. Cardinal among them was protection from Native Americans. As we will see below, rural Euro-Americans and Native Americans had good reason to fear each other. The harshness of life, the cruelty of climate, the endless assaults by whites on tribal lands, and the Native

Americans' occasional acts of retribution created a culture of violence which was unimaginable to Americans living in settled areas. Settlers ardently believed in their right to live where they pleased and in their racial superiority to native peoples. Thus they demanded that their state governments allocate enough money to protect their tiny settlements. Yet it never seemed that these governments did. Quakers in Philadelphia, for example, were especially diffident; the last thing these pacifists wanted to do was facilitate the extermination of Native Americans. The federal government was not much more responsive. When the American government finally sent troops west, as it did to parts of Pennsylvania and Kentucky in 1790, they were short of supplies, munitions, and common sense. The United States Army defeated the western Native Americans at the Battle of Fallen Timbers in 1794. The Treaty of Greenville in 1795 cleared the Appalachian and Ohio country for settlement. But by then the lives of many men, women, and children—Native American and white alike—had been lost in unspeakably horrible ways.

Americans on the trans-Appalachian frontier also worried about their local economies. Many had traveled from Germany, Ireland, and Scotland because speculators had promised that trade was plentiful, meadows bountiful, and their chance for economic autonomy secure. Like others before and after them, they were at once wedded to small producerism and local control of the community, its habits and traditions, and interested in participating in some broader market activities.[63] Neither aspiration turned out to be as easy to realize as they had planned. Predictably, the only bountiful parcels in most of these mountainous regions were held by speculators—including George Washington, as it turned out—and some of them refused to sell to settlers. Leases, of course, were available. As for trade routes, it was laughable in some sections to call the roads routes at all. Carved out of mountainsides or through forests, roads could be impassable six to nine months of the year, and impassable all year if carts were filled with heavy or bulky produce. Settlers on the trans-Appalachian frontier thus met disappointment, frustration, falling standards of living, illness, isolation, and poverty. Worst of all, they had a growing suspicion that no one in the East particularly cared that this was how they lived.

Trans-Appalachian settlers may not have been rich, but they were never without resources. They generated several proposals for regional economic improvement. For example, during and after the Revolution, western leaders pushed the federal government to procure navigation rights on the Mississippi River. For mountain people, particularly in the Ohio Valley, it was much easier to travel west to the mighty Mississippi than to struggle back overland to eastern seaports. In 1780, John Jay set forth to negotiate these rights with Spain but gave up trying almost immediately when it appeared such a proposal might prolong a resolution to the revolutionary crisis.[64] The Washington administration also promised to look into the problem, but decided that western counties would become even more alienated from the nation if they became accustomed to western trade routes. Moreover, western trade would diminish the business of eastern merchants and distributors. It took time, but slowly westerners came to realize that few eastern officials had ever been seriously committed to securing rights to the Mississippi.

A second but related proposal was secession—either from the Union entirely or from each individual state. In the 1780s leaders of western counties in Pennsylvania, Maryland, and North Carolina opened negotiations with rival European powers and British-controlled Canada. British spies planted throughout the region reported that the Union was about to crack into two parts—east and west. More sustained were the attempts by several western sections to be recognized as separate states, as Vermont was in 1791. Westsylavania (western Pennsylvania), Transylvania (western Maryland), Watauga (eastern Kentucky), and Franklin (eastern Tennessee) all demanded, but failed to receive, federal recognition. Eventually the Northwest Ordinance of 1787 resolved the question of when and how future western territories would become states, by ensuring that—with federal institutional support throughout the process—every western territory could eventually become a full-fledged member of the Union. Because it was adopted by the Federalist-dominated legislature, however, even this benign act demonstrated the hegemony of the central government over the settlers' lives. Hundreds of miles away, lawyers, merchants, and their representatives in Congress were setting the agenda for poor men's lives in territories that, as of yet, did not even exist.

Failing all else, the trans-Appalachian frontiersmen knew how to resist. Despite their disadvantaged and isolated lives, they held fast to their belief in liberty and to the tradition of mob action. State governments where they were still underrepresented and a federal government that usually ignored them and sometimes lied to them sparked interregional conflict in the early republic for two decades. The spark turned to flame in 1790 when Congress imposed a ten-cent-per-gallon tax on whisky—the most important product of the trans-Appalachian regional economy—and an additional tax on whisky stills. Resistance to these taxes would bring frontiersmen together, help define a new kind of opposition politics, and force the federal government to decide once and for all the place of mob violence in the American political system.

As Alexander Hamilton saw it, there was nothing wrong with congressionally imposed internal taxes, despite many Americans' pronounced hostility to them and their embarrassing resemblance to Parliament's recent impositions. If all state debts were to be assumed by the federal government and the entire national debt to be paid, the money had to come from somewhere. External taxes like customs duties and import taxes, which most Americans supported, could not pay for everything without restricting trade. Relying solely on external taxes, he feared, would also put an "undue proportion of the public burden on the merchant and on the [large] landholder."[65] Neither did it trouble him that many taxpayers could not vote and thus had no say in the passage of such a bill. Ordinary people without property could not be trusted with the vote, he believed. How much better it would be for the country to put its future in the hands of "inquisitive and enlightened statesmen . . . best qualified to make a judicious selection."[66] Eventually it would be these people—and the manufacturing centers and commercial interests they developed—that would forge the future of the country.

This was not the future small farmers and frontier people imagined, nor was Hamilton, a lawyer and sometime planter from the West Indies, a man they trusted to know anything about their lives. He certainly had no concept of the importance of whisky in Appalachian culture. Whisky was one of the only products that westerners could easily bring to market. Rather than having one or two big manufacturing distilleries, the Appalachian countryside was dotted with hundreds of tiny stills where groups of families cooperatively produced their own supply, which they used for domestic consumption and which they shipped down the Ohio River for sale. They even used whisky as a medium of exchange with day laborers, midwives, and local craftsmen. Moreover, Hamilton's prioritization of the burdens of taxation was exactly the opposite of the settlers'. As Thomas Slaughter has put it, "Opponents of the excise law *wanted* to put a heavier taxation burden on the merchant and the landowner. Because the government seemed to labor primarily for the interest of merchants and speculators, they should pay to finance it."[67] Finally, it seemed to frontiersmen that an internal tax like the one Hamilton had proposed was exactly what the British government had imposed on North America in the 1770s, which, once resisted by the colonists, had led to the use of military force. What was to stop this powerful, centralized, faraway government from doing exactly the same thing?

What indeed? As mob violence grew more and more common and the successful collection of the excise tax grew less and less so, Washington and Hamilton came to believe that only the imposition of troops would force frontiersmen to submit to federal authority. They exaggerated neither the extent nor the radical potential of the insurgency. Tax collectors and court officials including William Graham, Robert Johnson, and John Neville were kidnaped, tortured, and beaten by mobs; Johnson was blindfolded and tied to a tree for five hours. Neville's house and barn were both burned despite the protection of a dozen United States soldiers. Lives on both sides were lost. As months passed, mobs also targeted local merchants, speculators, and manufacturers. As a crowd of over seven thousand gathered to march on Pittsburgh, plunder its homes, and then burn it to the ground, one man rode through town shouting, "This is not all that I want: it is not the excise law only that must go down; your direct and associate judges must go down; your high offices and salaries. A great deal more is to be done; I am but beginning yet."[68]

In hindsight, we know that the beginning of the Whisky Rebellion's most radical period also marked the beginning of its end. In 1793 and 1794 moderates opened negotiations with rebels to try to reach a compromise. Indeed, resolutions had been passed in many rural districts promising that all settlers would "submit to the laws of the United States."[69] Moderate farmers and other citizens throughout Pennsylvania—for rural people were not the only ones who opposed the internal taxation—also organized political clubs called Democratic-Republican societies, through which they hoped to "collect, channel, and formulate public grievances so they would receive a full and sympathetic hearing."[70] But Washington was unaware of the early compromises and anything but sympathetic to these self-created societies. Thus he ordered the army to suppress the rebellion by force. Hearing that violence was spreading to Kentucky, Maryland, North Carolina, and the Ohio Territory and not wishing to wait another year before sending in troops, he ordered the deployment of fifteen thousand militia men. Overrepresented in this force were poor young men from the East who had so little to eat that the rebels soon called it the Watermelon Army. However undisciplined, hungry, sick, and tired the army was, its size alone sent rebels fleeing into the woods and mountains. To the generals' dismay only about twenty leaders of the rebellion were left to be captured. The overwhelming victory did not stop the army from treating their captives cruelly and in a few cases fatally, or from looting, plundering, and disrupting life in general while they supposedly maintained order over the winter months. Under such circumstances, the Whisky Rebels learned no new lessons about the fearful and corrupting power of a centralized government or the best ways to oppose it.

Except perhaps for one. The Democratic-Republican societies were the direct forerunners of political parties, described by Gordon S. Wood as those "impersonal and permanent organizations of professional salaried politicians that were designed solely to recruit leaders, mobilize voters, win elections, and compete regularly and legitimately with other opposition parties, that would mark the new political culture of the nineteenth century."[71] Of course, most members of the first Democratic-Republicans societies did not realize what the long-term impact of their extraconstitutional innovation would be.[72] Like many older leaders—including Hamilton, James Madison, and Washington—they believed that "factions" and competitive elections were unnecessarily disruptive, possibly even dangerous, and certainly only temporary. Even after the War of 1812, Thomas Jefferson still hoped that the final defeat of Federalism would result in the "complete suppression of party."[73] But within a few more years, such younger leaders as Martin Van Buren and Andrew Jackson would embrace the new community life that brought self-interested individuals together in party politics. Organized, loyal opposition could have a positive role in government, they believed. It would not bring disorder out of dissent but the very opposite. Party politics and competitive elections would prevent disorder by guaranteeing organized dissent a place within the political structure.

The election of 1800 ushered in a new administration without bloodshed or the disruption of governance. In one sense, it was a revolution of its own, a major landmark of structural and institutional change in American society. But periods of history are never entirely new but often overlap. So we can also see the election of 1800 as one logical endpoint of the revolutionary process begun in the mid-eighteenth century through which, despite a temporary rest stop to visit classical republicanism and aristocratic federalism, the liberal ideals of democracy, respect for ordinary men, and their private pursuit of happiness won the day. When Thomas Jefferson was inaugurated as president, he ushered in a new era in American culture by appealing to some of the oldest interpretations of the purpose and meaning of the Revolution. His administration honored small producers of all kinds, venerated farmers and rural life, and eventually made hundreds of millions of new acres available for settlers in the West. It shrank the size and the responsibilities of the federal government and by 1803 had abolished both internal taxes and the newly established circuit courts. All but three states granted universal manhood suffrage to whites by 1825.

But Jefferson and his followers did not choose to bring along into the nineteenth century every vestige of rural producer radicalism as it had been expressed in the eighteenth century—and for that reason, among others, the election of 1800 pointed as much to the future as it did to the past. Once all white men were granted the vote and access to a political party, they were to keep their protests off the streets. Throughout the nineteenth century, if any kind of domestic turmoil—interclass, interethnic, interracial, or interregional—ventured outside the structures of partisan politics, it would still be suppressed through the force of the standing federal army. The power of the state did not go away, even if the ordinary man had more rights. By exchanging extralegal strategies for extraconstitutional ones, then, many Americans—and rural Americans in particular—found themselves transformed from "ruffians and knaves" to "God's chosen people"— that is, as long as they played by the rules. Playing by the rules, however, left considerably less room for radicalism—and left rural people and their communities to the powerful men who wrote them.

The experience of insurgent farmers from mid-Maine summarizes the continuities, transformations, and contradictions of the colonial and early national eras. Beginning before the Revolution and continuing in earnest after it, farmers from the central counties of Maine, then a part of Massachusetts, struggled against the economic and political power of the Great Proprietors, rich men who claimed title to the lands and refused to sell it to squatters. Calling themselves Liberty Men and White Indians, settlers terrorized local men associated with the Proprietors, including merchants and court officials. Like the North Carolina Regulators, Massachusetts Shaysites, and Pennsylvania Whisky Rebels, the Maine farmers hated nonproductive citizens and lawyers most of all. Moreover, they insisted on the importance of small production and the corrupting influence of power and aristocracy. They even went so far as to say that any man who lived on land and improved that land ought to have the right to own it. Sporadically, but continually, these evangelical farmers struggled to achieve their version of the Revolution's promise.

In the early 1800s the insurgents from Maine helped to elect a new coalition of political leaders who called themselves Jeffersonians. In their platform, the Jeffersonians supported much of what the rebels had advocated for decades—including the end of state-supported clergy, the end of legal privileges for the elite, and universal manhood suffrage. Like their national counterparts, the new Maine leadership did not shun but instead embraced the settlers and their communities—the very things the Federalists had cared so little for in previous decades. According to Alan Taylor, the Federalists had been "undone by [their] reluctance to stoop to politicking among the common farmers and artisans at the mundane town meeting level, where [they] expected deference as a matter of course."[74] Such arrogance was political suicide. As in much of America, by 1800 the political culture in Maine had shifted drastically. No longer the property of a few educated lawyers or wealthy merchants, American government appeared to be in the hands of thousands of ordinary voters in ordinary towns.

But just because the Jeffersonians claimed to be the mid-Maine "settler's friend" did not mean that they themselves were, ever had been, or even wanted to be settlers. Like the wealthy planter Thomas Jefferson himself, they were far from any such occupation. Most of Maine's new leadership was merely a younger and more politically astute version of the old—doctors, shopkeepers, manufacturers, and large property owners. Some had even worked for the Federalist Great Proprietors. They also shared their opponents' commercial ambitions. Thus when the Jeffersonian leadership enacted the 1808 Betterment Act, forcing proprietors to sell their land but not below a fair market value and denying the claims of squatters, they protected both the proprietors and the more well-to-do settlers. Squatters who could not pay were evicted or chose to move on to another frontier. Thus in one fell swoop Jeffersonians remained committed at once to the rights of private property—even large holdings of private property—and to the ideal of the small farmer, but not to the most radical aspects of the producerist vision.[75]

As Maine went, so went the nation—at least to a certain extent. Pieces of legislation similar to Maine's Betterment Act were written in Kentucky and Tennessee. Land-reform acts were passed in Pennsylvania and, after more violence in the 1830s and 1840s, in New York. At the same time, however, Jeffersonian legislators tightened rules against squatters and organizers of extralegal protest. It was no longer necessary for people to see distinctions between rulers and ruled, they argued, as the "settlers' friends" were now in charge of government. Thus while Jeffersonian leaders would significantly advance the positions of small farmers, they would also deny the possibility for continuing radicalism in the patterns rural people had used for decades. When frontier rebels accepted a role inside the political process, they gave up their ability to protest outside it. And for this, all elites in America—the vanquished Federalists included—owed the Jeffersonian politicians "a debt of gratitude."[76]

And there was more. Despite its veneration of agrarianism and producerism, Jeffersonian politics also set the stage for a time when small producers would again feel isolated from and exploited by great men and faraway governments and would seek new forms of radical protest. By advocating the rights of property, the importance of self-interest, and the goal of material progress, Jeffersonians helped to establish what Pauline Maier calls a "new social order [wherein] property was to be widely distributed through a population of respectable 'independent' men; people of all ranks would be literate and informed, and a man's status would be determined by not wealth or parentage but individual merit."[77] They established, in other words, a liberal political culture within a capitalist economy. However familiar it might have initially seemed, such a culture ultimately promoted some values at odds with traditional rural life and small production—including unregulated competition, fragmentation of family and community life, and unrestrained individualism. According to Steven Watts it did not take long for the "the idealized figure of the independent republican producer [to] change shape into the striving self-made man," for the hero Daniel Boone to be replaced by the hero Andrew

Carnegie.[78] This shift would be a sharp break from both of the competing ideals of the eighteenth century: the Federalist vision of virtue and aristocracy, as well as the producerist vision of small, limited production, local control, and communal values. Jeffersonianism, in short, established many of the preconditions necessary for the transition to industrial capitalism.

So perhaps it was not Thomas Jefferson who had stood for the common man after all, but another man of the early nineteenth century, Andrew Jackson. While Jefferson had written about the yeomanry from the comfort and splendor of Monticello, Jackson had purportedly been born in a log cabin and had fearlessly fought Native Americans on the frontier. His political principles flowed from his association with rural producer radicalism—and indeed presaged many principles of the Populist movement of the 1890s. He linked farmers and workers as equals in the nation's productive life. Together, he argued, all workers were not just a class but actually the "bone and sinew of our country."[79] And he put his money where his mouth was. Jackson argued against monopolies; he fought with all his fiery will against the all-powerful Second Bank of the United States; he fought to keep western lands open to settlement, no matter the cost in life, liberty, or property to its indigenous inhabitants. By the late 1840s Jackson's vision would carry the Democratic Party from sea to shining sea, under the mantle of Manifest Destiny and the dream that ordinary (white) Americans might soon farm and work in every corner of the land.

But there were as many cracks in Jackson's log cabin as there had been in Jefferson's mansion, as it turned out. To begin with, Jackson's insistence on white equality sometimes served—despite his best efforts to the contrary—to further the dominance of the wealthy. Without a regulated national bank, for example, thousands of small banks rose up to provide services or disservices to settlers at their leisure. Likewise, as Alexander Saxton has shown, many of Jackson's common men were hardly common at all but were typical early-nineteenth-century "men on the make"—small businessmen, entrepreneurs, manufacturers, and wealthy southern planters.[80] Moreover, nothing could stop the burgeoning growth of cities and manufacturing in the 1830s and 1840s and the transformations of workplace, family, and leisure which ensued. In the end, the egalitarian democracy Jackson represented would founder on the shoals of its many contradictions, and on its support for slavery most of all. Northern and southern yeomen alike believed in the natural inferiority of Native Americans and African Americans. But some northerners also ardently believed in the free labor system, the one that helped many hired hands as well as tenant farmers to move up what was commonly called the agricultural ladder of success.[81] Before long, rural men in the North would come to see that the spread of slavery—just or unjust as the case may be—would fatally challenge free labor. These men would find a new rebel to vote for, one who really had been born in a log cabin. Then those who had joined together in the antiaristocratic army of Jacksonianism would face one another on the killing fields of the Civil War.

"A tongue of flame sat upon every man":

RURAL PRODUCER RADICALISM IN THE INDUSTRIAL ERA

When, in the midst of war, the United States Congress passed the Homestead Act in 1862 and opened up much of the Midwest, Great Plains, and Southwest for settlement, it set the stage for both the largest frontier migration in United States history and one of the most dramatic expansions of agricultural production in the world. Between 1870 and 1900 the number of farms in every region of the United States increased. Overall, the number of farms more than doubled, jumping from 2.7 million to 5.7 million. So did the numbers of acres of land in farms and the total value of farm property. More land was privately purchased and improved between 1870 and 1900 as had been privately purchased and improved in all the years between the European colonization of North America and the Civil War.[82] So huge was the growth in the Great Plains and Northwest that in 1889 six new western states entered the Union—more than at any one time since the Revolution. Even in the devastated South, economic progress was swift. Production of cotton expanded throughout the former Confederacy, increasing from four million bales to ten million bales in less than thirty years.[83]

But ironically, when this tremendous, multiregional expansion of agriculture began, the age of the farmer was already rapidly slipping away. In fact, conditions of life in the nation in 1865 were staggeringly different from what they had been in the time of Jefferson and Jackson, so recently passed. Some changes stemmed in small or large part from the division of the Union and the dawn of the bloody Civil War. Between 1861 and 1865 thousands of rural men and boys left the homes and communities where their families had lived for generations and never returned. This tragedy had an immediate impact on agricultural productivity and also had long-term effects on the distribution of the rural population. In the South, farms were ruined and families made homeless; poor white farmers who survived the devastation looked to Texas and Kansas to begin their lives anew. So did freed slaves whose dreams of "forty acres and a mule" would soon be replaced by a social oppression that was the moral equivalent of slavery. In the North, rural boys and men who went to war also experienced more of the world and its grim realities than they had ever planned. Some used these experiences as opportunities to migrate to places they had seen or heard about. Others migrated not because they wanted to keep marching but because they couldn't stop. Life would never get back to normal for them or for anybody else who lived in the United States.

But the Civil War accentuated and accelerated changes in American society other than the geographic distribution of its rural population. It also hastened economic, political, and cultural changes whose roots, as we have seen, lay in antebellum society but whose branches would now directly challenge the viability of small producerism. The postbellum era would bring new organizational structures to business, politics, and government. It would lead even more people to the nation's cities than to its farms, and it would encourage them to think about themselves and their futures in ways altogether foreign to rural ways of life. None of these changes, however, would escape the view of those Americans who still held fast to the dream of small production and local control. The changes would instead propel farmers—male and female—to seek out new ways to make their dreams come true. Moreover, the changes would encourage them to choose a strategy linking the futures of black and white and farmer and laborer together. At the intersection between urbanization, industrialization, and bureaucratization and a burgeoning and shifting agricultural population came the most widespread, articulate, and inclusive rural radical movement in the history of the United States.

Chief among all the challenges faced by farmers in the postbellum era was the consolidation of industrial capitalism. Most rural people in the United States had never been entirely self-sufficient, that is, without some rudimentary links to the market or cash economy. On the other hand, many had long been opposed to "bigness," the corruption that came with too much land, too much wealth (especially from non-productive labor), and too much political influence. And they had resisted all kinds of dependencies with their lives. Nevertheless, as early as the mid-eighteenth century, parts of the rural East and its people also served as a staging ground for the transformation of premodern capitalism to industrial capitalism, which was encouraged by Jeffersonian and Jacksonian liberal economics. In the same years that mid-Maine farmers fought for land from the Great Proprietors, they also began sending their daughters to work in the new textile mills in Lynn and Lowell, Massachusetts. Eastern Massachusetts farmers who may have sympathized with the western Shaysites took in piecework for shoemakers, hatmakers, and weavers. Even the cantankerous Whisky Rebels in Pennsylvania read, and perhaps answered, recruiting advertisements from a large manufacturer in Delaware. In this way, many farmers in the East were already both "in" and "of" the marketplace by 1800.[84]

The East was the vanguard of industrialization in rural America, of course. Because economic development never happens all at once, many pockets of the Far West, Midwest, and South remained immune to industrialization until mid-century. Some pockets in Appalachia may have even maintained a precapitalist economy of domestic consumption and barter. Nevertheless, between 1865 and 1900 the transition of the American economy to an advanced, centralized, and state-supported industrial-capitalist system was completed in every region—from the arid Great Plains of the West to the humid bayous of the former Confederacy. This meant that just as Americans on the frontier, freed slaves, and poor southern whites thought that they were beginning lives of economic independence, they became surrounded by what Patricia Nelson Limerick calls the new dependencies of the industrial era.[85]

Some of these dependencies came in unexpected packaging. For example, when the Republican Congress opened up many acres of the public domain to pioneer settlement in 1862, it also passed the Pacific Railroad Act, which provided hundreds of millions of acres of better land and substantial government loans to railroad corporations. Pioneers who could afford to bought land from the railroads instead of the government. But railroads also held monopolies on the transportation of their crops. Farmers in the West and South also became dependent on banks and furnishing merchants to finance seed, implements, and domestic goods. Some freedmen leased the same lands they had tilled as slaves and "shared" their crops with the same men who had owned them. All creditors pressured farmers to plant as much of their land in market crops as possible and as little in the traditional "safety first" crops grown exclusively for domestic consumption. To do so, however, required farmers to purchase even more domestic products from the merchant.

New labor-saving technologies complicated the postbellum farmer's autonomy as well. One hundred and sixty acres—the typical size of a homestead grant—quickly proved to be too small a plot to farm successfully in most of the West. As soon as possible, pioneer farmers bought more land either on credit or through the Timber Culture Act or the Desert Land Act. More land was more easily worked with horse-drawn machinery like the self-binding reaper and header, and in some places, the steam-powered thresher. These machines increased production but they did not contribute to an atmosphere of pastoral agrarianism. One Kansas observer thought that with the new technology his "vast farming region has more the appearance of an enormous manufacturing center than a quiet, unobtrusive, unparalleled grain-raising community."[86] Expensive machinery also required expensive financing, as did irrigation equipment in the Far West and new fertilizers introduced in the Old South. Increasingly, credit problems cost farmers both the ideal and the reality of autonomy. Tenancy—as feared as ever by small producers—increased in every region between 1870 and 1900. So did the number of former agriculturists employed in wage labor or extractive industry. Collapsing farm prices— common enough in the emerging global marketplace where speculators bought and sold crops as commodities—pushed many farm families to the brink of starvation.

American political culture also changed in the wake of the Civil War. By 1840 the partisan politics that Anti-Federalists had helped to fashion had thoroughly captured the political imagination of white men in America. In fact, in a time of increasing mobility and urbanization, political parties served as new kinds of collective communities. As a result, nineteenth-century men were not interested in politics only at election time as they are today—if they still are at all. They considered partisan politics to be part of their personal identities and part of the ongoing civic culture of their communities. Huge percentages of eligible Americans voted in the smallest local and the largest national contests. Moreover, the location of most political activity moved from indoors, the traditional location of the elite, to out-of-doors, the traditional location of the people, thus incorporating that space within the political structure. Lavish parades, festivals, songs, and pageants accompanied the electoral process. Millions of Americans including Native Americans, Asian Americans, African Americans, and women were still disenfranchised, of course, and their disenfranchisement still upheld the independence of white men. Nevertheless, as Michael McGerr notes, "American politics from roughly the 'thirties to the 'nineties demanded the legitimacy conferred by all classes of the people."[87] Governance by a few wealthy aristocrats who thought that they knew best for all the rest was the politics of the past, as far as nineteenth-century men were concerned.

The war did not change the fervor with which men participated in politics but it did change the reasons why they felt allegiance to their parties. In the 1830s and 1840s men essentially voted with their pocketbooks: those who associated themselves with the needs of small producers, including farmers and urban artisans, voted with Jackson or, after 1840 in the North, with the Whigs. Those associated with large business voted decidedly Republican. The war that broke so many bodies also crushed these economically and ideologically based political divisions. Between 1860 and 1880 seven of the eight major voting blocks in the North and South "waved the bloody shirt" with their ballots.[88] Although voters in the Far West were somewhat less partisan in their voting patterns, for a quarter of a century after the Civil War the Solid South and Republican North could not be broken by interregional economic or political issues. As late as 1892, an Alabama congressman who dared to change his party allegiance remarked, "My own father would not hear me speak and said he would rather make my coffin with his own hands and bury me than to have me desert the Democratic Party."[89] In time, many would come together and vow to "join hands against a common foe . . . without regret for the past or fear for the future."[90] Such a feat would be anything but easy, however.

The form and function of the government also began to change in these years, as it mirrored the emerging centralization and subsequent fragmentation and bureaucratization of the modern corporation. We often locate the origin of the modern bureaucratic state in the Progressive Era or the New Deal, but in fact the modern state was beginning its work in the 1870s by increasing its capacities, fragmenting its organizational style, and relying on a new class of white-collared experts and professionals. Just as rural areas had been the staging grounds for industrial capitalism, so did they (particularly in the West) become what Richard White calls the "kindergarten[s] of the American state."[91] In the last three decades of the nineteenth century, the federal government expanded its power in land reclamation, irrigation, public education, Native American affairs, scientific agriculture, and forest management. Likewise, it created new centralized bureaucracies, staffed not by the political cronies of the Jacksonian era but by civil servants, professional government workers. Desperately in need of capital for development and practical information for survival, Americans on the frontier did not turn the government away. Instead, they began to imagine that they could potentially refashion the federal government into something they could recognize, something that would directly serve their interests and ideals. Until it did, however, they would continue to fear federal control of local affairs and scorn the intrusion of outsiders in their business.

Finally, between the end of the Civil War and the dawn of World War I, the dominant outlook of most Americans shifted from production to consumption. Again, this was not a trend that came out of the blue, or one in which rural people had not participated. Part of the currency crisis that led the United States into economic depression during and after the Revolutionary War was caused by the spending spree that Americans—settlers among them—went on to satisfy their pent-up demand for consumer products.[92] In fact, there is evidence that ordinary colonists sought luxury items like fine china and fancy linens from Great Britain by the end of the seventeenth century. But after the Revolution, especially, farmers used consumption patterns as a way of demonstrating their status in the emerging American middle class.[93] Late-eighteenth-century farmers' daughters increasingly understood the importance of including store-bought goods in their hope chests; farmers' sons understood the importance of obtaining manufactured implements for their farms. These needs and desires increased in the antebellum North as access to mass-produced goods improved. Pioneer families of the 1840s and 1850s set out on their overland journeys to California and Oregon in wagons overloaded with furniture, bedding, and clothing that their parents and grandparents would not even have imagined owning.

But a culture dedicated to consumption is more than a society of men and women who enjoy consumer products. It is one that begins to judge individual worth in terms of possessions and material goods rather than of work products. And this shift—among the most important in American history—took place first in the burgeoning cities of the nation in the late nineteenth century, not on its farms. As Robert McMath has put it, in the late nineteenth century farmers understood farming to be "more than a way of making money; it was still a way of life."[94] Before the violent conflicts of the 1870s, 1880s, and 1890s, many urban artisans felt the same way and fought for the rights of workers to own the wealth that their labor created. But as the century wore on, the vacuum that meaningful work had occupied was increasingly filled with the activities of consumption: shopping, fashion, amusements, shows, professional sports, vaudeville. Urban and rural reformers and political organizers decried this trend, but to no avail. Like the children of immigrants, the children of farmers could see with their own eyes (thanks to the mass distribution of magazines, catalogs, and novels) that urban life was more exciting and more colorful than rural life. Backcountry people thus increasingly felt, as David Danbom puts it, "that the nation was passing [them] by, leaving [them] behind, ignoring [them] at best and derogating [them] at worst."[95]

Despite these changes and perhaps because of them too, rural people held more steadfastly to the dream of producerism in the late nineteenth century than they ever had before. When northerners traveled west, for example, they responded not only to the promise of free land but also to the corresponding vow of free labor. New Englanders on failing soil and sons of Ohio who had to move on believed that in the West it was still possible to be one's own boss, to control the affairs of the local community, and to maintain the age-old habits of mutuality associated with agrarian life. To the astonishment of some observers, this dream was strong enough to bring millions of immigrants from Europe as well. Swedes and Norwegians whose land could not sustain another generation; Germans in Russia experiencing persecution; Czechs, Bohemians, and Irishmen whose peasant villages were filled with the warmth of tradition and the cold of famine—all sent favorite sons and daughters to the American West. No matter where they hailed from, however, the new frontiersmen carried with them the same fervent desire for economic autonomy and personal liberty which had propelled British subjects into the wilderness two hundred years earlier.

The dream of rural producer radicalism survived the desolation of war in the American South as well—indeed it stretched its meaning to include many who had been disenfranchised before. For African American freedmen, the period between 1865 and 1890 was among the only times in African American history that such dreaming would be possible. On the Sea Islands off Georgia, for example, Union troops divided plantation lands among former slaves and watched as they learned to manage their own farms. Elsewhere, freedmen set up small farms and, with the arduous labors of their wives and many children, sometimes earned enough to profit from them. But African Americans did not seek simply to imitate white economic culture. Indeed, evidence suggests that freed slaves were more cautious and conservative about "safety first" agriculture, when they could afford to be, than whites were. Moreover, they maintained different crops, different management styles, and different leisure activities associated with the farm. Some of these, when seen through the eyes of whites, would be called lazy and used to demonstrate the futility of allowing African Americans economic or political independence. Nevertheless, some African Americans prospered and many learned to survive from year to year by conjoining producerist ideals and autonomous cultural patterns and traditions.

Whites in the Old South who did not own plantations were also determined to labor on the soil—despite the very small, even tiny size of their holdings. Eventually some would move to Texas and Kansas to find new lands. Those who stayed behind worked harder than ever to maintain productivity on their homesteads. Many switched all their acreage to production of King Cotton and gave up the safety net of self-sufficiency. In the Carolinas a new king was born of blue-flue tobacco. But surviving the economic turmoil of the period would prove nearly as difficult for small farmers in the South—sometimes called the "devastated generation"—as surviving the war had been. In time they would wonder whose lot in life they really shared—that of small farmers in other regions and even of different races, or that of the wealthy Democratic planters and politicians who seemed to have utterly forgotten them and their sacrifices.

None of these rural people—westerners, southerners, blacks, whites, Yankees, or Europeans—expected rural life to be easy. And after a few years, nearly all knew they had been right. The harsh plains environment taught new survival lessons by brute force: how to clean a house made of dirt; how to reach the barn in a blizzard and avoid freezing to death yards from shelter; how to clean grasshoppers inches deep from floors, cupboards, fields, and wells; how to endure illness, accident, and childbirth miles from medical care; how to maintain sanity in a one-room house with no trees, no water, and no neighbors anywhere in sight. In the South, drought, prairie fires, boll-weevil infestations, and unexpectedly early frosts could also mean the difference between food on the table or another year of hunger. Sometimes, when times were at their worst, farmers humbled themselves and requested aid from their local and state governments. Usually they were turned down by officials like Minnesota's Governor John Pillsbury, who worried that if he provided more than five dollars to a starving family of nine who had lost three years of crops to grasshoppers, they would be reduced to "habitual beggary" and "confirmed mendicancy."[96]

As devastating as these natural disasters were and as much as rural people hoped that the government would help them, hard times were not by themselves sufficient cause for radicalism. Like Pillsbury, many rural people also felt that poverty was the result of personal failure like a lack of planning or enough hard work.[97] For generations farmers had faced natural disasters of one kind or another and carried on in the hope that "next year" would be better. The kinds of disasters that rural people did not agree simply to endure were the peculiar economic problems of their time. These problems—a shortage of currency, a high rate of credit, a grossly inequitable system of rates on transcontinental railroads, the monopolization of industry, and the corruption of political parties—were anything but acts of God. They were, more and more farmers came to believe, the deliberate acts of greedy men, aided by an unresponsive and undemocratic government that had lost its concern for small producers. Before long, farmers in all sections would rise together to fight these man-made plagues and create an upheaval that, as one observer described it in 1890, could "hardly be diagnosed as a political campaign. It was a religious revival, a crusade . . . in which a tongue of flame sat upon every man, and each spake as the spirit gave him utterance."[98]

The Populist movement was more than a political campaign, that much is certain. When it began it had little to do with institutionalized politics and a great deal to do with the anger and courage of ordinary men and women who had suffered too much for too long at the hands of wealthy men they had never met. These leaders combined common-sense economics with a vision of truly democratic politics to spark a cyclone of activity, education, and recruitment. As Lawrence Goodwyn has put it, Populism was a "spirit of egalitarian hope expressed . . . not in the prose of a platform, however creative, and not ultimately even in a third party, but in a self-generated culture of collective dignity and individual longing."[99] Indeed, by the time the Populist movement waged a conventional political campaign within the two-party system in 1896, it had lost much of its initial radicalism. Nevertheless, the broad-based organizing strategies and nationwide programs developed by the Populists could never have been sustained—or even imagined—in the isolated settlements of colonial and revolutionary America.

In spite of all the things farmers were afraid they had lost to industrialization and modernization, they had gained some new resources that allowed them to work outside the two-party system but still on a nationwide scale. First and foremost, they had the voluntary association, a mainstay of American civic culture in the nineteenth century which brought isolated communities together through national organizations. Even in rural communities where neighbors customarily helped one another in the time-honored habits of mutuality, voluntarism thrived. Churches, schools, literary societies, secret clubs, and philanthropic organizations all brought self-interested Americans of the nineteenth century together in a new kind of community life. Every small town in the South and West was full of voluntary organizations like these. Webster, South Dakota, for example, whose population reached only a few thousand in the early twentieth century, hosted the Odd Fellows, Woodmen, Knights of Pythias, Catholic Order of Foresters, Royal Neighbors, and A.O.U.W.[100]

Closely related to the growth of voluntary associations was the changing roles of women within the workplace and family. In urban areas where work and family life had become distinct, the ideology of separate spheres for men and women suggested to middle-class white women that their abilities, duties, and desires were also unique, defined by their capacity to nurture others and to understand moral issues with clarity. This role did not make women unimportant, however. Within the conventions of separate spheres women were free to acquire more education, to become more involved in their churches, and even to form associations with distinctly political orientations. Some urban women followed the logic of separate spheres all the way to radical abolitionism and feminism. In this way, the bonds of womanhood both kept women separate from and inherently unequal to men and also empowered women to achieve distinctly political acts of sisterhood.[101]

The lives of nineteenth-century rural women were very different from those of urban women. As a very practical matter, they did not have, as Nancy Grey Osterud reveals, a separate sphere. They did not tend the home while men went to work in a factory or office or shop. They worked with men, sometimes even in the barns and fields with men, in a family-based business. Moreover, they were productive on their own terms, not only reproducing and training the farm's work force but also growing vegetables, selling dairy products, and running chicken and egg operations. Off the farm as well they sought to enact cross-gendered activities and to empower themselves through community-based habits of mutuality and reciprocity. At quilting bees, barn-raisings, and a host of other activities, rural women linked families and communities together and encouraged menfolk to do the same. Of course, they still did not own the value of their labor. Nevertheless, they actively pursued more egalitarianism within their activities.[102] And yet the ideology of a separate sphere did not escape them entirely, especially by the end of the century. Rural women, too, formed voluntary associations at their churches and in their neighborhoods. Some were affiliated with men's groups, where they influenced men's activities, and some sought change strictly through a woman's perspective.

The first organizations that tried to modify the economic problems of the industrial age in rural America took the form of voluntary organizations that mimicked women's habits of mutuality and that included women and women's interests within their frameworks. The Patrons of Husbandry (more commonly referred to as the Grange) was founded in Ohio and Missouri in 1867 by Oliver Hudson Kelly as a social and educational club for farmers and their families whose lives were isolated and perhaps even a little bit dull. Kelly himself was a thirty-second-degree Mason, and it was in the Masonic tradition that he organized the club, leaving his job to recruit across the countryside. The growth in membership was slow, but the format was sure. As Kelly saw it, the Grange would have a men's and a women's division, have four ranks within each local division, and two more at the state and national levels. It would maintain secret initiation rites, rituals, and memberships. Its agenda would include monthly meetings, lectures on agricultural improvement, and picnics hosted by a women's auxiliary.

In many ways, however, women's lives were not merely auxiliary to the Grange's agenda. An early Grange credo read, "Woman was intended by our Creator to be the help meet, companion, and equal of man—the perfecting half added to his hemisphere—thus completing the fully globed orb of our common humanity."[103] In 1893 the national headquarters of the Grange would announce what many state Granges had years earlier—that it was in full support of women's suffrage. Women and men who worked together on the farm were among the first to believe that they ought to vote together at the polls.

During the depression of 1873 the membership of the Grange began to accelerate—there were one and half million members by 1874—and its agenda began to include prescriptions for economic change. Reform of the railroads in particular came into its sights. Grangers complained that railroads had monopolies on their business, charged exorbitant rates, and charged the highest rates of all to farmers west of the Mississippi. Because railroads charged more per mile to westerners than to easterners, farmers in the West suffered simply because they lived in the West—where it was hard enough to live anyway. In 1890 it cost farmers as much to ship from Fargo, North Dakota, to Minneapolis as it did to ship from Minneapolis all the way to New York City. Likewise, farmers had to pay mileage to the farthest eastern point on the line, whether or not that was their destination. Other corporations, including creameries, processors, and banks, had comparable strangleholds on small producers and took huge bites from the profits the farmers saw as rightfully their own.

Grangers also complained about another vexing problem in rural America—the shortage of currency. Between 1865 and 1890 the supply of money in circulation in the United States remained the same, despite the increasing population and burgeoning business activity. The declining money supply meant that each dollar was worth more, and thus it became increasingly expensive for farmers to pay off their debts. A farmer who borrowed a thousand dollars in 1865 at 10-percent interest would have to pay back the equivalent of a hundred bushels of wheat. By 1880 he would have to produce twice as much to pay the same bill. And, like railroad rates, westerners paid higher interest rates than easterners did. In currency matters as in all economic affairs of the

This 1873 lithograph, "Gift for the Grangers," reveals both the interest of Grangers in agrarian production and their commitment to farm women.
Courtesy of the Library of Congress.

era, one historian notes that "the farmers' stick had two short ends."[104] Grangers, like the members of the Greenback Party—a third party organized in the 1870s—encouraged the government to increase the supply of money either by returning to a bimetallic money system or by printing more paper money.

Antirailroad and soft-money factions existed as minorities in both major parties, but in a voluntary organization like the Grange, Republicans and Democrats found that they could come together and increase their influence. They succeeded in getting some regulation of the railroads when the Supreme Court upheld so-called Granger laws in *Munn v. Illinois* in 1876. Despite a reversal in *Wabash v. Illinois* in 1886, the Interstate Commerce Act of 1887 made railroad regulation a lasting item on the American public-policy agenda. In the area of currency, however, the Grangers and their allies had significantly less success. When supplies of silver became scarce in 1873, the bimetallic money system was changed to a gold standard. But soon thereafter, much more silver became available through strikes in the Rocky Mountains and the Southwest. Still, wealthy businessmen and some urban laborers were resistant to increasing the money supply in any way. Not until 1890 would the Sherman Silver Purchase Act permit purchases of silver, and then only in very limited quantities. Meanwhile, the farm economy improved somewhat and most Grangers returned to the organization's social agenda. It would remain to another voluntary organization to bring farmers together in a sustained, nationwide, political program.

That organization was the Farmers' Alliance, begun in Texas in the mid-1880s when a severe drought and plummeting crop prices brought hard times back with a vengeance. A nonpartisan organization for a "farmer, farm laborer, a country mechanic, a country merchant, a country school teacher, a country physician, or a minister of the gospel," the Farmers' Alliance took on more than the railroads and developed into more than a club.[105] It became a radical political organization dedicated to changing the direction of American capitalism toward sustained, cooperative producerism. Southern leaders Charles Macune and S. O. Daws focused on a host of economic problems, including railroad rates, credit rates, the monopolization of markets for their goods, and the high prices charged to them by retailers. Borrowing ideas and strategies from earlier organizations including the Agricultural Wheel and the Grange, they preached cooperation among farmers to overcome what Daws called the encroachments of monopolies.[106] Soon Texas farmers began to do just that, by purchasing, selling, and distributing credit in their cooperative, nonprofit organization. Looking forward to the day when he too might be able to walk right past the local merchant's store, one Nebraska farmer wrote, "We'll have an Alliance Store too, at Hayes Center and back these merchants off the track. You just wait till we control things and we'll make you town leaders hump yourselves."[107]

"Alliance" was a good title for the new group, because it demonstrated the broad and inclusive attitude of its founders. As they were in the Grange, women were included in the Populist movement, and their experiences with community and kinship networking were reflected in the language of cooperation and reciprocity which defined the organization. Populists supported women's suffrage; many women were among its best-known and farthest-traveled leaders. Likewise, although whites debated over and over whether African American farmers should be allowed membership in white alliances, no one debated whether they should become part of the movement. Indeed, white recruiters were sent into African American communities to stress the commonality of economic problems which white and African American farmers faced. The most radical believed that class interests transcended racial interests. In the end, African American farmers formed segregated "colored alliances." The fact that they existed at all, however, demonstrated the inclusiveness of Populism as well as the continuing relevance of radical producerism to freedmen and their children.

Ultimately Populists would also try to make alliances with industrial workers. Although their difference of opinion over free coinage of silver would make it difficult, the reality of a farmer-labor alliance seemed possible for a time. Populists believed that farm workers and industrial workers were caught in the same trap of exploitation and underrepresentation. They also did not necessarily equate rural with agrarian and urban with industrial work. There were, after all, burgeoning centers of industrial and especially extractive industry in both the West and South. The Knights of Labor recognized the importance of rural industry to their organization in the 1870s and 1880s. In the 1890s the Western Federation of Miners (WFM) would become one of the most radical unions in the country. Like farmers, miners were isolated from centers of economic and political power, and they did the most dangerous and difficult work in America. The WFM organized first to empower workers, and then to protect them. For example, the WFM created a network of union-supported, community-operated hospitals. They also attempted to negotiate issues of health and safety with corporations. To Populists, the twin ideals of workplace democracy and radical producerism were no different from the egalitarian and cooperative commonwealth for which they were struggling already.

After the St. Louis convention of 1889, which formally brought the northern and southern halves of the Alliance together, Populist leaders took on a specifically political, third-party agenda. They recruited new members, entered Alliance candidates in local, state, and national elections, and conceived of national programs. One of the most radical of these proposals was the subtreasury plan, whereby the federal government would buy farmers' crops and store them until the price was high, thus taking the middleman's profit out of the marketing process. This was one of the first articulations of an agricultural program whereby the federal government would essentially act as a low-cost lender to farmers and take away potential profits from large corporations. Equally original were the recommendations for a graduated income tax, a ban on land speculation, and the nationalization of the railroads. With leaders such as Ignatius Donnelly of Minnesota, Tom Watson of Georgia, and Mary Lease of Kansas, Populists also began to reimagine a political process that would be more responsive to the people. Direct election of senators and the initiative and referendum were two ways by which they believed the people's voices might better be heard and the party bosses', so often influenced by businesses and wealthy contributors, might be silenced.

Ironically, as the Populists sought to remake democratic politics, they also relied on its favorite out-of-doors rituals. It was difficult, terrible even, for some Populists to leave their political parties. Saying goodby to the party of their fathers, however, did not mean giving up the power or pleasure of partisanship. As they campaigned for state offices, Congress, and the presidency, Populists inherited the ability to organize politically and to make politics meaningful at the local level.[108] In small towns and country fields, the rituals of conventional nineteenth-century politics were used in an attempt to overthrow what was left of conventional nineteenth-century politics. Speeches, parades, rituals, bands, glee clubs, picnics, orations, fireworks, banners, and unrestrained references to Thomas Jefferson, Andrew Jackson, Abraham Lincoln, the Declaration of Independence, the United States Constitution, and the

Bible all evoked an older style of political community among people who believed—no, they knew—that they could think and vote and imagine a new day for America and help make it come true.

The rhetoric and ritual of the People's Party was powerful but its political success was short-lived. James Weaver won more than a million votes in his bid for the presidency in 1892, but nearly all of them came from voters in a handful of western states. In many of the same ways familiar to us today, third-party candidacies in the late nineteenth century were limited by the structures of politics as usual. Thus some Populist leaders reluctantly came to believe that only fusion with a major political party would bring long-term success. In 1896 the Populists endorsed the candidacies of Democrat William Jennings Bryan for president and Populist Tom Watson of Georgia for vice president. While Watson stayed in the South, Bryan crisscrossed the Midwest by train traveling thirteen thousand miles and giving four hundred speeches. He warned crowds at every stop of the "cross of gold" upon which they were nailed. He also advocated the public ownership of the railroads, the free coinage of silver, the direct election of senators, and the imposition of a graduated income tax. But most of all he reminded rural voters of the eternal importance of farming and the high moral character of all producers. As Bryan told it, "There are but two sides in the conflict that is being waged in this country today. On the one side are the allied hosts of monopolies, the money power, great trusts and railroad corporations. . . . On the other are the farmers, laborers, merchants, and all other people who produce wealth and bear the burdens of taxation. . . . Between these two there is no middle ground."[109]

Meanwhile, William McKinley sat on his back porch entertaining the press and giving interviews to prominent party leaders. He traveled nowhere, gave few speeches, and left most of the public-relations work to his assistant, Mark Hanna. When McKinley was elected, with a majority of 600,000 popular votes and nearly a hundred electoral votes, many observers believed that the distance between producer radicalism and industrial capitalism as well as that between participatory politics and modern consumer politics was measured by the miles between Bryan's train and McKinley's porch. Truth be told, however, the most radical of the Populists' ideals had been abandoned at the moment when the Alliance supporters had chosen to fuse with the Democrats. Democratic Party regulars and officials—even ordinary voters—cared a great deal more about the free-silver issue than they did about the trans-

formative vision of an egalitarian and inclusive cooperative commonwealth. Thus the election was never really about the Populists' broader
vision for America. In 1896 modern politics prevailed, as the modern industrial system had already. For another century the impact of the dual
victories would be felt throughout rural America.

"Treat the banker like a chicken thief.
Shoot him on sight":

RURAL PRODUCER RADICALISM IN THE AGE OF REFORM

Most historians, whether they admire the Populists or not, have agreed
that when the Populists met defeat in the 1896 election rural producer
radicalism also came to an end. After that, they imply, farmers abandoned their dream of an egalitarian, cooperative, and participatory
democracy and, like so many other Americans, settled for the waxy and
tasteless fruits of prosperity, consumption, and passive partnership in
politics. Rather than visionaries, farm leaders became lobbyists, advocates for an interest group that benefited from the expansion of the liberal state in the Progressive, New Deal, and the Great Society eras.
Individual farmers, likewise, became comfortable beneficiaries of the welfare state. By creating a compromise with modern liberalism, then, farmers admitted that they no longer dreamed of transforming American
culture and society. All they wanted was to get the biggest possible share
of the burgeoning federal pie. The metamorphosis was so complete that
most farmers today can no longer even imagine the radically different
America that their great grandparents believed was so close at hand.[110]

Although fusion with the Democratic Party weakened rural producer radicalism considerably, reports of its demise were premature.
The persistent hostility of farmers to the Department of Agriculture,
the renewed calls for an overhaul in farm-subsidy programs, the recur-
rent threats of farmers to vote out the very system that supported
them, and the growing hostility of all rural people to anything to do
with the federal government suggest that some part of the transformative pact between liberal America and the farm belt did not take root.
In the United States more generally, the anticorporate, antieastern, and
antiparty basis of neo-Populist rhetoric has had lasting appeal, and in

the last twenty years it has found its way into several third-party organizations, including George Wallace's American Party and Ross Perot's
Reform Party. Finally, the enduring strength of rural producer radicalism is reflected in the continued admiration Americans have for the
values and lifestyles they associate with traditional rural life. It may
surprise some Americans to learn that Laura Ingalls Wilder wrote her
classic *Little House* series to protest the coming of the New Deal.[111] It
would surprise few of us, however, to learn that the television show
based on the books was among the most successful series of the 1970s
and early 1980s, when political conservatism and traditional values
were making a powerful national comeback.

Understanding the contradictory and confusing relationship between rural people and modern liberalism requires a return to the moments in time when it was forged. We must try to understand the
reasons why farmers agreed to put down their swords and bludgeons,
their threats of third-party politics, and their hopes of re-creating the
American political economy to act as advisers to the very government
they had resisted for so long. What were the ideas and who were the
leaders in the period that led up to this consolidation? Which organizations, if any, continued to stand outside the conventional political
structure? How did they fare? How did individual farmers respond to
the growing power of the state? When we can answer these questions,
we will be in a much stronger position to understand why, today, the
very people who have benefited so much from the modern liberal state
are now so interested in taking it apart. We may also discover what
parts of rural producer radicalism survived the election of 1896 and
how they are made manifest in America today.

The movement toward agrarian liberalism grew logically from the
fusion of the People's Party and the Democratic Party. Once farm
leaders began to work with the federal government, many did not want
to turn back to political isolation. And in some places during the Progressive Era, it seemed possible to combine the Populist agenda with
conventional party politics. Wisconsin's Robert La Follette, for example, a leading figure in the midwestern Progressivism of the early twentieth century, had not been a Populist but had nonetheless learned the
lessons of radical producerism at an early age. "As a boy on the farm . . .
I heard and felt this movement of the Grangers swirling around me,"
La Follette wrote in his 1913 autobiography. "I suppose I have never
fully lost the effect of that early impression."[112] He was also impressed

by the power that businessmen and industrial leaders held in the Wisconsin Republican Party—including one, Philetus Sawyer, who he believed had tried to bribe him. Before long, La Follette was campaigning for governor on the promise to crush the political machine and democratize politics and the economy. To the many farmers who voted for him, including a large group of German immigrants and their children, La Follette seemed to defend plain people rather than corporate elites.[113] After winning the election, he pushed for a direct primary rule, for state regulation of the railroads and water, gas, electric, and telephone companies, and for inheritance and income taxes. Similar laws were passed by Iowa governor Albert Cummins, Minnesota governor John Johnson, and Missouri governor Joseph Folk. Contemporary political observers did not miss the connection between midwestern Populism and midwestern Progressivism. These new governors, one wrote, "caught the Populists in swimming and stole all of their clothing except the frayed underwear of free silver."[114]

More important, agrarian liberalism developed from growing divisions within the agricultural sector itself—divisions between small farmers, tenants, and sharecroppers and larger, more sophisticated landowners and their allies in agribusiness. As early as the 1880s, but increasingly in the 1910s and 1920s, some wealthy farmers and speculators began to try to buy huge sections of land and supervise hired labor for its production. In the Dakotas and California, for example, bonanza farms and early versions of today's super farms were growing more wheat and produce than settlers had dreamed possible. In small towns also, businesses, banks, mills, mines, and other small manufacturing centers came to be owned by outside investors and corporations. Chain stores replaced some corner stores; shopping from a Sears-Roebuck catalog became easier than ordering from a local merchant. Thus locally owned stores and businesses that valued their independence felt pressured to modernize in order to remain competitive. Before long, these divisions would also appear in the ways in which particular farm organizations interacted with the federal government. Those whose members were interested in modernization and the development of the rural sector saw a natural alliance with the white-collared professionals of the federal government. Those who still imagined a different world remained for a time outside their grasp.

In 1909 the *Report of the Country Life Commission* reflected these new divisions and ambitions in rural America. President Theodore Roosevelt considered himself a friend of the farmer, but he was also a major supporter of "improving" life in the countryside and making it more like urban living. In the early 1900s many political advisers were worried about the long-term health of the agricultural economy. Some, for example, were concerned that the best and brightest rural youths were leaving the countryside for the city because they were dissatisfied with their lives. Others worried that farmers were becoming increasingly inefficient and contributing to an ever-increasing cost of living for all Americans. Thus the 1909 report presented several suggestions for improving rural life and rural productivity, including beautifying rural homes and improving their facilities, consolidating one-room schools and modernizing their curricula, and establishing agricultural agents at state land-grant colleges who could disseminate innovations in scientific agriculture. This emphasis on consumerism and progressive education differed significantly from the production-oriented values of rural communities. Nevertheless, the many social workers, industrialists, ministers, and educators on the commission heartily endorsed the report.

Many ordinary rural folks, however, did not like it one bit. As it turned out, they valued their one-room schools and thought additional subjects like music and art were totally unnecessary for their children. They believed that the most important thing to teach children—boys and girls alike—was the value of hard work, not the best ways to beautify a farmhouse. They disliked county agents, many of whom had never been farmers but who still thought they knew what was best for farmers. They wondered why it was that so many urban outsiders seemed to believe that they knew so much about what was wrong with other people's lives.[115] Their resistance slowed the reform of country life and frustrated many who had thought that rural people would have been grateful for their assistance and advice. Moreover, it stood as a warning to others who would "help" farmers to "improve" their lives. Independent, strong-minded, and proud, farmers have not always welcomed assistance even when they sincerely needed it. They believed that they could help themselves and handle their own affairs. And most of all, they never wanted to be anybody's objects of concern. That would remain true even when they became desperately concerned about themselves.[116]

It was these kinds of people that carried on the legacy of Populism and earlier rural producer radicalism. Despite the temptations of "progress," a handful of rural Americans, scattered across several states, still remembered what the Populists had really meant—before fusion, before Progressivism, before the first inklings of agrarian liberalism, before suggestions that if farmers lived in prettier houses they would have prettier lives. Throughout the 1900s, 1910s, and 1920s westerners and southerners, blacks and whites, Europeans and Americans, men and women were struggling to achieve a different kind of democratic community, one in which every vote counted as much as every other vote, in which the great accumulation of wealth by middlemen and corporate men would not be tolerated, in which the affairs of local communities would be handled by those local communities, and in which farmers would still be honored for what they had made by the sweat of their brows. To bring such a transformation about, many of them turned for new ideas and plans to the leaders of American socialism. This alliance they did not in any way, however, consider to be un-American. To the contrary, they maintained that their dedication to small producers and the common good was the most ardently American agenda of them all.

The Farmers' Union, the American Society of Equity, and the Non-partisan League were the most influential of the early-twentieth-century radical farm organizations. Each created itself in the mirror image of the most powerful farm organization of all—the American Farm Bureau Federation (AFBF)—which was directly tied to the land-grant colleges, agribusiness leaders, and wealthy landowners and which worked closely with Congress throughout the 1920s to begin to create federal farm programs for agriculture. To radicals, the AFBF did not seem like a real farm organization. After all, what real farm organization would have palatial offices and salaried officials in Chicago and Washington? What real farm organization would allow multinational corporations like International Harvester to provide start-up money for local bureaus? What real farm organization would permit nonfarmers, including businessmen, to be members? What real farm organization would encourage county agents to recruit members—agents whose salaries were paid by all taxpayers? The feud between these groups was not a simple matter of various clubs vying for the same limited membership. It reflected a difference in world view: a difference in the degree of defiance of corporate power and of resistance to federal control and to the idea of the farmer as a consumer rather than as a person dedicated to the values of small production.

Arthur C. Townley addresses farm men and women in the Nonpartisan League outside Steele, North Dakota.
Courtesy of the State Historical Society of North Dakota.

All three of these organizations addressed the perpetual difficulties farmers experienced marketing their products and paying their debts. Whether prices were relatively high, as they were before World War I, or they were plunging downward, as they did in the late 1920s, the high costs farmers paid to middlemen felt like salt rubbed in an open wound. The Farmers' Union, begun in Texas in 1902 and 400,000 members strong in 1908, dedicated itself to one-crop cooperation on a grander scale than had ever been tried before. President John Barrett reminded members that cotton was "the one indispensable article of civilization and heathendom. . . . Without it, unnumbered millions of Christians, Mohammedans, Buddhists, black, yellow, and brown hordes . . . would go naked, hungry, and without shelter."[117] In the next decade, however, the union practiced a brand of vertical integration of the cotton industry which would have made implements tycoon John Deere himself proud. It owned and operated, according to Theodore Saloutos, "1,628 warehouses, . . . a large number of elevators and terminal agencies . . . ; 245 packing houses; dozens of newspapers; coal mines; several banks; several hundred stores; flour mills, creameries, pickle factories, an implement factory, a phosphate plant, tobacco factories and warehouses; produce exchanges, fertilizer factories, many cotton-grading schools; and cooperative life and fire insurance companies."[118]

The Nonpartisan League was also dedicated to wresting control of marketing away from middlemen, but it sought to do so in a significantly more radical way—by proposing and implementing state ownership of many marketing facilities. A. C. Townley may have been the most persuasive and charismatic farm organizer in American history. Beginning as a socialist organizer in the 1910s but breaking off to organize his own farmer association in 1914, Townley set the force of his personality, the tradition of farmer grievance, the Scandinavian heritage of rural radicalism, and the strength of several Model Ts to fuel a major rural revolt. His platform included state ownership of terminal elevators, flour mills, packing houses, and cold-storage plants; state inspection of grain and grain dockage; exemption of farm improvements from taxation; state hail insurance; and rural-credit banks for low-interest loans.[119] After twelve straight months of Townley's one-on-one salesmanship in farmers' yards, fields, barns, and kitchens, the league boasted forty thousand members. Its newspaper, the *Nonpartisan Leader*, had the largest circulation of any newspaper in North Dakota.

The NPL scored a major victory in the 1918 elections when North Dakotans reelected the plain-speaking but politically astute farmer from Hoople, Lynn Frazier, as governor and the cunning and ambitious lawyer, William Langer, as attorney general. Next, the state supreme court ruled in favor of many of the laws proposed by the NPL-dominated legislature. Soon plans for a state-owned elevator and a state-owned bank were under way. Spreading regionally, the NPL called for increased rights for industrial workers, the end of monopoly, national ownership of public transportation and communication, steeply graduated income and inheritance taxes, and women's suffrage. Meanwhile, opponents were lining up and waiting to retaliate. Republicans who opposed the league began the Independent Voters Association (IVA); investors in the East refused to buy state bonds; patriotic citizens of all stripes accused the league of disloyalty when it did not immediately support the war effort in 1918. The strength of these criticisms as well as the NPL's own inept management would bring down its reign— temporarily. In the 1930s "Wild Bill" Langer would return to power and to league principles with a vengeance. In his person would be represented the problem Roosevelt faced in organizing radical farmers for participation in the liberal state.

Elsewhere socialist ideas also blazed a path through the American countryside. In the mountains and forests where the WFM had fought in the 1890s, an entirely new and avowedly socialist union, the Industrial Workers of the World, appeared in the 1910s to organize unskilled laborers from many industries. One of the IWW's leaders was the WFM's William ("Big Bill") Haywood, another Eugene V. Debs. Both believed it was time for American workers to take back their workplaces and end the power of industrial capitalism. In Oklahoma likewise "farmers voted red" from the earliest days of statehood through World War I. More than one in six voters in Oklahoma voted for Debs for president in 1912. In the Midwest rural socialists and communists began to organize an entirely new regional party, the Farmer-Labor Party, which explicitly conjoined the interests of all workers. In the 1924 gubernatorial elections, Farmer-Labor candidates won between a quarter and a third of the votes cast in Minnesota, Nebraska, South Dakota, and Washington.[120] As the economy began to slip—and it slipped much sooner in rural than in urban America— even more Americans questioned whether industrial capitalism was meant to last.

But the 1930s were, of course, the hardest times of all.[121] Prices for crops and values of land had steadily fallen in the 1920s while the costs for credit and consumer goods stayed the same or increased. Bank failures were commonplace in rural America well before the stock-market collapse. But the worldwide depression that began in 1929 sent this slow decline into a full-scale tailspin. Total farm income in the United States dropped 60 percent between 1929 and 1932. Prices on corn, wheat, cotton, and hogs plummeted to levels never seen before. On a single day—October 24, 1929—wheat dropped ten cents a bushel.[122] In 1932 farm families in North Dakota had an average annual income of $145.00—only 47 percent of the income for the average American family.

On the Great Plains the economic depression was accompanied by a devastating drought. Year after year, in counties in the Dakotas, Kansas, Oklahoma, and Texas, new records were set for heat and lack of rain. Crops died in the fields before they had grown a foot. Watering holes dried up and animals died from thirst. When the wind began to blow in the summers of 1934, 1935, and 1936, dust storms covered the sun, carried tons of topsoil to the Atlantic Ocean, and ruined lives forever. Before the dust storms began, relief workers had visited families who had only one blanket, one set of good clothes, no shoes for children's feet, and failing health from malnutrition. Even farms that had survived the economic collapse of the late 1920s strained under the pressure of the ecological disaster of the 1930s. Up and down the Plains hundreds of thousands of farms were lost to foreclosure. Hundreds of thousands of families packed up and left their homes, hoping that in California or Washington or Oregon they might prosper again. If there were ever circumstances under which proud rural people would rise up in protest, these were they. But if there ever were circumstances under which proud rural people would accept the help and assistance of "urban outsiders," these were they as well.

Not surprisingly, farm leaders and farm organizations that had chosen to work within the two-party system in the Progressive era continued to do so in the 1930s. Advisers to Franklin Roosevelt included Henry Wallace, whose grandfather had been a member of the Country Life Commission and whose father had been President Warren Harding's secretary of agriculture. Wallace, Illinois businessman George Peek, and rural economist M. L. Wilson all had strong ties to the land-

grant colleges, county agents, and the AFBF. In the 1920s they had supported the McNary-Haugen plan to regulate distribution of agricultural
surplus, but increasingly turned their attention now to regulating agricultural production. If prices were too low, they argued, then farmers
were producing too much. Given that other nations would continue to
place high tariffs on imported goods, only a system of domestic allotment and careful centralized planning could realign supply, demand,
and price. Thus in 1933 the Roosevelt administration introduced the
Agricultural Adjustment Act. Under its auspices, farmers would be al-
lotted a certain number of acres to plant and would be paid a subsidy
for leaving the rest fallow. The subsidy in turn would be paid through
a tax on processors.

The way this story is commonly told, as soon as Roosevelt announced the domestic allotment plan, desperate farmers lined up for
miles to sign up for it, happy to take what they could and relieved that
the government was not going to force them to abandon their arid
lands.[123] Although it is true that most farmers did agree to participate
in the AAA, the story is actually much more complicated than that. As
we have seen, not all farmers or farm leaders were as comfortable as
Wallace and the others were in working within the federal government and in supporting the modernization of agriculture and rural
life. Since the 1900s they had held more firmly to the radical legacy of
Populism. These men were not at all happy with the government's
new plan. John Simpson, head of the Farmers' Union, for example,
was frankly appalled by the proposal. In it he saw "an army of bureaucrats"—perhaps as many as 200,000—supervising and regulating
the business activities of every farmer in the land. Like the county
agents before them and the entire Roosevelt "brain trust," these "nin-
compoops" were likely to know little if anything about the realities of
farming.[124]

Despite the overwhelming power of the forces behind domestic
allotment, Simpson presented to Congress and to a conference of
nine farm-state governors his own plan for farm relief: "cost-of-production." Under this scheme, the government would not restrict production but "turn the farmer loose" to produce as much as he was
able. He would be guaranteed a fixed price for produce for domestic
consumption—a price to be paid at licensed processors—and then
would be free to sell the rest at world market prices. Farmers would
get paid without the army of bureaucrats poking around in their

fields and their account books. In fact, the burden of supervision would fall on the processors, middlemen whom farmers had always encouraged the government to regulate more attentively. And if prices went up, Simpson argued, production might even go down, because farmers would begin taking the vacations and shopping trips they had already put off for years. Farmers could be consumers, he seemed to be saying, but only after they had their productive affairs in order.

In the early 1930s rural people who supported Simpson but had heard enough debates in Congress to know what usually came of them began to take action of their own—action that hearkened back to a time before conventional politics set the standard for dissent in America. As one farmer from Dickinson, N.D., put it, "A worthy farmer cannot be expected to sit back and watch his work of a lifetime taken away from him without raising his hand in protest."[125] So protest they did. In Iowa, two violent insurgent movements developed in the years when incomes were slipping and allotments being negotiated. First, the "Cow War" broke out when health officials at Iowa State University in Ames ordered all cattle tested for tuberculosis, because they believed that an increase in childhood tuberculosis was linked to tuberculosis in milk. State officials ordered that all milk-giving cows be tested and that those identified as carriers be destroyed, with the farmer carrying one-third of the financial burden. The testing was carried out not by local veterinarians but by state-employed veterinarians from the Iowa State Agricultural College in Ames. These officials, of course, were not only strangers but associates of the hated AFBF.

The Iowa farmers, most of whom belonged to the Farmers' Union, distrusted the veterinarians. They also distrusted the test itself, which had been shown to be inaccurate from time to time. Most important, they felt strongly that the state order infringed on their rights as small property owners. As local Farmers' Union leader Milo Reno put it, "[The farmers'] property is no longer their own. Any little shyster who has come out of a certain agricultural college in this state can go to a farmer's property and conduct a test that is more apt to be wrong than right."[126] They pointed out that a daughter of one of the farmers whose cattle had been condemned had been named "America's healthiest girl." She attributed her good health to drinking a quart of farm-fresh milk every day.

To protest the testing, Iowa farmers petitioned the governor and organized the Farmers' Protective Association. They marched on Des Moines carrying placards that condemned the "cow squirters" as "fake, fake, fake."[127] Later, when veterinarians came to a farmstead, large groups of neighbors gathered to make it uncomfortable at best for the testing to proceed. In Tipton, West Junction, and Liberty, Iowa, mobs of up to five hundred men were armed with eggs, mud, and clubs. Governor Daniel Turner dispatched three regiments of the Iowa National Guard to guarantee the safety of the veterinarians. Later, he also promised to allow farmers to select their own testers and potentially to receive more compensation for their livestock at the meat-packing sites. This compromise silenced the farmers' protests—for a time. Nonetheless, it did not change the suspicion farmers felt toward outside experts who would challenge their right to run their businesses as they saw fit.

These feelings and frustrations led to the organization of the Farmers' Holiday Association, a national organization of farmers established by veterans of the Cow War in the summer of 1932. As its name implied, the organization hoped that farmers would take a holiday from marketing their goods, just as the bankers had taken a holiday from finance. They hoped that a well-coordinated farm-products strike would drive up prices to the cost of production, at least. The slogan for the organization was "Stay at home—Buy nothing—Sell nothing." As another leader put it, "We'll eat our wheat and ham and eggs and let them eat their gold."[128] On August 15, 1932, farmers in Iowa, the Dakotas, and Minnesota set up roadblocks to keep farm products from market. In Sioux City and Denison, Iowa, in Milwaukee, Wisconsin, in Omaha, Nebraska, and in western Minnesota, violence erupted at the roadblocks. One farmer's son was shot with a .38-caliber bullet in Racine, Wisconsin.

The Farmers' Holiday Association—and especially its women's auxiliaries—also fought to stop foreclosures on farms. They did so in several ways. Women sponsored letter-writing campaigns to state governors and to Eleanor Roosevelt, explaining the danger they believed foreclosure represented to farm women and girls.[129] Together with menfolk, they also staged direct actions. In Le Mars, Iowa, for example, farmers kidnaped a local judge in an effort to force him to sign a pledge not to foreclose on any more property. They led him out of town, tied him, blindfolded him, and beat him, threatening to kill him. He refused to sign the pledge. More frequent were demonstrations of community and cross-gender solidarity at the sites of foreclosures themselves. In the Dakotas crowds blocked access to foreclosure sales to anyone interested in purchasing the property. Others then bid extremely low prices (these became known as "penny auctions"), and when the sale was concluded gave the property back to its original owner. In support of the farmers, the governor of North Dakota was rumored to have said, "Treat the banker like a chicken thief. Shoot him on sight."[130]

"Wild Bill" Langer, now governor of North Dakota, was the highest-ranking government official who supported the goals—and the tactics—of the Farmers' Holiday Association. Indeed, he forwarded their actions through legislation by passing a farm-foreclosure act and by attempting to put an embargo on all wheat leaving the state of North Dakota. He ordered the North Dakota Terminal Elevator to outbid the asking price for wheat by thirty-five cents and forced the price up across the nation. Most of all, he spoke out bitterly against the Roosevelt administration. Despite his three trials on conspiracy charges, a conviction, prison sentence, and more, Dakota voters were dedicated to the man they saw as unafraid to stand up for small farmers no matter what the cost. Some say they voted for Langer for years after they knew he was already dead.

But farm families in the upper Midwest were not alone in their radicalism in the 1930s. Across the South, sharecroppers and tenant farmers, including many African Americans, were equally disappointed by the provisions of the New Deal. In fact, as far as sharecroppers and tenant farmers were concerned there were no provisions of the New Deal. Money that came to landowners through the AAA or other programs almost never trickled down to the poorest farmers. As they had in the Populist movement, African Americans mobilized to increase their share of federal relief. The Southern Tenant Farmers' Union, for example, began when African Americans and whites in Arkansas gathered to protest sharecroppers' working and living conditions. Soon the STFU spread to neighboring states, where poor farmers courageously spoke out against mistreatment and demanded full participation in government programs. For doing so, they were threatened, beaten, and jailed. The way whites saw it, African American farmers did not get the checks because they did not deserve them. And if they had to move on and live somewhere else, in a town or a city far away, that suited many of them just fine.[131]

Farmers' Holiday Association members gather to prevent eviction
of a local farmer in Cass County, North Dakota.
Courtesy of the State Historical Society of North Dakota.

Finally, like urban Americans, rural Americans had simply to turn on their radios to hear the voices of other Americans who believed that the New Deal was heading down the wrong path. Father Charles Coughlin of Detroit and Francis E. Townsend of California, for example, exhorted Americans to redistribute wealth more equally among all rather than establish elaborate bureaucracies and welfare programs. Huey Long of Louisiana, however, presented the most serious threat to Roosevelt's presidency. Long told his audience again and again of his rural heritage, his days as a boy on his family's small farm. Thus he seemed to be a reliable source of criticism of wealth and corruption in the United States. Moreover, he insisted that he was not a socialist or a communist. "Just say I'm *sui generis* and leave it at that."[132] His sharp criticisms of Roosevelt and his own plan for reconstruction were just as original. He argued that taxing the rich would make it possible to provide every family with $5,000 as well as a home, pension, education, and automobile: "every man a king." Although Long was assassinated before he could run for president, he claimed 7.6 million members in eight thousand community-based organizations in 1935. Much of his support came from rural men and women and those who had recently moved to urban areas, those for whom the Great Depression was just the final chapter of a long, sad book of personal and regional defeat.[133]

In the end, nearly every one of these radicalized Americans—the Cow Warriors, Farmers' Holiday members, Langer supporters, southern tenant farmers, and followers of Huey Long—made their peace with the Roosevelt administration. They signed their contracts with the Agricultural Adjustment Administration or were helped to relocated to a new state by the Resettlement Administration. And despite the 1936 Union Party candidacies of Long ally Gerald L. K. Smith and Langer ally William Lemke, most rural Americans cast a second ballot for Roosevelt. They did so for obvious reasons: their families were hungry, their crops dried up in the fields, and they were thankful that someone was doing something to help them. Even so, farmers' concerns about the intellectual imperialism of the "brain trust" and the arrogance of the county agents did not disappear entirely. In many states the return to local conservatism came as early as the 1938 congressional elections. In others it came with the advent of anticommunism in the 1940s and 1950s. Meanwhile, evidence suggests that even those farmers who agreed to cooperate with the government's programs practiced a kind of passive resistance to federal authority. Finding loopholes, lying, or simply cheating the government was an act of noncooperation as surely—but significantly less radically—as refusing to sign in the first place.

In the moment of its construction, the compact between rural radicals and the liberal state was built on shaky ground, fashioned from the inequity of power and need. Perhaps in the New Deal and subsequent farm programs, radical farmers found something they had sought for so long: an acknowledgment that their difficult labors were important and that their concerns deserved to be heard in the highest halls of government. Even so, the programs took the form of something they had struggled against equally long: interference by a centralized authority that knew little about the realities of their lives and that increasingly would think of them as potential consumers rather than as heroic producers. In this light it is not difficult at all to understand why some farmers today—like those in the Iowa Farm Bill Study Group—would ask the federal government to dismantle farm programs and set the farmers loose in the international marketplace. They want to make their own way, to feed the world, to make decisions for themselves in their own communities, and to earn their pay. The early rebels of New Jersey and New York, of North Carolina and Vermont, of Massachusetts, Pennsylvania, and Maine did not fight for economic or political change in the industrial or the Progressive age. They would not recognize the rhetoric, the farming techniques, or the politics of farmers in contemporary society. But they would recognize what lies most deeply in their hearts.

2

THE CULTURE OF VIGILANTISM

IN 1982, Jim Jenkins, the owner of a small farm in southern Minnesota, faced losing all he had to bank foreclosure. Jenkins had been encouraged by high prices for crops and land to take out loans and buy more livestock and farm equipment in the early 1970s. When crop and land prices fell, when inflation and interest rates soared, and when the Carter administration placed an embargo on agricultural exports to the Soviet Union, Jenkins could no longer meet his financial obligations. He was anything but alone in his plight. With nearly a third of all small- and medium-sized farms at risk of foreclosure, the 1980s marked the most serious agricultural emergency in the United States since the Great Depression. Even so, to Jenkins this farm crisis remained a deeply personal experience. It required him to endure his neighbors' gossip, to take menial jobs off the farm, and to go back to his banker to ask for more money when he knew he would be turned down. Even federal farm subsidies could not make up his losses. By the fall of 1983, he had realized that nothing could.

As long as American agriculture has been fully integrated into market capitalism, farmers like Jim Jenkins have known the frustration of struggling to stay afloat when larger economic and political forces were working against them. No matter how long they worked or how thrifty they were, in hard times they lost their meager profits to taxes, retail costs, and interest expenses. Jenkins resented all the middlemen whom he believed were responsible for his failure, but he hated his banker, Rudy Blythe, most of all. Not a long-time member of the community, Blythe was originally from Philadelphia and had lived for many years in Des Moines. He had bought the Buffalo Ridge State Bank in Ruthton, Minnesota, to achieve a dream of his own—to be self-employed and become a revered and beloved member of a small community. But it did not work out that way. From his clients' perspective, Rudy would never fit in, no matter how hard he tried. Local bankers never had fit in anyway—and Rudy was the quintessential banker, right down to the plaid pants and the golf clubs. His wife did not fare much better, especially after she put an expensive addition on their house and suggested that corporal punishment be outlawed at their son's school. After several years in town, she still had only a few friends. When her husband's bank started to fail, Susan Blythe took a job in Houston.[1]

If Jim Jenkins shared economic grievances with his rural forefathers, he did not choose to share their strong and active political heritage. As we have seen, after the Populist defeat of 1896, radical farm groups became increasingly marginalized and isolated from one another. At the same time, groups representing wealthy farmers and agribusiness firms worked with Congress until the farm bloc and the federal government reached an uneasy accord in 1933. In the late 1950s and especially in the early 1980s, many farmers would realize that the liberal state could not protect their livelihoods and that, perhaps, it had never intended to in the first place. After years of political marginalization and liberal hegemony, however, they found it difficult to rebuild an effective political infrastructure in the tradition of rural producer radicalism. The American Agriculture Movement, for example, tried to alert federal officials to the impending crisis in the late 1970s, but was ridiculed for maintaining an uncompromising political position and for threatening violence. Grass-roots organizations like the Iowa Farm Unity Coalition did better in the 1980s by helping farmers and their wives gain access to social services, food, medical care, and even marriage counseling. Such programs would not have appealed to a man like Jenkins, however. His own marriage had failed and, some people surmised, may have turned violent near the end. Not particularly comfortable with women—and there were plenty of women activists during the farm crisis—Jenkins preferred the company of his teenage son, Steve, who sported a boot-camp-style haircut, dressed in camouflage gear, and collected guns.

Even without a political organization to join, however, Jenkins was not alone. He still laid claim to a second tradition of rural life in the United States—collective vigilante-style justice performed in the name of community self-defense. From the earliest days of settlement on the continent, rural Americans have taken the law into their own hands. They have done so, in defiance of provincial, state, and federal governments, to uphold community standards and protect themselves, their families, and their property. Their actions have fallen under the rubric of three distinct but inevitably overlapping categories. First, Americans on the frontier have attacked deviants, criminals, poor people, and others whose behaviors or beliefs threatened the physical safety and/or economic stability of their communities. Second, settlers and other rural Americans have targeted people whose racial heritage they deemed intolerable. Third, they have joined with urban Americans to pursue those they believed to be "un-American" in some way, because of religious or ethnic heritage or political beliefs. And within all three contexts, rural men have worked to protect their power and control over women and to reinforce patriarchy and heterosexuality. Rural people have not been responsible for all the atrocities that have taken place in America. Nothing could be further from the truth. Urban Americans have done more than their fair share of hating and killing throughout the American past. Likewise, urban Americans have acted collectively to repress those they have found intolerable. Nevertheless, over three centuries, the isolation and deprivation of the frontier, the enforced homogeneity of the small town, and the wide availability and reverence for guns have combined to create a distinct heritage of radical rural vigilantism.

It was with no sense of contradiction then but with a deep connection to rural Americans who had gone before him that Jim Jenkins and his son murdered the banker who foreclosed on their dream. Coolly, calculatedly, Jenkins and his son called Rudy Blythe and pretended to be potential buyers for Jenkins's farmstead. They insisted on meeting him at the property rather than in his office. This request seemed strange to Rudy, but he was so desperate to unload the Jenkins place that he agreed and brought his chief operating officer, Toby Thulin, with him. No sooner had they arrived, however, than a shotgun blast ripped through Thulin's skull. In a cold, driving rain, Blythe ran for his life. He was only fifty yards from the county road when a hail of bullets cut him down. In the 1980s an angry white rural man like Jim Jenkins could not turn to the Farmers' Holiday Association or appeal to a governor like "Wild Bill"

Langer. But he could pick up his army-issue rifle. And, after a long chase through parts of the rural Midwest and Texas, when capture by police and agents of the FBI was imminent, he could turn it on himself.

Perhaps Jenkins felt no contradiction between the dual traditions of rural producer radicalism and the culture of vigilante violence because the distance between them had never been as large as we would like to think it was in the first place. Jenkins would have fit in quite comfortably in a mob of colonial men armed with clubs, demanding access to free land or fair representation in the government. He would have gladly burned the home of an excise collector during the Whisky Rebellion if his and his community's independence were at stake. He would have been happy to vote against political parties steeped in wealth and corruption in anticipation of the Populists' "cooperative commonwealth." And he would have been more than willing to get his gun to try to stop a foreclosure on a neighbor's farm. Even more important, however, if Jenkins had joined any of these organizations that predated agrarian liberalism, he would have learned that rural producer radicals—the heroes of dozens of history books—shared both his fondest aspirations and some of his deepest hatreds and resentments. Jim Jenkins was a cold-blooded killer. But like other rural men whose acts of violence usually stopped short of murder, he had wanted to be respected for his honest, ordinary labors. When his dream turned to a nightmare, he did not have to go far to find someone to blame.

"Industry was Restor'd":

VIGILANTISM AND THE POLITICS OF CLASS

Whether we would admit it or not, most Americans are attracted from time to time to the idea of vigilantism. When the court system moves too slowly or a recognized criminal is acquitted of a heinous crime, we consider acts of retribution by the victim or his or her family or community as necessary and just. We also remember fondly the frontier West's brand of do-it-yourself justice, reprocessed again and again by Hollywood. Far from courts, sheriffs, or jails, brave men willing to act outside the law seemed to have been the only people who could save a community from lawlessness. We are not the first Americans to feel this way. So heroic, in fact, did this vigilante tradition seem to men in the late nineteenth century, when the West was nearly settled and the future of the much-vaunted strenuous life seemed in doubt, that elite easterners, including future president Theodore Roosevelt, sought out vigilante groups to join. Likewise, men who participated in vigilante activities often capitalized on their exploits. Several became governors, congressmen, and diplomats. Dr. John Osborne, a physician who served as governor of Wyoming in the 1890s, proudly displayed items—including a pair of ladies' shoes—that he had made from the tanned skin of his best-known victim, George "Big Nose" Parrott.[2]

However justified it might sound in retrospect, vigilantism in rural America was more often than not a brutal act of violence which, in its broadest manifestation, sought out men and women who threatened the safety and economic stability of their communities. Vigilantes pursued criminals, of course, including counterfeiters, horse thieves, robbers, and murderers. But they also "brought to justice" people whose behaviors or beliefs more subtly threatened their futures. In the colonial era, they attacked the "lower sort," people whose poverty or idleness threatened the productivity of more established frontier families. In the early nineteenth century, they targeted Mormons because, among other things, they dared to challenge the emerging doctrine of liberal individualism in the age of the farmer. In the industrial era, miners and farm workers moved against Chinese and Mexicans for working too hard and being paid too little. The tables were turned, however, when miners and lumberjacks tried to unionize to protect their rights. Then they became the victims of vigilante violence themselves. Across three centuries of time, deviant, poor and working-class Americans experienced the horror of verdict without trial and punishment by committee. Nor could they appeal their sentences when the judge, jury, and executioners included the "best men" in town.

The first recorded instance of organized and sustained vigilantism against the "lower sort" in colonial America occurred on the rugged, dangerous, and politically isolated South Carolina frontier in 1767. There frontiersmen took the law into their own hands even when provincial authorities directly ordered them to desist. Because they turned from targeting criminals to seeking out poor people in general, they set the pattern for much of the more explicitly class-based vigilantism of the nineteenth century. Because they defied the government and demanded fuller representation in it, they also begged the question of the relationship between rural producer radicalism and rural vigilantism. If a South Carolina Regulator had conferred with a North Carolina Regulator, he would have discovered how much they had in common. However, he might not, as most historians have not, have remembered it that way.

Settlers in South Carolina lived the roughest sort of existence in the 1760s. Few men owned more than one hundred acres and, as Richard Maxwell Brown says, to cultivate these they "depended mainly on [their] own stout back[s] and the toil of [their] considerable famil[ies]."[3] Women married early and might have seen as many children die as survive to maturity. And the settlers were poor. In an economy dominated by slave labor in the East, settlers in the West usually could not afford to buy any. Thus a labor shortage combined with the increased distance they had to travel to market put them at a distinct economic disadvantage. Worst of all, they lived in constant fear of Native American attack. In 1760 and 1761 in particular, the Cherokee War devastated the countryside. Again and again, in tiny frontier communities such as Long Canes and Ninety Six, Cherokee warriors ambushed settlers and their families. Forty were killed in a swamp on February 1, 1760. When Patrick Calhoun, the father of John C. Calhoun, returned to the site to help bury the dead—including his own mother—he found mangled and mutilated corpses. After another attack, children with missing scalps and huge gashes on their faces and heads were found wandering in the woods.[4] For months, demoralized and terrified settlers huddled in squalid forts, ignoring crops, subsisting on the most basic rations, and stealing and looting simply to survive.

A haphazard system of law and order made difficult conditions even worse. Saint Mark's Parish claimed only two of forty-eight seats in the provincial assembly. Moreover, it was far too large to govern effectively, and the colony refused to create any new counties until the settlers agreed to support the Anglican church—an unlikely occurrence given the diversity of dissenting and evangelical Protestant sects and Scots-Irish parishioners there.[5] As a result, few courts were in operation. If the local militia somehow succeeded in capturing a gang of outlaws, the officers could not try them but had to hold them in a local jail until they could arrange transportation to Charleston, two hundred rough-trail miles away. Even the local justices of the peace did not maintain order. They mostly attended to their responsibilities regarding stray livestock and bounties for "wild beasts." Drinking, card playing, dancing, and shooting matches accompanied their hearings.

Thus when an outbreak of crime threatened the frontier in the summer of 1767, settlers believed that they had nowhere to turn. Outlaws had long been attracted to the rough and unregulated frontier conditions. In the words of a local Anglican minister and the soon-to-be-leader of the Regulation, Charles Woodmason, "Gamblers Gamesters of all Sorts—Horse Thieves . . . United in Gangs and Combinations" filled the woods.[6] They were joined by runaway slaves and mulattos, as well as prostitutes and other "women and Girls . . . very deep in the foulest of Crimes . . . aiding, abetting—Watching—Secreting—Trafficking and in ev'ry Manner supporting and assisting these Villains."[7] Outlaw gangs were even known to kidnap young girls from settlers' families to act as fresh recruits. Settlers periodically attempted to rescue the girls; in one instance they recaptured thirty-five but later determined that most had been too fully corrupted to live in regular society again.

Widespread attacks on life and property in June and July of 1767 were the last straw. Gangs of men descended on isolated frontier cabins and stores and demanded money, horses, livestock, and any other goods on hand. Having—or being believed to have—as little as fifty pounds put settlers at risk. Men were tortured with hot irons until they told where they kept their money. Dennis Hayes was tied to a chair and forced to watch as his store was looted and his wife and ten-year-old daughter were raped. Charles Kitchen was robbed, tortured, burned, and had an eyed gouged out. On each occasion when the regular militia attempted to end the violence, criminals either escaped or simply outran the troops. So frightened were some officials in the backcountry that they agreed to act as spies and undercover agents for the outlaws.

At first, the citizens who gathered to oppose this outbreak simply called themselves a "Mobb." But by early November 1767 everyone in the backcountry knew them as the Regulators. And they knew of their determination to take "the most vigorous measures . . . to clear the country of the whole gang."[8] Their strategies were varied, unabashed, and potent. They burned cabins of known outlaws and those thought to harbor them. They rounded up gang members and their families, tied them to trees, and whipped them. They gathered their guns, followed gangs, and opened fire on them without warning. They captured runaway slaves and, if returning them was too much trouble, executed them on the spot.

Elite eastern planters were aghast. Quickly Governor Charles Grenville Montagu issued a proclamation ordering the Regulators to

disperse. But the Regulators did not care what the governor proclaimed; after all, he had issued acts of clemency to some outlaws they
had brought to trial in Charleston earlier that spring. Joined by official
Ranger units of the provincial army, the Regulators dispatched local
criminals and their allies with relish and aplomb until nearly all had
been killed or dispersed. Still they were not finished. Indeed, they had
only begun the most important part of their defense of the community. In the spring of 1768, the South Carolina Regulators chose a new
set of victims—the "lower sort" of people who lived on the edges of
their communities but who had never actually committed a crime. Beginning in the spring of 1768, Regulators turned their vicious attention
to "Vagrants—Idlers—Gamblers, and the Outcasts of Virginia and
North Carolina."[9] And for this they did not bother with support of the
Rangers or any other officials.

The Regulators said that they condemned their poorer neighbors
because they were in some way immoral. For example, they attacked
"lewd" women, unfaithful husbands, and neglectful fathers by hauling
them from their homes, tying them to trees, and flogging them. But
beneath the moral judgments lay a defense of the economic interests of
the leading men, for the Regulators also targeted people who did not
measure up in economic terms, who were "nonproductive" or who potentially could diminish the "better" settlers' prosperity. They victimized people, for example, who had chosen a subsistence or nomadic
lifestyle that conflicted with the emerging tenets of market production
or who refused to work for wages despite the labor shortage. "Having
no property or visible way of living," hunting on public land without a
permit, squatting, drifting, owing money and not paying up, these behaviors separated the poorest settlers from the rest of frontier society
and made them potential victims of the Regulation.[10] In 1768 a self-
proclaimed Congress of Regulators enacted a new vagrancy law that
forced landless men to work for others six days a week or be flogged. To
clean up the backcountry and to get free labor at the same time was a
deal that most settlers simply could not resist.

Both a legal and an extralegal force brought the South Carolina
Regulation to an end. First, South Carolina's provincial assembly and
the British Parliament passed the Circuit Court Act of 1769 to provide
a more effective infrastructure of courts and magistrates for the backcountry. Because a dearth of governmental services had influenced the
settlers' desire to police themselves, an increase led to a reduction in

vigilantism. In the years following passage of the bill, only a few instances of Regulator action occurred. Likewise new lands opened in the trans-Appalachian frontier and provided opportunities for poor men to own their own farms. The backcountry remained a rough part of South Carolina. Nevertheless, its leading citizens prospered when Native Americans, outlaws, and vagrants were controlled. After three years, Charles Woodmason reported that "tranquillity reigned. Industry was restor'd" in the South Carolina backcountry.[11]

But the Regulators also ended their vigilantism because counter-vigilantes—men who called themselves the Moderators—challenged them at their own game. As the Regulator violence became more brutal—two-hour floggings accompanied by beating drums and dancing fiddles—and targeted some well-respected members of the community, other settlers turned against them. Leading men who had stayed outside the movement came to see that the Regulators were providing no more protection to their communities than the outlaws had. They did not quibble, however, with vigilante-style justice. Indeed, they adopted it themselves. With little or no official authority, the Moderators launched attacks on the Regulators. They began a new round of kidnaping, flogging, and imprisoning without warrants or trials. On March 25, 1769, nearly seven hundred Moderators and Regulators faced one another, prepared for all-out civil war. Just as the first shots were fired, however, two highly respected militia leaders who had not participated on either side of the dispute rode up and offered a truce agreement. Its provisions required the abolition of the name "Regulators" and the promise, sworn by both sides, "that, for the future, the law should take [its] course without opposition."[12] Reluctantly, all men agreed to put down their arms.

And so the first episode of frontier vigilantism came to an end. It would hardly be the last. Many more so-called social bandits and many more vagrants would be shown the way to the flogging tree or the hangman's noose before all the West was settled. Each episode of vigilantism was, of course, unique to its particular moment in time. Yet each also adhered—to a greater or lesser extent—to the basic themes and patterns set forth in South Carolina. For example, vigilante groups throughout the frontier West targeted criminals in their communities. In fact, some vigilante organizations disbanded as soon as they had successfully suppressed a particular gang of thieves or murderers. Other vigilante groups, however, targeted people in their communities who had no criminal records but clung to economic behaviors that threatened the long-term stability of the community and the long-term interests of its elites.

What's more, many vigilantes resembled rural producer radicals more than they—or their observers since—have realized. In the cases of the two different sets of Regulators from the Carolinas in the 1760s, for example, settlers were frustrated by very similar sets of problems: difficulty establishing an effective economy, threats from local Native Americans, and an unresponsive and unrepresentative central government. They responded in very different ways, however: North Carolina Regulators attacked the government itself; South Carolina Regulators ignored the government and attacked one another. Because Governor Charles Montagu, unlike Governor William Tryon, was never the direct target of Regulator violence, he more willingly provided the increased governmental infrastructure and representation the Regulators demanded. Thus, in many ways, the South Carolinians won a battle in the finest tradition of rural producer radicalism. The trouble was that they never came to understand it as such. Instead, as Richard Maxwell Brown has pointed out, South Carolinians from Edgefield County glorified their heritage of righteous violence and popular sovereignty. Moreover, they deepened and augmented this heritage with every passing decade.[13] In lieu of an articulated politics of rural producer radicalism, South Carolinians were left to embrace a much deadlier tradition of the countryside.

Whether they realized it or not, other rural Americans also engaged in a vigilantism that resembled rural producer radicalism. In the territories of the trans-Mississippi West, for example, where governments were far away, unavailing, or filled with do-nothing federal appointees, men who took the law into their own hands also took it away from the authorities and long remembered their independent antistatist heritage. Close ties also linked the Whisky Rebels to a group of Indian killers called the Paxton Boys, the Populists to the Ku Klux Klan, a few of the leaders of the Farmers' Holiday Association to leaders of anti-Semitic and protofascist movements of the 1930s, and the grassroots coalitions of the farm crisis of the 1980s to the militants of the contemporary far right. However contradictory we might see the urge to protect freedom and democracy and cruelly and violently to deny it to others, many rural Americans have not. Just before or just after participating in vigilantism, rural Americans have also participated in actions dedicated to the pursuit of equality and justice. Of course, to the victims of vigilantism, such intriguing ambivalence and contradiction mattered little. Whatever the multiple meanings of vigilante violence might have been in any given time or place, they were thoroughly subsumed to its barbarity and terror.

Vigilantism that targeted criminals who destabilized frontier communities spread across the continent with the path of Euro-American settlement. Between 1767 and 1902 more than 326 identifiable vigilante organizations were responsible for at least 729 deaths.[14] Nearly all of these incidents occurred in the small towns and emerging cities of the frontier. Wherever vigilantes went, however, they treaded the same fine line between community protection, community self-definition, and community decimation which the South Carolina Regulators did. In the Regulator-Moderator War in Shelby County, Texas, between 1840 and 1841, for example, local men became fed up with the preponderance of murderers, thieves, and counterfeiters in their communities. The trouble was that they were not such peaceable fellows themselves. Charles Jackson, who led the Regulators against the criminals, had himself murdered a man back in Louisiana. When Jackson was murdered, the Regulators chose a new leader with even fewer scruples. A group called the Moderators gathered to oppose the Regulators. Soon every man in the county had to choose one side or the other, until the area was arming two small forces. Finally, Republic of Texas president Sam Houston sent a six-hundred-man militia into Shelbyville and forced ten leaders from each side to sign a peace treaty. Hostilities were not easily forgotten, however. When Shelby County organized units to fight in the Mexican-American War in the mid-1840s, both Regulator and Moderator factions volunteered. In fact, lasting peace did not come to Shelby County for several generations.

In the 1860s, in Montana, the desire to protect the local community also devolved into a long-standing feud. In the mining areas of western Montana, a combination of a young mobile male population, an abundance of alcohol, and an occasionally booming economy led to near social anarchy. Henry Plummer secretly headed a notorious gang that robbed miners of their gold and murdered any who spoke against them. Whenever members of the gang were arrested and brought to trial, Plummer's men would intimidate the jury so completely that they were acquitted time and time again. After one trial, some community members, unaware that Plummer was the leader of the gang, asked him to take over as sheriff and clean up the town. After that, Plummer's men could rest even more comfortably in the knowledge that they could terrorize the citizenry without reprisal.

Soon the "better men" in town—those trying to establish a community, institutions of government, and their own fortunes—had had all they could take. In the fall of 1863, local Masons laid the groundwork for a vigilante organization. When one member of Plummer's gang was tried for murder, the Masons took turns standing in court with their firearms at their sides. This time they got the verdict they wanted. Rather than ship the prisoner to a distant jail, the vigilantes hanged him that very night. Success bred more attempts at justice. The Committee of Vigilance murdered Plummer and executed twenty-one of the suspected gang members in thirty-seven days. So hell-bent were they on retribution that some vigilantes traveled six hundred miles to exterminate the last vestiges of the Plummer gang.[15]

Even such apparently legitimate and Hollywood-ready organizations moved from targeting criminality to targeting those they did not like for other reasons. The most dubious achievement of the Montana vigilantes was the execution of Thomas Slade for disorderly conduct. He was a poor man who refused to go along with the vigilantes, and the Montana men believed that it was important to "make an example" of him. Even so, many Montanans recalled this vigilante episode as one of the proudest in their history—and it has become a part of the usable past as well. In advertising for recruits for the Militia of Montana—which was formed after United States marshals killed Vicki and Sammy Weaver in Ruby Ridge, Idaho, in 1992—the Weavers' friend John Trochmann reminded the people of Montana of their heritage in the all-American vigilante past.[16]

If disorderly conduct could cost a man his life, criminality had clearly become a subjective category in many rural communities. In fact, as in South Carolina, vigilantism became more revealing when frontiersmen turned from solving crimes to pursuing people in their communities whose behaviors or beliefs more subtly threatened the economic stability or political control of their communities. But again, as in South Carolina, these disputes were rarely presented in the explicit language of class. More often questions of economic difference were linked to religion, morality, or racial entitlement. Among the most important instances of frontier vigilantism, then, are those that combine several deviations from community standards. For their communal economy, authoritarian political system, and polygamous marriage practices, for example, the Mormons suffered more than any other religious group in the United States. And this was true despite the fact that they were, more completely than any other religious group of the time, born in America.

Mormonism began within a society flush with the excitement of reform, revivalism, and evangelism and the anxieties of a new economic and political era. Throughout the first decades of the nineteenth century, northern New York provided some of the most fertile ground for the massive religious revival known as the Second Great Awakening. The region was home not only to farm families, like Joseph Smith's, who were struggling to make ends meet after a series of crop failures, but also to newly urbanized families who had moved to the industrial centers of Rochester and Utica to seek their fortunes away from the vicissitudes of nature. All were concerned with protecting their place in the emerging middle class and in taking control of their economic destinies. Thus they were also attracted to revivalist preachers like Charles Grandison Finney, who told them to reject the rigidities and hierarchies of orthodox Calvinism, seek conversion experiences, and take control of their spiritual destinies. The preachers were, in a sense, completing the job of transforming American society which had begun in the revolutionary and early national periods. They told farmers, small businessmen, and skilled workers that the old hierarchies and authorities were gone. Now any man could make himself into anything he wanted to be. Moreover, any woman could take charge of her spiritual life and that of her children and community. Economic, political, and spiritual life now lay singularly, if precariously, in the hands of the "common" man and woman.

Joseph Smith's mother and father did not join any of the new revivalist sects organizing around Palmyra, New York, but Joseph undoubtedly heard their calls and felt their magnitude. He attended many local camp meetings and brooded about which path to take. On a beautiful spring morning in 1820, he went to a familiar spot in the woods to pray. Suddenly, he claimed, "[I] was seized by some power which entirely overcame me, and had such astonishing influence over me as to blind my tongue so that I could not speak."[17] Visions and voices were common parts of the Protestant conversion experience, but what came next most definitely was not. In a series of revelations, Joseph learned that God did not recognize any of the current sects as his church. In fact, the entire idea of pluralism within Protestantism was utterly incorrect. There was only one true church after all, the church of ancient man in North America which waited for a new prophet to recreate it. After a visit on September 21, 1823, from a messenger named Moroni, Smith learned that the church's complete history and teachings were written on plates buried on a nearby hillside. For the next five years, Smith translated the plates from behind a curtain while scribes wrote down his words. The resulting document, *The Book of Mormon*, was published in 1829.

From 1830 until 1839, Smith and his converts worked to establish a new religious community. Although founded in America for Americans, the Mormon community would be significantly different from most American communities of its time. Rather than persevere and prosper as individuals, for example, Smith asked converts to give over all their worldly possessions to the church and to work cooperatively under his sole authority and direction. Rather than decide things for themselves in the liberal political tradition, he asked them to vote as a bloc in local elections. Rather than submit decisions to a democratic forum, Smith made all decisions regarding the future of the church himself and appointed whomever he pleased to local assemblies.

These practices rankled his fellow New Yorkers from the outset. They were intrigued by Smith's conversion, yet horrified by what they saw as his money-grubbing. Soon they concluded that every word Smith said was blasphemy. If so, they could not tolerate Mormonism as they did most other new sects. For an early meeting of thirty converts, the town of Palmyra denied Smith the use of the town hall. A group of men tore out a dam that had been built for baptisms. Smith patiently rebuilt it. When the baptisms were performed, however, a mob of men surrounded Smith's house. Twice in the summer of 1830 Smith was arrested on a charge of disorderly conduct.[18]

Smith realized that he would have to leave New York if his community were to survive. But even as his flock prospered in their new home in Ohio, trouble was never far away. Insisting that following *The Book of Mormon* was the only path to salvation, missionaries spread out throughout the Northeast seeking converts. Ironically, the same circumstances that turned some New Yorkers against the Mormons turned others into believers. In an age of economic and social insecurity and rampant revivalism, many Americans were searching for certainty in their lives. Many found what they were looking for in the Church of Jesus Christ of the Latter-day Saints, and by 1831 Smith had authorized two Ohio locations and envisioned a third, a New Jerusalem, in Independence, Missouri. The Missouri township took root under the direction of Edward Partridge, and only new converts who had traveled from outside the region would reside there. Such devout believers were more than willing to give all they had to the church and follow the teachings of their prophet to the letter.

They would also have to sacrifice their lives. In both Ohio and Missouri settlers continued to resent the Saints' communalistic economic and political behavior. Mormons traded exclusively with other Mormons; likewise, they used their community capital to buy more large plots of land at public auction—a calamity for local settlers who had been waiting for years for the land to become available. Frontiersmen also did not like their political power or the suppression of free speech and free press within the church. They resented the Mormons' belief that that Native Americans should be assimilated into white society and that slavery should be abolished. But what they said they hated most of all was the Mormons' practice of "celestial marriage," or polygamy. The settlers believed, first and foremost, that having multiple wives violated God's teachings. But they also thought that polygamy assailed the dignity of the marriage contract, which, in the view of many nineteenth-century men and women, distinguished women's unpaid labor from slavery. Moreover, they worried that polygamy gave male Mormons an economic advantage through the unpaid productivity of their wives.[19] All these differences were too much on a frontier troubled by economic depression and growing sectional rivalries, steeped in the heritage of republican politics, liberal economics, and emerging but controversial notions of women's role in the republic. Again and again, in town after town, setters decided the Mormons had to go.

But there was nowhere for them to go. In Ohio a disgruntled ex-convert and a gang of local men used a barrel of whisky to smash their way into a home where Smith was staying. Fawn M. Brodie describes how they dragged him out of bed, "stripped him, scratched and beat him with savage pleasure, and smeared his bleeding body with tar from head to foot. Ripping a pillow into shreds, they [covered] him with feathers . . . and dragged him into unconsciousness over the frozen ground."[20] Frontier people in Missouri were even more determined to keep Mormons out of their communities. On July 20, 1832, five hundred men swarmed the courthouse in Independence and demanded that all Mormons leave Jackson County. The meeting shortly turned into a mob that marched to the office of the Mormon newspaper and wrecked its entire contents, including all existing copies of Smith's revelations, *A Book of Commandments*. Finally, they tarred and feathered Partridge and another leader, Charles Allen. When they came back on July 23, they carried rifles, pistols, clubs, and whips and compelled Mormon leaders to assemble in the public square. Slaves were told to burn the Mormons' crops, while their masters burned the Mormons' homes and stores. "We will rid Jackson County of the Mormons, peaceably if we can, forcibly if we must. If they will not go without, we will whip and kill the men; we will destroy their children, and ravish their Women."[21]

Smith and the Mormons were determined to remain in their promised land. They petitioned the governor for protection of their property and even armed their own fighting force. In a skirmish be-

Violence followed Mormons wherever they moved in the Mississippi Valley. This lithograph shows a mob tarring and feathering Joseph Smith in 1830.
Courtesy of Brown Brothers.

tween Saints and Missouri militia men, several Mormons were killed. Still the attacks continued. In one community, mobs burned all Mormons' homes, forcing several families to live in the adjoining forest. Many died of exposure, exhaustion, illness, and starvation. In another town, mobs prevented any Mormons from voting in local elections. Nineteen more Mormons were killed at Shoal Creek when two hundred state militia men fired on Mormon women and children hiding in a blacksmith shop. Even when the Saints agreed to leave Missouri and move across the Mississippi River to a town they renamed Nauvoo, peace did not last long. Although Illinois settlers had initially welcomed the Saints, soon they too came to resent and fear them. In 1844 officials ordered the press of the Mormon *Nauvoo Expositor* destroyed and Smith arrested. For their "protection," Smith and his brother Hyrum were moved to a jail in Carthage, but on June 27, 1844, a mob broke into the jail and shot and killed both men. Shortly thereafter, Mormon homes were once again burned to the ground by angry mobs of nightriding, torchbearing Gentiles.

Given this terrifying history, it is not surprising that the new leader of the Saints, Brigham Young, chose the most remote place he could find in North America for his people. Utah was not even a part of the United States when the surviving Mormons settled there. Although Mormonism was the most completely and indigenously American religion ever practiced, with its optimistic and progressive outlook as well as its admiration of the United States Constitution and the natural environment, Young believed that the Mormons could not live among United States citizens or under the jurisdiction of the federal government. Likewise, while Mormons eventually prospered, symbolizing the self-made man of the American bourgeoisie and, as Klaus J. Hansen remarks, even "out-Jackson[ing] the Jacksonians by proclaiming that the common man could become a god," they were not perceived as capitalist individualists in their years of persecution.[22] Frontiersmen in the Mississippi Valley were struggling themselves to adapt to and fit into the complex and contradictory antebellum era. People who would not even try to participate in this culture and whose counterculture threatened the strength and viability of the mainstream were beyond the pale—or more precisely beyond the confines of toleration.

The culminating episodes of frontier vigilantism took place in the industrializing Rocky Mountain West and Southwest. There, white

miners and farmers targeted, in the time-worn habits of collective violence, Chinese and Mexican workers who threatened the control and
success of their so-called white republic. They forcibly deported these
workers, or murdered them and burned their homes, all to achieve a
semblance of control over their economic destinies. But even when
they succeeded in ridding the West of some ethnic competitors, they
still did not prosper. When many then turned to unionization to ac-
complish their goals, they experienced a reversal of roles. The "best
people" in nineteenth-century mining communities, like those on the
South Carolina frontier, were still not too wealthy, too sophisticated, or
too proud to organize as vigilantes themselves. They attacked the
union activists with the same ferocity that the miners had attacked the
Chinese. Thus two groups of small producers turned against each other
instead of working together to support democratic reform. Eventually
only industrial corporations and their ally, the federal government,
would come out on top.

When news of the gold strike at Sutter's Mill outside Sonoma, California, finally leaked out, it spread around the world as fast as men
could shout it. Before long, miners in quest of their fortunes were sail-
ing, walking, and riding to California from all corners of the globe. Soon
it became apparent that few if any miners were really going to get rich
quick; instead, they would compete for the few good sections of river
and the few well-paying jobs at the large mining companies. As early as
1850, then, white miners in California struggled to exclude others they
deemed intolerable—in particular the Chinese—from the mining economy. They believed that the Chinese in particular seemed to be willing
and able to work longer hours for shorter wages than whites and thus
diminished white workers' authority and remuneration. In camp after
camp, Chinese miners watched as their few possessions were destroyed
by angry mobs. Soon the anti-Chinese violence became even better organized. Anti-coolie clubs put pressure on politicians in California cities
and Caucasian clubs enforced the Foreign Miners' Tax and other dis-
criminatory policies in the countryside. Indeed, anti-Chinese violence
brought together such ethnically diverse whites that without it they
might never have believed that they had anything in common.

Attacks on Chinese miners increased with the economic hardship
of the 1880s. Over the summer of 1885 in Rock Springs, Wyoming, for
example, resentful white workers at the Union Pacific coal fields who
believed that the company was replacing them with Chinese miners

waited for their chance to gain revenge. On September 2, a fight broke out between a white miner and two Chinese miners and ended with injuries to all three. According to one witness, "No sooner had the miners finished their dinners, than they began to assemble in the streets, and 'Vengeance on the Chinese!' was the universal cry, even some of the women joining in the demonstration. A vote was then taken, and the immediate expulsion of the Mongolians was determined upon." Seventy-five armed men proceeded to march on the camp's Chinese section "yelling like wild men, and shooting every Chinaman who was in sight." Chinese fled, some without shoes or hats, into the mountains with the miners in hot pursuit. Later the men went back to the Chinese section, looted the houses, and set them on fire. "The flames forced out quite a number of Chinamen who had, until then, eluded detection. These poor fellows were either murdered outright, or fatally wounded and thrown into the burning buildings there to be roasted alive."[23] Encouraged by the "success" in Rock Springs, several other towns erupted in anti-Chinese violence in the next days and weeks.

Chinese who fled the killing zones of the mines met with more success, but no less prejudice, performing agricultural labor. As Cletus E. Daniel put it, large farm owners were often interested in making the Chinese be to California "what the Africans had been to the South."[24] White farm workers and small landowners wanted nothing of the kind. In 1876–79 and again in 1893–94, whites formed vigilante-style organizations dedicated to forcing the Chinese off the land. Some organizations resolved that they would not use mob violence but only "lawful and honorable means."[25] After a mob in Wheatland, California, had broken into the cabins of several Chinese workers, burned all their possessions, and turned them loose without a penny to their names, one newspaper reporter observed that "mob violence and incendiarism is neither lawful nor honorable and will not be countenanced by the people. . . . The eastern press is impressing the people with the idea that all the Western slope is a mob, and occurrences such as that at Wheatland only strengthen the assertions."[26] As if in counterpoint, a few days later workers in Nicolaus, California, forcibly marched a group of forty Chinese men to a nearby barge and sent them to Sacramento. They paid the $125 fare themselves.

Elsewhere, however, vigilantism went far beyond "lawful and honorable" means. Throughout central California, Chinese workers were physically assaulted and their homes and belongings burned. In March 1877, five men who were members of the Order of Caucasians, a com-

bination union and voluntary fraternal association—planned a reign of
terror in the countryside outside Chico, California. They began by en-
tering the cabin of four Chinese workers at the Lemm ranch at gun-
point. Then one of the men, Eugene Roberts, decided that each white
should pick one Chinese to execute. Next he threw kerosene on the
wounded men's bodies and set them on fire. The five men were tried
and sentenced to long prison terms for the murder. All who observed
the trial understood, however, that their sentences were light. Even
seventy-five years later, a Yuba City reporter recalled that "had their
victims been white men they would have been hanged."[27]

But Chinese were not the only workers targeted by frontier-style
vigilantes. Mexican workers too aroused the resentments of white Cal-
ifornians—even as whites also intermarried with the elite landowning
californios. In the early 1850s whites tried to expel Sonorans and Mexicans from the mines just as they had expelled Native Americans and
Chinese. Unlike the Chinese, however, some Hispanic miners did not
look for alternative sources of employment, in the railroads, in agricultural work, or in urban factories. Instead they organized in bandit
gangs—reminiscent of those in South Carolina—to prey on miners and
seek revenge for the injustices they had incurred. Fear moved one
white Californian in 1854 to advise, "When I see a Mexican approach-
ing, I cock my rifle and cover him with it. At the same time calling him
to raise his hand away from his lasso which hangs at his saddle-bow. In
this way, I keep my rifle on him until he has passed and gone beyond
lasso distance."[28] According to Richard White, in Los Angeles anti-Mexican violence "brought Los Angeles to the brink of race war between
1850 and 1856."[29] Although there were only 2,300 people living in Los
Angeles County in 1850 and 1851, there were forty-four murders. Most
were acts of violence targeting Mexicans, whether they had been justly
accused of wrongdoing or not. Even more widespread anti-Mexican violence would occur with the increased immigration of Mexican farm
workers in the 1920s.[30]

In Texas, tensions between whites and *tejanos* did result in a race
war, with vigilantism on both sides. The Texas Rangers was a vigilante organization with a twist—it had been officially funded by the Republic of
Texas to fight Native Americans and Mexicans in the 1840s. After Texas
became a state and protection of the frontier reverted to the federal government, the Rangers became a fully voluntary and self-supporting organization. The Rangers became notorious for their raids on Native

Americans and Hispanics. But in 1859 in southern Texas, the Rangers got a tåste of their own medicine when Juan Cortina shot the Brownsville sheriff for pistol-whipping a drunken *vaquero*. He escaped, but returned with sixty more angry *tejanos* who let all the Hispanic prisoners go, gathered provisions in white-owned stores, and murdered four Americans they accused of killing Hispanics. Cortina and his allies escaped capture both in Texas and south of the border. The Texas Rangers satisfied themselves with reprisals against most other Hispanics in the region.[31]

By attacking Chinese and Mexican laborers, white workers tried to secure their economic authority in the emerging industrial economy. But, as we have seen, they also did so by organizing and promoting unionization. In the mines and fields and forests of the Far West workers mobilized local cells of the Knights of Labor, the Western Federation of Miners, and the Industrial Workers of the World. When they did, however, they themselves became, in the eyes of the "better men" in their towns, the very sort of lazy, criminal "lower sort" whom they had victimized before. When they struck for higher wages and safer working conditions and suggested that industrial capitalism had not kept its promise to all members of the work force, least of all to its essential producers, miners became the victims of state and federal militia, detective agencies, spies, imported strikebreakers, and, of course, vigilante organizations of local citizens.

The most notorious attacks by local citizens on organized miners came in Cripple Creek and Ludlow, Colorado. Although separated by fifteen years, the strikes bore several important resemblances. In both cases, middle-class shopkeepers and professionals fought alongside mine owners and state officials to undermine the growing power of strikers and union activists. Earlier in the century, such men and women had sympathized with the strikers, who, after all, were their clients and patrons. At the 1892 strike in Coeur d'Alene, Idaho, local businessmen had even been arrested and thrown into open-air bullpens with the strikers. By the late 1890s and the early 1900s, however, mine owners had succeeded, in Richard White's words, in "driving a wedge between middle-class and working-class members of the mining towns."[32] Open class conflict like this served to radicalize some workers even more, encouraging them toward the avowed socialism of the Industrial Workers of the World. At the same time, however, this conflict so horrified business leaders and politicians that they began to look for a way to replace it with harmony.

To be fair, the miners were not exactly pacifists themselves. Strikers armed themselves fully, made use of explosives, and murdered scabs. But middle-class citizens' use of vigilantism and their support from state and federal authorities proved stronger than the workers and eventually broke the strike. In Cripple Creek, for example, merchants and shopkeepers organized the Citizens' Alliance, a vigilante organization in which membership was mandatory. By March 1904 they began the forcible deportation of strikers from the town. When a bomb exploded at a railroad station killing thirteen scabs, the Citizens' Alliance went to work in earnest. They began to deport all union members by train and even abandoned one carload of men in the middle of the Kansas prairie. At the Ludlow, Colorado, coal mines owned by John D. Rockefeller, strikebreakers, militia men, and citizens' deputies launched an attack on a tent colony of strikers' families. When the strikers fought back, the deputies set the tents on fire. Thirty-nine people were killed, including eleven children who suffocated in their burning tents.

Such tactics were well in place in the West when the most feared union of all, the Industrial Workers of the World, gathered strength among miners, lumberjacks, dock workers, and farm workers. Community members in such industrial towns as Everett, Washington, and Bisbee, Arizona, were horrified by the appearance of thousands of "bums" and "bindlestiffs" arriving in town for IWW rallies or strikes. They were even less pleased with the IWW's fiery language of sabotage and destruction of the industrial system. But they knew what to do to stop it. In 1917 vigilantes from Butte, Montana, kidnaped IWW organizer Frank Little and murdered him. In Bisbee, Arizona, other citizens deported "Wobblies" into the desert. In Everett, Washington, sheriff's "deputies" tried to run all the Wobblies out of town. When some returned on a boat from Seattle, they stood on the dock fully armed and ready for a fight. Not long after, five Wobblies lay dead and fifty-one other men were injured. Given the perceived threat of socialism in the United States and around the world during World War I, many Americans believed that vigilante justice against labor organizers and other radicals was an act of patriotism. Thus when a group of Wobblies dared to fire a shot into an American Legion parade in Centralia, Washington, in 1919, near civil war erupted. Among other cruelties, legionnaires dragged Wesley Everest into the forest, forced him to run the gauntlet, then castrated and murdered him.[33]

Acts of violence like these, as well as the carefully orchestrated assaults and arrests by the United States Department of Justice, brought the Wobblies to their knees. Never again in the United States would so many workers take such a radical vision of worker democracy so seriously. But, of course, they would not again believe that they had to. Within two decades, economic prosperity and federal recognition of the rights of workers and their unions would make many Americans, rural and urban alike, believe that the promise of freedom and democracy and a classless society had come true. The Wagner Act of 1935, like the Agricultural Adjustment Act of 1933, sought to smooth the rough edges of capitalism and spread its benefits more broadly to all Americans. It provided the foundation for significant increases in wages, benefits, and protections for industrial workers after World War II. As the strikes by migrant workers and other unskilled laborers in the 1950s and 1960s proved, however, initial benefits from the marriage between labor and the liberal state were won by whites. Moreover, as the shrinking of industry in America in the 1980s and 1990s has shown, the broadening of capitalism was not the transforming of capitalism. Nothing the liberal state could do or say could prevent corporate employers from scaling back wages, benefits, and workplace safety regulations or even from leaving the country altogether. By the 1980s and 1990s, the "lower sorts" in rural America would discover just how low they could go.

"For that they were all Enemies":

VIGILANTISM AND THE POLITICS OF RACE

When white miners met up with Chinese miners in the rugged hills of California, they saw competitors for their daily bread, coffee, and beans. But they saw—and objected to—much more than this competition. The Chinese "had to go," they would say, not only because they worked so hard but because they were Chinese, members of a different, inferior, and dangerous race whose offenses included lusting after white women and keeping their own women as slaves. Thus it would be foolish and naive to explain all or even most of the vigilantism in rural America in strictly economic terms or even in the simple terms of frontier self-defense. The most significant episodes of rural violence in

the United States have pitted white frontiersmen and their rural prog-
eny against enemies they have defined by race, particularly Native
Americans and African Americans. In fact, rural communities supported and rewarded racial violence so completely and over such long
periods of time that entire subsections of the West, Midwest, and South
became akin to vigilante committees of the whole, primed and ready
for action at any time, and caring little what the official authorities of
government might think of them. Historian Joel Williamson describes
such attitudes as racial radicalism.[34] But ordinary people knew what
they meant too. As one outspoken critic of lynching put it in 1895,
"The South is a pretty good organized mob, and will remain so until
bursted by the federal government."[35]

If the colonists who came to British North America were, by custom and memory, potential producer radicals, so were they also potential racial radicals. Although most Europeans did not own slaves and
had not yet developed the strict institutions of racism which they
would in the New World, they had nonetheless established sophisticated notions about the relationship between skin color and culture.
Early travel narratives portrayed Native Americans, for example, as bar-
baric and untrustworthy. And although Native Americans could also be
admired for their physical grace, nobility, and honor, they were nevertheless understood to be as different as any people could possibly be
from Europeans.[36] Such presumptions of racial superiority and difference lay in wait, ready to take root and grow on the North American
continent, where the two cultures would meet face to face.

Even if they were only *potentially* racist—and this is a matter of
some debate—Europeans were undoubtedly and unabashedly ethnocentric.[37] Englishmen who came to Massachusetts and Virginia were
absolutely certain that what they brought to the New World was vastly
superior to anything (other than gold) they might acquire here. They
had a powerful arsenal of political, economic, social, cultural, and military weapons. Gunpowder, guns, navigational instruments, horses, attack dogs, armor, colorful pieces of cloth, bright beads, sturdy shoes, a
permanent system of government and a code of law—all these gave Europeans a powerful sense of superiority. Moreover, everything that Europeans possessed and believed could be represented and reproduced
through writing; this ability gave them an advantage of the highest order.[38] As Stephen Greenblatt remarks, "Such was the confidence of this

culture that it expected perfect strangers . . . to abandon their own beliefs, preferably immediately, and embrace those of Europe as luminously and self-evidently true. A failure to do so provoked impatience, contempt, and even murderous rage."[39]

Europeans did not simply consider their culture to be superior to native culture, however. They believed that Native American culture was so vastly inferior that it actually represented the mirror image, or a cultural contradiction, of their own. Europeans were a people of God; Native Americans were godless. Europeans were a people with a written history; Native Americans were a people without any history at all. While Europeans, as James Axtell notes, "participated in a capitalist economy of currency and credit, the natives bartered in kind from hand to hand. While [they] were governed by statutes, sheriffs, parliaments, and kings, the Indians' suasive politics of chiefs and councils seemed to be no government at all. . . . While [European] time shot straight ahead into a progressive future, Indian time looped and circled upon itself, blurring the boundaries between a hazy past, a spacious present, and an attenuated future."[40] In short, native people helped Europeans define themselves by showing them who they were and were not.

By focusing so entirely on what Native Americans lacked, Europeans overlooked what they did have, including the ideals, skills, and ways of life that would prevent their immediate acceptance of European culture and would instead promote resistance throughout the countryside for hundreds of years. Not the least of these was the Native Americans' own well-formed sense of superiority. "There is no Indian," said a Micmac chief, "who does not consider himself infinitely more happy and more powerful than the French."[41] Although they envied, accumulated, and sometimes transformed for their own purposes many aspects of European culture, they saw no need for others. Moreover, Native American culture proved remarkably flexible. The Iroquois and Catawba and other tribes allied, cooperated, and traded with some European settlers while maintaining their own integrity. Other tribes used their knowledge of the land and skills in war to halt European advancement and ruin attempts at Native American enslavement. By the end of Metacom's War in 1676, warriors had forced New Englanders to abandon one-fifth of the towns in Massachusetts and Rhode Island and killed one of every twenty males. Although the end of the story is well known, for at least one hundred years along the Atlantic Coast and much longer in the Mississippi Valley, the Europeanization of the continent was—at best—a draw.[42]

This drama of resistance, synthesis, transformation, and conquest played itself out on the frontier of Euro-American settlement. The leading edge of white settlement everywhere predated the final battles and treaties that officially allowed it. Indeed, settlement was in some cases intended to force those final acts of cultural encounter. Thus representatives of two ardently ethnocentric cultures came together on the frontier with a great deal to win, lose, and fear from each other. Over and again, whites demonstrated their determination to take Native American land by whatever means necessary, through rape, murder, massacre, disease, and enslavement. Over and over, Native Americans fought back. In Jamestown, Virginia, Deerfield, Massachusetts, Long Canes, South Carolina, New Ulm, Minnesota, and countless other isolated frontier outposts, raiding parties of angry Native Americans attacked, killed, and captured men, women, and children in an effort to force them off the land.

Fear of personal violence alone might have radicalized frontiersmen's underlying racism and ethnocentricity. But they were afraid of more than death. Unlike easterners, who lived far enough away from the edge of settlement to develop generous and sentimental attitudes about "noble savages," men and women of the frontier struggled to maintain "civilized" ways of life in a wilderness of both literal and figurative temptation. As John Demos has said of eighteenth-century Puritan New Englanders, "At some deeper (mostly unacknowledged) level, [they worried] that the process might reverse itself—so as to make the currents of change run the opposite way. Instead of their civilizing the wilderness . . . the wilderness might change, might *uncivilize them*. This they [feel] as an appalling prospect, a nightmare to resist and suppress by every means possible."[43] In New England—and other regions as well—stories of whites who had been captured by Native Americans, crossed over into the world of the savage, and then returned were wildly popular. Told less frequently and with considerably less relish were the stories of captives who refused at all cost to return to their old lives. Among them were women who married into Native American tribes and refused to return their bodies or souls to the white men who claimed them.[44]

In fear for their lives, their cultures, and their claims to manhood, frontiersmen met Native American people better prepared for violence than for compassion. Of course, sometimes their acts of violence were legitimated by the provincial, state, or federal government's official proclamation of war. At other times, however, rural people went beyond the government's command, explicitly defied the government's treaties, or forced a change in government policy through the use or threat of violence. For example, rural people tended to overlook the distinctions between peaceful and hostile, treaty and nontreaty, Christian and non-Christian Native Americans—distinctions that helped governments establish trade, transportation, and defense capabilities on the frontier. To many frontiersmen, a Native American of any kind was better dead than alive. Likewise, settlers who killed Native Americans rarely considered themselves to be disloyal. To the contrary, they believed that they were the true defenders of Euro-American ways of life. As James Axtell has written of colonial New Englanders, Indian fighting was the first experience that brought colonists together and helped them see that they had more in common with one another than they had with the British.[45] Killing an Indian, thus, marked a colonist as being a fully initiated American—and it would continue to do so for many years to come.

Colonial Virginia provides our first example of racial radicalism among rural people. In Bacon's Rebellion, the racial animus of frontiersmen went so far beyond that of government officials that it is often remembered as the first important colonial rebellion against the British. Yet it was not initially understood that way by the men involved. Bacon's Rebellion began in 1676 when freed servants and other small farmers in western Virginia tired of a negotiated peace with local Native Americans whose lands they coveted and whose ways of life they deplored. By that time the famous Powhatan empire had been defeated but the British had still not consolidated its own power in the region. Wars between and among colonists and Native American nations in Virginia, Maryland, Carolina, and even as far away as New England created a constantly changing landscape of alliances, treaties, trading partners, and potential violence. For example, in July 1675, when warriors of the Doeg tribe stole hogs from a wealthy Virginia planter named Thomas Mathew and subsequently killed one of his servants, Virginians followed them across the Potomac and killed ten Doeg tribesmen as well as fourteen Susquehannock people, whom they conveniently forgot were long-time British allies. Retaliatory raids by the Native Americans led to a full-scale assault on one hundred Susquehannock people caught within the old Piscataway Fort and the capture and execution of two Susquehannock kings. When the other Native Americans escaped the fort, they began raids that this time would provide lessons in terror. Virginians could not tell where the warriors might strike next or even how many there were. It seemed that there were "so many that none can guess at their number" and even worse, that they "had joined a 'confederation' to destroy them."[46]

A confederation to destroy all Native Americans—peaceful or not—was what Nathaniel Bacon organized when he heard that Governor William Berkeley planned to protect the countryside with a series of upriver forts. Every settler knew that forts were an unworkable solution: Native Americans disappeared into the forests as soon as they struck, and the most vulnerable settlements were far removed from the rivers. Moreover, the governor planned to pay the soldiers stationed there more than poor farmers could earn in a year—and tax local residents to pay for it. Why not simply be rid of the Native Americans for once and for all and distribute their lands to poor white farmers, Bacon and his allies wondered. After all, there was no real difference between a "good" or a "bad" Indian. As he explained to Governor Berkeley later, Bacon wanted to kill "all Indians in general for that they were all Enemies."[47] Without an official commission, Bacon gathered local men together and went on the offensive. He marched first against the Susquehannock. A friendly tribe, the Occaneechees, offered prisoners, food, and shelter to the Virginians. After killing the prisoners, Bacon turned on his hosts and quickly dispatched most of them as well.

Governor Berkeley was not amused. Appalled at the massacres and worried about their effect on trading alliances with friendly tribes, Berkeley removed Bacon from the council and declared him a rebel, a threat to the government of the colony. When Bacon arrived in Jamestown to take his seat, Berkeley's men captured him and presented him to the assemblymen on his knees. Next he tried to compromise with Bacon by suggesting other ways in which the lives of western Virginians could be improved. Such coy strategies only enraged Bacon more. He returned to Jamestown with even more volunteers and announced his intention to continue the assault on Native Americans with or without an official commission. His allies raided the camp of the peaceful Pamunkey nation, murdering, plundering, and capturing as they went. Some Pamunkey prisoners were marched through the streets of Jamestown. Finally, they turned on the elite of Jamestown itself, who had never done enough to help the backcountry men. While terrified planters and officials waited on ships offshore, Bacon's men looted their homes and burned the capital to the ground.

When Bacon died of dysentery on October 26, 1676, the rebellion came to an abrupt conclusion. Discussion of its significance, however, had only just begun. Three meanings have been widely agreed upon. First, along with the devastations of Metacom's War in New England, Bacon's Rebellion captured the attention of the British government and brought about increased supervision and taxation of the colonies. Second, the rebellion convinced some local tribes not to trust a British treaty, no matter who presented it, and thus increased the possibility of serious retaliation in the Southeast during the next century. Most important, Bacon's Rebellion demonstrated the powerful way in which hatred of an alien race could bring economically diverse white men together and help them see one another as more alike than different. Such experiences would ultimately lead to the quintessential American paradox: the coexistence of a society devoted to personal liberty and a society that legalized slavery.[48] In the dirty work of Bacon and his men we can see the vague outlines of a culture that could glorify the use of violence in the name of freedom and equality and not see any contradiction at all.

Wherever a colonial or early American government was perceived as caring more about protecting Native Americans and providing for eastern elites than protecting settlers, trouble was sure to follow. Nowhere was this more true than in eighteenth-century Pennsylvania. As they would be in the Whisky Rebellion, Pennsylvanians were strictly divided by region, ethnicity, and religion. The wealthy, subdued, pacifist Quaker elite in Philadelphia had little time for the rowdy, violent, poor Scots-Irish Presbyterians who were under constant assault from Native Americans. Over and again the elite denied these westerners funds for defense or even bounties for scalps—a practice common in the colonies. The westerners were also denied equal representation in the provincial assembly; only one in every five seats belonged to them.

Between 1753 and 1767 Native American allies of the French raided Pennsylvania cabins and farms every summer and fall. Eventually these sallies led to the larger French and Indian War and, finally, to yet another set of frontier assaults. Hostilities unfolded this way: between 1755 and 1763, French and Native American troops battled British regulars for control of the entire Ohio River valley. Although the French troops held their ground initially, British troops eventually prevailed and forced the French from the continent once and for all. For Native Americans who had grown accustomed to the French government's liberal attitudes, the sudden transfer of authority was shocking. Many British officials cared a great deal less about keeping the peace than they did about pacification—by whatever means necessary. For example, General Jeffrey Amherst, commander-in chief of British forces in America, held Native American people in utter contempt. He cut off supplies of food and ammunition, as well as the French custom of gift giving. Such expenses were completely unnecessary, he believed. "The only sure method of treating the savages," he instructed his officers in the field, "is to keep them in proper subjection and punish, without exception, the transgressor."[49]

When the French and Indian War ended in 1763, thousands of land-hungry colonists who had endured the demographic explosion of mid-eighteenth-century America poured into the newly opened West. Just as they did, however, those areas exploded in warfare again. After consulting Neolin, a Delaware prophet who had learned in a vision that the Ohio River tribes should unite against whites and forsake their ways, the great Ottawa chief Pontiac called for a sweeping military movement against the victorious British. But this time he meant *all* the British—the ones wearing the elaborate costumes of battle and the ones wearing the ruder garments of cultivation. Pontiac's forces attacked every fort between Pennsylvania and Green Bay, Wisconsin— seven in two months alone—effectively isolating settlers from their only defenses. Then they laid siege to the new settlement communities. In less than two years, as many as two thousand colonists were killed or captured.[50] Thousands more fled their homes. In some places, Pontiac's War pushed back the line of settlement one hundred miles.

Still the Quakers in Philadelphia maintained their pacifism. In fact, they continued to provide refuge and protection to scattered remnants of Native American nations from the coast that had long since been defeated in battle and converted to Christianity. One such group was the Susquehannock, who lived as Christians near Conestoga, Pennsylvania. Frontiersmen, on the other hand, would have laughed at the idea of protecting Native Americans if they had not believed the consequences to be so deadly. As the raiding continued into 1763, rumors raged that "friendly" Indians were actually spies and were providing important information and supplies to warring nations. If true, something had to be done—something like what General Amherst was suggesting was the best way to "extirpate this execrable race": distribute blankets infested with smallpox or unleash a pack of specially trained dogs.[51]

But mob action was an option too. On December 14, 1763, a group of frontiersmen from Pennsylvania's "Paxton District" led by a Presbyterian minister attacked the village at Conestoga. The fifty-seven armed men had little trouble finishing off six Native Americans, including two women and one boy. According to a witness, "these poor defenseless Creatures were immediately fired upon, stabbed and Hatcheted to Death! The good [chief], among the rest, cut to pieces in his BED. All of them were scalped, and otherwise horribly mangled."[52] Then the frontiersmen set all the Native Americans' huts and possessions on fire so that when other tribesmen returned from a trading expedition they would find no food or shelter. A victory celebration for a job well done commenced immediately.

The party stopped when the frontiersmen learned of the government's plan to move the surviving Conestoga to a secure facility in Lancaster. This they felt was an unacceptable insult to whites. The government had never provided a secure facility or food or shelter for them when Native American raiding parties had terrorized the region. More frontiersmen gathered and followed the Conestoga to Lancaster. On December 27, they broke into the workhouse and attacked every man, woman, and child they could find. As a witness described it later, "When the poor [Indians] saw they had no protection . . . nor could possibly escape, and being without the least weapon for defense . . . they divided into their little families, the children clinging to the parents; they fell on their knees, protested their innocence, declared their love to the English, and, that, in their whole lives, they had never done them injury; and in this posture they all received the hatchet!"[53] When they were done, the Paxton Boys "huzzaed their triumph, as if they had gained victory and rode off—unmolested!"[54]

Still unsatisfied, in February an even larger group of frontiersmen marched on Philadelphia, demanding the execution of all Native Americans. As they trudged through the countryside, carrying knives, tomahawks, and pistols, their backcountry fellows gathered to cheer them on. So frightened were the people of Philadelphia that they formed militias in preparation. To avoid civil war, Benjamin Franklin offered to meet the incoming troops in Germantown. There the Paxton Boys presented him with a proclamation of their grievances against the government, including in particular their demand that more money be spent on western defense. Franklin promised to consider the petitions, the rebels went home for planting season, and the provincial assembly conveniently dropped the entire matter. For twenty more years, Native American raids against frontiersmen in western Pennsylvania continued unrestrained. By 1790 Pennsylvania frontiersmen who had always known that they should not trust Native Americans believed that they should never have trusted the government either. When the Washington administration added a tax on whisky to the other insults of frontier life, a new rebellion began, with many old faces in attendance.[55]

Even in the age of Jackson, when government policy explicitly sought to remove Native Americans to a so-called Permanent Indian Frontier and politicians boasted of their Indian-fighting exploits, rural people still took radical action against Native Americans. In the 1830s, southeastern cotton growers could hardly wait to burn homes, loot property, and wave good-by to their Cherokee neighbors, who were starting on their enforced and fatal Trail of Tears to Oklahoma. In southern Oregon, Indian extermination became a stated goal of many communities. In August 1853, for example, whites in Jacksonville, Oregon, executed a seven-year-old boy because, as they put it, "nits breed lice."[56] In California in the 1850s and 1860s local organizations raised money for bounties for scalps. Men who went over the limit simply lined their blankets and coats with the surplus. Likewise, when surviving Native Americans raided livestock or retaliated against settlers' families, vengeance was swift and sure. The total Native American population of California was reduced by 80 percent in less than twenty-five years. By 1915 several California tribes had been completely destroyed.[57]

Two manifestations of racial radicalism on the nineteenth-century frontier so shocked the nation that they caught the attention of a president who had had little time for Native American affairs and opened the door to major changes in federal policy toward native peoples. As in Virginia in 1676 and Pennsylvania in 1763, in Colorado and Minnesota in in 1860s, settlers were outnumbered and under attack from Native Americans angry at the encroachments of white settlers and the corruption of government officials. In Colorado, Cheyenne and Arapaho warriors refused to honor an 1858 treaty they considered unjust. Instead, they raided, looted, burned the homes and murdered the families of settlers on the isolated high plains. In Minnesota, in the summer of 1862, Santee Sioux under the leadership of Little Crow attacked settlers to avenge the corruption and cruelty of agency officials near New Ulm. For more than three terrifying months, warriors killed and captured white settlers and their families. In the end more than eight hundred settlers had been killed; more were captured, tortured, and forcibly marched through the countryside.

Horrible as these assaults were, Abraham Lincoln was even more appalled by what the settlers did to retaliate. In both cases frontiersmen attacked Native Americans after they had already surrendered and had been promised protection from the state. In Colorado, frenzied frontiersmen volunteered to serve in a makeshift militia under the leadership of former minister John Chivington. He told the fresh recruits that "the Cheyenne will have to be soundly whipped before they will be quiet. . . . kill them, as that is the only way."[58] But one band of Cheyenne under Chief Black Kettle had signed a peace agreement in Washington, agreeing to live under the government's protection along Sand Creek. That is where they were when Chivington's militia attacked at dawn on November 30, 1864. Black Kettle waved a white flag, then the American flag, all to no avail. The frontiersmen viciously attacked every Native American they could find. They dragged children out of caves, split open pregnant women, mutilated and mangled the corpses of all. It was not until five o'clock in the evening that they rode off triumphant, leaving the few survivors without food, shelter, or blankets on a bitterly cold night. Later, the militia men paraded the Cheyenne's severed body parts in front of cheering crowds on the streets of Denver.

The Minnesota crowds gathered to cheer as well—but did not do so quite so loudly as they had planned. On December 26, 1862, the largest mass execution in United States history took place in Mankato, Minnesota, when thirty-eight Santee warriors were hanged on a specially made gallows. One hundred more would have been put to death, if Lincoln had not commuted their sentences. Despite the demands of the Civil War, Lincoln and his staff reviewed the transcripts of the trial of the vanquished warriors and discovered that the Minnesota courts had followed few if any customary legal procedures. So egregious were the proceedings, in fact, that Lincoln would have commuted even more of the sentences if Governor Alexander Ramsey had not pleaded with him to let them stand. He argued that executions alone would protect the safety of innocent Santee. Already mobs of Minnesotans had attacked the prisoners—when they were marched from the agency to the courthouse, for example—by hurling boiling water and shooting

Thirty-eight Santee Sioux are hanged together in Mankato, Minnesota, on December 26, 1862, while crowds of settlers watch. Leslie's Illustrated Newspaper, January 24, 1863, p. 285
Courtesy of Minnesota Historical Society.

into the crowd. Many spoke of a mass retaliation against them if the execution did not go forward. The only answer, Ramsey believed, was a public execution of a just number of warriors and then the permanent removal of the Sioux from Minnesota. The Santee Sioux could never be assured of their safety in Minnesota again.[59]

Lincoln commuted the Santee sentences and ordered a congressional inquiry into the Sand Creek massacre. It would be left to his successor, Ulysses S. Grant, however—under the guidance of a new group of kindhearted Quakers—to propose federal policies that would prevent future attacks like this on Native Americans. They included the restriction of all Native Americans to reservations far away from white settlements and on land they believed no white could ever desire, the allotment of former Native American lands into homesteads for white settlers, and the forced assimilation of Native American children into white culture. Because Native Americans resisted these new programs, the killing continued. In fact, there were more battles in the era of Grant's "Peace Policy" than there had ever been before, including the most famous of all, the Battle of Little Big Horn. But as time went on in the late nineteenth century, more and more of the Indian killing was done by army regulars in battle against hostile Native American resisters, and less by roving mobs of frontiersmen against any and all Native Americans they could find. Thus the Peace Period, for all its own cruelties and failures, marked the beginning of the end of rampant genocidal violence between Native Americans and white settlers who had once stood face to face in the wilderness.

Rural violence against African Americans began in much the same way that rural violence against Native Americans did: with European cultural stereotypes about people with dark complexions and the fears that turn arrogance and greed into murderous rage. But it took a different chronological and regional course because of the imposition of African slavery. Whereas in the postbellum years Native American people were forced to move farther and farther away from whites and lost a great portion of their freedom, African Americans gained power and moved both literally and figuratively closer to whites. Thus just as the worst of the vigilante violence against Native Americans began to abate, the worst of the vigilante violence against freed African Americans was just beginning. Nevertheless, the same dynamics of rural life influenced both sets of assaults. Fear and resentment of the federal government, the struggle to maintain economic independence, a desire to control local affairs, an association of heterosexual manhood with sexual conquest, and a tradition of collective action all played a part in rural white men's determination to maintain racial superiority by whatever means necessary.

Colonists held preconceptions about Africans well before a large number of Africans arrived in British North America. European folklore, religious liturgy, travel narratives, and even Shakespeare plays described Africans as closer to beast than man, naturally lascivious, profoundly unintelligent, and permanently savage.[60] These racial prejudices both set the stage for the introduction of African slavery and were reinforced by it. Africans were sold into slavery because they could be—that is, they were available through slave traders, were unfamiliar with the American landscape, and were divided from one another by language and culture—and also because many whites thought they should be. Once they were, the racism that allowed African slavery to exist was hardened, consolidated, and codified by it. A variety of laws governing slavery were passed by the Virginia House of Burgesses between 1670 and 1705. Among other things, they allowed for the corporal punishment of a slave by his/her owner, and even the slave's murder if the owner felt it was justified. According to historian George Frederickson, the movement to abolish slavery accentuated this trend. As northern abolitionists argued for the equality of all men, southern intellectuals began to articulate their racist assumptions more completely.[61] In short, from 1700 until 1865 racial radicalism and the violence necessary to perpetuate it were the official and conventional—unradical—policies of half the states in the union.

Groups of racial radicals first appeared in the American South in the late-nineteenth century when, for the first time, the future of race relations (and of much else as well) was in doubt. Beginning in the immediate aftermath of the Civil War, accelerating with the coming of industrialization to the South, and continuing into the modern era, rural whites created a climate of terror for blacks. As one Atlanta minister described life in the early 1920s, "In many of the rural sections of Georgia . . . [a black person leads] a life of constant fear. . . . To him the beat of horses' hooves on the road at night, the rustling sound of a motor car, or the sudden call of a human voice, may be his death summons."[62]

*This poster, from the late 1860s, shows the popular
southern image of the Ku Klux Klan as the champion of
white supremacy over the recently emancipated slaves.*
Courtesy of the Rutherford B. Hayes Presidential Center.

The best-known manifestation of southern racial radicalism began
in December 1865 in the town of Pulaski, Tennessee, when six well-
educated but unemployed Confederate veterans who were looking for
something to do decided to form a club. The name they chose—Ku
Klux Klan—came from a division of the Greek word for circle, "kuklos,"
and the Scottish word "clan" spelled with an extra "K" for consistency.
In the pattern of fraternal organizations, so popular throughout the
United States in the nineteenth century, the young men met in secret
and developed elaborate rituals. One night they took bed linens from a

closet and made costumes. Then for fun they got on their horses and galloped around town in the dark. An unexpected result of this horseplay changed the nature of the club forever. As one observer put it, "The superstitious Negroes [in Pulaski] had not been amused by the spectacle, but, instead, had taken the riders for ghosts of the Confederate dead."[63] By November 1866 the Klan had spread through much of Tennessee; so had its custom of nocturnal visitations and threats to freedmen.

By 1867 the KKK had a constitution and an elaborate hierarchy; it expanded to nine states in the Piedmont and upcountry regions of the South when the Reconstruction Congress of the Radical Republicans ordered new governments installed throughout the South to limit the power former Confederates held in their home states. These new governments empowered southern sympathizers with the North (known as Scalawags) and local freedmen. For example, Radical Reconstructionists encouraged freedmen to form militias and to run for public office. They also established schools for the freedmen and encouraged African American suffrage. These goals were, of course, anathema to the members of the Klan. The new purpose of the Klan became to secure complete political and social subordination of all African Americans.[64] Nightriders now attacked the black militia men, whipping some and murdering others, threatened or killed African Americans who tried to vote, and burned schools, whipping, torturing, and hanging teachers at the new schools. With the most vengeance, they sought out African American men who they believed had engaged in or merely desired sexual contact with white women. Even after the first Klan had been disbanded by its leader Nathan Bedford Forrest in 1872, the suggestion of miscegenation by an African American man very often proved fatal—despite the fact that white men had raped African American women for centuries without reproach.

Indeed, it was a perceived increase in attacks by African American men on white women which fueled an explosion of radical violence against African Americans in the industrial era. Although many complex transformations occurred in the South between 1880 and 1915—including the completion of the railroads, the construction of mills, the influx of people to cities, the loosening of sexual mores, and the collapse of cotton prices—it was the increased mobility of a new generation of African Americans which most fully enraged rural whites. These were not the familiar blacks of an earlier time who had personal ties to whites, but "strange" and "bad" blacks whose identities and characters were unknown.[65] It would be hard to minimize the importance of this transformation from the point of view of most southern white men. As Nancy MacLean writes, Klansmen "could not discuss issues of race, class, or state power apart from their understanding of manhood, womanhood, and sexual decorum."[66] Any attack on the South—by the federal government, the power of an industrial economy, or the vagaries of global prices for crops—was submerged by many southerners into the rhetoric of gender and race.

For a few years, lynchings were not reserved for African Americans but were also used to control intolerable whites. Nevertheless, between 1890 and 1915 lynching became a predominantly interracial phenomenon in the South. In the 1890s, 75 percent of all people lynched were African American. In the 1900s, 90 percent were. The peak in absolute numbers came in the early 1890s: nearly seven hundred people died at the hands of lynch mobs between 1889 and 1893. In 1892 twice as many people were lynched as were executed legally in the United States. The highest rates were in the areas with the most recent increase in African American population—the gulf plains and cotton uplands regions. In these places lynchings became almost commonplace, despite its very real horror and brutality.[67]

A lynching was as cruel and savage an act of terror as any massacre of Native Americans on the frontier, and the lynch mob's methods of pursuing justice made those vengefully adopted in southern Minnesota in the aftermath of Little Crow's War look like the height of modern jurisprudence. "Black beasts" were accused of all manner of crimes, but particularly of rape, and were found guilty through forced confessions or none at all, with eyewitnesses who were certain of the identity of the perpetrator or not so certain, and for crimes that had not necessarily even been committed. Punishments were equally varied yet absolute. Before the victim was killed, he might be dragged behind a horse or car, forced to run a gauntlet of clubs, or flogged. Death could then come by a riddle of bullets, a hanging tree, or a pack of hungry hunting dogs. Mutilation of body parts—particularly castration—could come before or after execution. Other acts of torture could be added in certain cases. Death by fire—a slow or quick one—was popular in some communities. In fact, in their variations on the theme of inhumanity, lynchings were, in historian Edward Ayers's words, both "depressingly similar" and "monotonous," both truly extraordinary and fundamentally banal.[68]

Lynchings did distinguish themselves from frontier massacres and discrete episodes of vigilantism in one respect—the degree to which they were supported and sustained over many years by most or all members of the white community, including women. Lynch mobs were not sudden, irrational actions provoked by years of frontier assault and revenge, nor were they organizations that took on an immediate problem and then (sometimes at least) disbanded. They were instead, Ayers says, "madness . . . with a method."[69] Moreover, communities did not simply condone lynchings as sheriffs, jurors, women, and children looked the other way; they actively participated in them. One early-twentieth-century lynching was delayed until more people could arrive from out of town to watch. After another lynching women collected mutilated body parts as souvenirs. Sometimes men posed for pictures with the corpse and allowed sound recordings to be made. Everywhere lynchings were justified by the call to a higher power than the state, particularly when it came to the defense of white womanhood and the patriarchal family. As a mob in Maryland pronounced in an official statement of its purpose, "Before God we believe in the existence of a higher code than that which is dignified by the great seal of a Commonwealth and that the high and holy time to exercise it is when the chastity of our women is tarnished by the foul breath of an imp from hell and the sanctity of our homes invaded by a demon."[70] That African American women's chastity had not been tarnished by the foul breath of a white rapist only suggests that they were not women, but objects of white men's lust for power and violence.

The lynching of Leo Frank in 1915 exemplifies the certainty with which southern men believed that their moral code was above—well above—the law of the state or federal government. It attracted national attention and helped to accelerate an antilynching movement among Progressives throughout America. But the lynching of Leo Frank—who was not an African American but a Jew—also helped to revitalize the Ku Klux Klan, whose targets now included a wider variety of Americans than the first KKK did. By 1925 the new Klan boasted a membership of over four million whites from all over the country desperate to strike out at those who threatened their claims to power. Many were from urban areas like Portland and Denver with burgeoning immigrant and working-class populations.[71] Others were those who had stayed behind to tend the farms and shops of their parents and grandparents. Still others fell between rural and urban life. Perhaps they had just moved to a smaller metropolitan area in an agricultural state and were searching for a guarantee that nothing had really changed in their lives or in the society at large. The vast majority of new Klansmen, however, hailed from the South, Midwest, and Far West, bastions of Protestant fundamentalism, white racism, and, in a nearly forgotten time, widespread support for a brand of radical rural producer politics called Populism.

Leo Frank was a Jewish factory owner from the Northeast accused of murdering a thirteen-year-old girl named Mary Phagan in the basement of the Atlanta factory where they both worked. Her family had once been prosperous landowners in Cobb County, Georgia, but, like so many farmers in the New South, had fallen on hard times. Eventually Phagan's widowed mother moved the family to Atlanta and sent her daughter to work for wages. She made certain, however, that Mary still attended church and participated in other Christian activities. Mrs. Phagan described Mary as "very pretty" with "dimples in her cheeks."[72] Although no evidence of forced intercourse existed, Frank's accusers insisted that rape, or attempted rape, accompanied the murder. Phagan thus came to symbolize every white woman, rich or poor, who, as one contemporary put it, "yet holds pure the priceless jewel of virtue and surrenders her life rather than yield to the demands of lustful force."[73]

As Phagan came to symbolize female purity, Frank became a lascivious, hardhearted beast. This role was, as we have seen, usually reserved for African American men in the South, while it was played out in reality by white men. But in the Frank case, even though significant evidence existed that an African American janitor may have been the killer, accusers preferred to believe that only Frank was evil enough to have committed the grisly crime. In an increasingly complicated time, when industrialization had transformed the southern economy and many of its families' lives and when northern progressives accused southerners of barbarity in labor and race relations, Frank represented more of those complications: northern economic and political power, industrial labor relations, and progressive ideas. Most damning of all was his Judaism. As one accuser explained after the case concluded, the death of a local black janitor "would be poor atonement for the life of this innocent little girl," but "a Yankee Jew . . . here would be a victim worthy to pay for the crime."[74]

The history of anti-Semitism, like that of many racisms, goes beyond the boundaries of any one city, state, region, or even nation. For centuries Christians around the world have demonized Jews for their purported role in the crucifixion of Christ. But in the United States, and in the industrial era in particular, Christians also associated Jews with the economic forces that exploited small producers. Many Populist leaders, including Ignatius Donnelly of Minnesota and Mary Lease of Kansas, warned farmers of the sinister plans of "Jewish bankers" to turn them into serfs and peasants. William "Coin" Harvey's popular *Coin's Financial School* told of a Jewish banker named Baron Rothe whose plan was to "bury the knife deep into the heart" of America.[75] Some Populists also maintained that Jews dominated the "nonproductive" classes, those who drew profits away from productive labor like farming. Finally, they believed that Jews, like African Americans, lusted after Gentile women and, as employers, took advantage of the vulnerability of young girls who worked for wages. Like their racism against Native Americans and African Americans, rural Americans' anti-Semitism was informed by their economic fears, religious beliefs, and stalwart claims to traditional gender roles.

Industrial-era producer politics and Progressive-era race relations were not simply linked in the realm of ideas, however. They were linked by the leadership of white men, especially Tom Watson of Georgia, the Georgia Populist who had run for vice president in 1896. In the height of his powers as a Populist, Watson seemed to believe that class interest superseded racial difference. Yet even then he seemed to support race mixing only in the abstract. After his defeat, his racial radicalism became more pronounced. He supported Jim Crow legislation that segregated whites and blacks in all public facilities and effectively disenfranchised African American voters.[76] Moreover, he turned vehemently and unambivalently anti-Semitic. Then, in 1911, he formed the Guardians of Liberty, a small organization that sought to restrict immigration of Catholics from southern and eastern Europe. In 1915 he became a leader of the assault on Leo Frank. Watson wrote extensively about the case in his popular publication, *Watson's Magazine*. He emphasized Frank's purported sexual perversions and promiscuity, his connections with big money in "Jew-Owned" New York, his large nose and thick lips. He associated Jews with unproductive finance capital, greed, and the vice trade. And he reminded his readers of the right of popular sovereignty and vigilante justice when they no longer trusted the state to protect their best interests, warning that "the next Jew who does what Frank did, is going to get exactly the same thing that we give

*In 1915 members of the Knights of
Mary Phagan pose for a commemorative
photograph around Leo Frank's corpse.*
Courtesy of Georgia Department of
Archives and History.

to Negro rapists." When the governor of Georgia commuted Frank's
death sentence, Watson wrote, "RISE! PEOPLE OF GEORGIA!"[77]

Little more needed to be said. Thousands of supporters from
around the nation had battled to save Frank's life; twenty-five men
from Phagan's home town who called themselves the Knights of Mary
Phagan were all it took to end it. On August 16, 1915, they kidnaped
Frank from the prison, drove him hundreds of miles to her home community, and hanged him from a tree. Many white Georgians were not
just pleased but jubilant. When newspapers around the country wrote
in protest, Watson made his position perfectly clear. "All power is in
the people," he explained. "When the constituted authorities are unable, or unwilling to protect life, liberty, and property, the People must
assert their right to do so."[78] Many Georgians took the opportunity to

threaten Jews in their own communities. Watson saw an even broader lesson. On September 2, he wrote that "another Ku Klux Klan" should be organized "to restore HOME RULE."[79]

Once again, little more needed to be said. Exactly two months after the lynching of Frank, the Knights of Mary Phagan returned to Atlanta and burned a huge wooden cross on top of Stone Mountain. The spectacle galvanized many others to action, including Colonel William Simmons, a revivalist Methodist from Harpersville, Alabama, who had failed at ministry but dreamed of founding his own fraternal organization. After hearing about the cross-burning and the concurrent release of D. W. Griffith's *Birth of a Nation*, which celebrated the first Klan, he declared his calling. On Thanksgiving Day, 1915, Simmons and sixteen other men, including some of the Knights of Mary Phagan and two members of the original Klan, climbed the large granite crest of Stone Mountain and burned another cross. As Simmons recalled it later, "Bathed in the sacred glow of the fiery cross, the Invisible Empire was called from its slumber of half a century to take up a new task and fulfill a new mission for humanity's good."[80]

Within a few years, the new Klan had grown by leaps and bounds. Its primary base continued to be in the South. After Georgia, the first state in the new empire was Texas, where the next leader of the Klan, Hiram Evans, would also emerge. Then Klansmen began to organize in Louisiana, Arkansas, and Alabama. Throughout the South, African American men remained favorite targets of the Klan. In parts of Georgia where lynchings had nearly disappeared, they now returned, accompanied by intimidation, parades, arsons, floggings, and kidnapings—and especially cross-burnings.[81] In Texas, Klansmen branded some African Americans on their foreheads with acid, publicly whipped others, and castrated a doctor who was believed to be dating a white woman. In Aiken, South Carolina, in 1926, two African American brothers and their sister were murdered by "parties unknown." The woman begged for her life so ardently that, one man recalled, "It was almost hard to murder her."[82]

But southern Klansmen, like the Knights of Mary Phagan, believed that many more people—indeed, in their view, many more important people—were to blame for the problems of modern society. What else could explain the burgeoning cities, smokey speakeasies, speeding automobiles, scantily clothed women, and strange new economic and political ideas that filled the air? Thus Klansmen in the South began to target other intolerable members of their communities and then spread their wide swath of hatred north and west. As the early 1920s became the middle 1920s, it seemed as if the Klan was nearly unstoppable. In Indiana, the head of the Klan even dreamed of becoming the president of the United States. More than a movement or a fraternal association, the second Klan came to resemble a religious revival, a crusade to reclaim America for Americans and to restore the traditional values that had been eclipsed by urbanization, modernization, and pluralism. Of course, Populism had been described that way too. But unlike Populism, this crusade dedicated itself to excluding, rather than including, others from achieving their dreams.

"Jews, Juggers, and Jesuits" was the slogan of the Oklahoma Klan, and it well summed up the characteristics of the white victims of the second Klan. First, like Leo Frank, Jews were harassed, intimidated, and boycotted. Articles in Klan publications underscored and intensified Klansmen's beliefs that Jews, who formed a significant percentage of the new immigrants to the country, were "insoluble and indigestible" in Protestant America. Among others, titles read: "The Mightiest Weapons for the Jews Are Dollars and Cents" and "Jewish Rabbi Gets Rabid."[83] Klansmen blamed Jews for the demoralization of the public schools and the business community. In Athens, Georgia, where three members of the board of education were Jewish, Klansmen encouraged one another to boycott Jewish businesses and vote against Jewish politicians. They also blamed Jews for creating the World Court and the League of Nations, which they feared would establish a "Super State" or a "gigantic trust" that would "rule the world . . . in the interest of a few."[84]

Unlike those in Athens, however, many rank-and-file Klansmen did not know a Jew. They lived in such places as Mentone, Indiana, which boasted on a sign outside the city limits which read "With a population of 1100, Mentone has not a Catholic, foreigner, Negro, nor Jew living in the city. Practically every man in the city belongs to one or more fraternal organizations."[85] On the other hand, every Klansman knew or believed that he knew whites whose behaviors threatened the morality of his community—and who deserved to be punished for it. Along with African Americans and Jews, then, the new Klan targeted bootleggers, prostitutes, divorced men and women, adulterers, and neglectful parents. In Taft, California, for example, a crowd of Klansmen gathered to watch a doctor who was suing for divorce get what he deserved. Klansmen stripped him naked, hanged him, revived him, flogged him with knotted ropes and wire whips, revived him again, and cut his back before leaving him on the ground. In other places whites were deemed intolerable when they did not support actions like these. In Mer Rouge, Louisiana, two men who had spoken out against the Klan were dragged from their cars, bound with wire, crushed, dismembered, and tossed into an alligator-infested lake.[86]

But the second Klan saved its loudest and most sustained attacks for Roman Catholics. Of course, anti-Catholicism was as old as the United States itself and had been the source of violence on and off throughout the nineteenth century. In the 1920s, however, increased immigration from southern and eastern Europe, the growth of parochial schools, and the hardening of official church dogma renewed Americans' fears that Catholics were trying to take over the United States. So strong were these beliefs that when a minister in North Manchester, Indiana, proclaimed (metaphorically) that the pope was coming to town on a train from Chicago the very next morning and warned his parishioners to "Prepare! America for Americans! Search everywhere for hidden enemies, vipers at the heart's bloom of our sacred Republic! Watch the trains," more than a thousand people took him seriously and gathered at the train station. When one passenger, a stranger, disembarked, it took him nearly thirty minutes to convince the mob that he was not the pope but a ladies' corset salesman. Even so, they put him on the next train out of town.[87]

Klansmen objected to Catholicism in the 1920s for many of the same reasons other rural Americans had objected to Mormonism in the 1840s. First and foremost, they believed that free, republican government was endangered when one group of voters answered to a higher authority than the Constitution. If Joseph Smith could tell his flock how to vote, why wouldn't the pope do the very same thing? Klansmen also objected to what they believed were immoral or dangerous gender relations practiced by some Catholics. Klansmen reveled in stories of sex-starved priests who kidnaped, tortured, and raped nuns and then buried their unfortunate infants deep in the convents' walls. But the Klansmen also believed that Roman Catholics were plotting to take over the United States and kill all Protestants who would not convert. "The Pope will sit in the White House when Hell Freezes Over" read one banner at an Indiana Klan rally.[88] Some Klansmen also thought that Catholics were collaborating with communists and that the communists hoped that the tyranny of Catholicism would help bring about a bolshevik revolution.

Although rarely murdered—Catholics were, after all, the neighbors, even friends, of many Klansmen—Catholics suffered from economic and political intimidation in the 1920s. In Grand Forks, North Dakota, for example, where the senior minister of the First Presbyterian Church was also the Grand Dragon of the Ku Klux Klan, Klansmen succeeded in removing Catholics from all important municipal committees. There, and in hundreds of other midwestern towns and small cities, shopkeepers posted special signs that indicated they were "100 percent" for the Klan. Elsewhere Klansmen protested the celebration of the "pro-Catholic" Columbus Day, the singing of the "anti-Protestant" "Star Spangled Banner," and the religiously inclusive policies of the Boy Scouts of America. They were galvanized in particular by the nomination of the Democratic "wafer worshiper," Al Smith, for president.[89] Although in retrospect some attributes of the Klan—including its costuming, hierarchy, and ceremonialism—might seem oddly suggestive of Catholicism and its activities distinctly homoerotic, the Klansmen never seemed to notice. According to them, Catholics threatened the strength of freedom in the United States as much as any African American or Jew did. But they were no longer worried about the future. Standing around a huge burning cross, with arms outstretched and voices raised in song, Klansmen believed that American freedom had finally found its guardian angels.

"Shut up or get out":

VIGILANTISM AND THE POLITICS OF PATRIOTISM

When Klansmen accused Catholics of being unfit to be Americans, they enacted and reinforced a third theme within vigilantism in the countryside: vigilantism in the name of extremist nationalism or radical patriotism. As we have seen, other rural people also justified their violence in the name of freedom and "100-percent Americanism." Sometimes their participation in vigilantism was in itself a way of becoming an American. Nevertheless, until the dawn of the twentieth century, issues of criminality, economic hegemony, race, morality, and religion primarily motivated vigilantism. Beginning in 1915, however, rural Americans began to target those whom they believed were a danger to the nation at large. During World War I, for example, rural Americans attacked people in their communities who they believed were disloyal to the war effort. In the 1920s they expanded their search to include other kinds of radicals, socialists, and anarchists. Although as usual they went beyond the spirit of the law, they were generally immune from prosecution because the enemies they sought were also the official enemies of the federal government. In the 1930s, however, some rural Americans began to wonder whether the government itself had not become an enemy, an un-American agent in their midst. Claims that the government was an enemy of the people hearkened back to the uprisings of producer radicals in the colonial and early national periods. Even more, they set the stage for rural radicalism in our own time, which does not only defy the government as an abstract entity but directly targets the men and women in its employ.

Although throughout the nineteenth and early twentieth centuries the list of "unassimilable" and "un-American" immigrants grew longer and longer, few Americans would ever have put Germans, especially German Protestants, on it. In fact, after suffering from discrimination in the eighteenth century, Germans had a relatively successful immigration experience. Many German immigrants headed to rural areas, set up farms, and prospered by maintaining culturally specific land-management and inheritance practices and avoiding speculation and indebtedness. In the Dakotas, Illinois, Minnesota, Nebraska, and Wisconsin, Germans continued to keep farms in their families and to increase their acreage long after Yankee families had moved into town. Clusters of German families in country communities encouraged the establishment of German-language schools, churches, and fraternal organizations. Despite conflict over gender roles and the Germans' use of alcohol, Germans and Yankees cooperated in economic and political life with little of the violent conflict that marred other relationships in the countryside.[90]

Such relatively peaceful relations came to an abrupt halt with the onset of World War I. Throughout the 1910s, Allied powers flooded the world market with propaganda against the Germans. Americans who believed reports that German soldiers bayoneted Belgian babies and strapped women to machine guns also began to look askance at the German Americans in their communities. And it was true that some Germans—like some other Americans—had questioned the entry of the United States into the war. Some had supported Germany because they felt they could not support Great Britain, a long-time rival. Other German Americans, including the Amish and the Mennonites, were pacifists and refused to fight on religious grounds. But many Americans did not differentiate between those Germans who remained loyal to Germany for a time and those who did not. Instead, as David Bennett explains, they turned against Germans who valued their heritage in any way at all. "German-Americans were now seen as an arm of the official enemy. . . . Their sin was not their religion but their nationality."[91]

State governments led the way in disarming German Americans of their culture. In many midwestern states, new laws forbade schools from teaching German, presses from printing German, and churches from offering German-language services. Laws making alcohol illegal and women's suffrage legal were passed in part because they defied traditional German cultural practices. And where laws left off, mobs of "100-percent Americans" took over. In Yankton and Faulkton, South Dakota, men, women, and children gathered all the German-language books they could find and burned them in great piles on the street. In North Dakota farmers turned in their neighbors for joking about or threatening the flag. In Kansas armed men tarred and feathered Mennonites. In Texas a mob of men publicly flogged a German Lutheran pastor for preaching in German. Bennett says that with the outbreak of hostilities in Europe and the agonizing deaths of Americans in foxholes, "it was now a mark of patriotism to throw a rock through butcher Schultz's window."[92]

Anti-German hysteria reached an apex on April 5, 1918, when a vigilante mob lynched Robert Prager in Collinsville, Illinois. A group of miners, convinced that Prager was a spy, abbreviated their drunken evening at a local saloon because they wanted to go hunting for "their German." They found him at home, where he told them, "Brothers, I am a loyal U.S.A. workingman."[93] The crowd told him that he had ten minutes to get out of town. But for some of the vigilantes, that was not enough. They ripped off most of his clothing, made him kiss the flag and sing patriotic songs. The local police jailed Prager and closed the saloons for his protection. The plan backfired. Soon hundreds of angry men gathered outside the jail and seized the prisoner. After holding a mock trail, botching the hanging once, and allowing Prager to write a letter to his mother, they finally hoisted the noose ten feet in the air and killed him. Later a jury would take only forty-five minutes to acquit the men accused of his murder. The defense claimed the murder was justified under "unwritten law."[94]

Disloyalty took on a broader definition when Americans took notice of the Bolshevik Revolution in Russia. Beginning in 1917, many Americans turned their attention to potential radicals in the United States—including socialists, anarchists, labor organizers, pacifists, and feminists. Kicked off by Attorney General A. Mitchell Palmer's raids on leftist organizations including the Communist Party of America, the 1920s became a prototype for right-wing extremism in the twentieth century. While many urban Americans participated fully in the Red Scare, some rural Americans played an important part by using vigilantism to carry out their deeds. And they looked for radicalism in their own communities. Thus they began to target other rural organizations—including the Alabama Communist Party and the Nonpartisan League—that themselves had grown out of a tradition of producer radicalism but now seemed dangerously un-American. The potency of anticommunism was proved when political vigilantes forced fellow rural Americans to disband or deny the true meanings of their politics.

Among the best-known antiradical organizations was the second Ku Klux Klan. Although, as we have seen, the KKK concerned itself with African Americans, Catholics, and Jews, it also attacked socialists, communists, anarchists, and labor radicals. Klansmen associated socialism with tyranny and believed that its proponents wished to bring the downfall of republican government—a disloyalty of the worst kind. In fact, many Klansmen concluded that it was disloyal for an American to criticize the government in any way. No "man or woman who opposes the government," wrote a Klansman from Georgia, "has any right to protection." He "should be deported or placed behind prison bars."[95] The official position of the national Klan was similar. Critics of the United States "must either shut up or get out." To some even this was not enough. One Grand Dragon supported the death penalty for communists. Socialism was "without a possible exception . . . the most destructive philosophy preached by thinking men," another believed. "The Red is the most dastardly creature infesting the earth, the worst menace to civilization."[96]

Such strong antagonisms provoked equally strong actions. For example, because they assumed that all strikes were unwarranted and probably the result of infiltration by foreign agitators, Klansmen worked to end strikes and to break up union organizing wherever it appeared in their communities. They opposed the United Mine Workers' strike in West Virginia in the 1920s, for example, by volunteering to act as auxiliary members of the company-owned deputies group. Likewise, they used force to prevent the organization of citrus workers in Lakeland, Florida. One organizer working in Lakeland responded to a call for help one night but never returned. Other bodies had purportedly been dumped in swamps and old phosphate mines.[97]

Klansmen were especially fond of terrorizing African Americans who were associated with labor movements, sharecropper associations, and communist organizations. For example, Birmingham, Alabama, was the site of several strikes in which communist organizers took part. In 1934 forty-four new klaverns were founded to demonstrate to African Americans the danger of association with communists. The organizers themselves got more than a warning. Historian Robin Kelley reports that "Clyde Johnson survived at least three assassination attempts. Steve Simmons suffered a near fatal beating at the hands of Klansmen in North Birmingham, and a few months later his African American comrade in Bessemer, Saul Davis, was kidnapped by a gang of white[s], . . . stripped bare, and flogged for several hours. These examples represent only a fraction of the anti-radical terror that pervaded the Birmingham district in 1934."[98]

The Oklahoma Klan had to work particularly hard to protect America in the 1920s. Many businessmen in small towns and cities joined the Klan, determined to make Oklahoma the most "American" state in the union. In Atoka and Balk Knob, they formed posses and assaulted union organizers and members of the IWW. To the talk of forming a Farmer-Labor Party, they answered a resounding "no," with floggings and lynchings reaching an all-time high. Oklahoma's rural left, however, did not give up so easily. Newspaper editors accused Klansmen of being allied with the nonproducing classes who every day stole the rightful property of ordinary workers. Oklahoma farmers also would not be intimidated. In the 1924 and 1928 gubernatorial races, defiantly anti-Klan candidates won in many counties. And they did so by ascribing to the Klansmen the worst of the old Populists' approbations. As one farmer put it in song, "These Coo-coos what's singing is the Ku Klux Klan / A tyin' up the farmer like a sackful of bran! / These Kukes have gone loco, it's affectin' their health, / they've eaten too much of the farmers' wealth! / We might say it different / there's nothing in a name / These Ku Klux are grafters / they're one and the same!"[99]

On the northern plains, antiradicalism successfully snuffed out the power and authority of the Nonpartisan League, but North Dakotans did not require the Klan to do the job. In 1916 thousands of North Dakota Republicans, especially Yankee Protestant Republicans from large towns and cities, had organized the Independent Voters Association (IVA) to fight the Nonpartisan League. During the war, charges of disloyalty and socialism gave them new and even more powerful ammunition. Members of the IVA, for example, charged the NPL with disloyalty because the NPL had ardently opposed American entry into the war, opposition that in turn had derived from the NPL's critique of industrial capitalism. League leaders believed, as North Dakotan Elwyn Robinson puts it, that "the war was being fomented by eastern financiers and industrialists for their own selfish advantage. They believed that the war would destroy progressive reform, [and] that it was not really a just one for democratic ends."[100] "Who are the men who are fighting for us in France?" asked NPL organizer Walter Thomas Mills in Fargo in 1918. "They are not the sons of members of chambers of commerce; they are not sons of commercial travelers; they are not bankers' or merchants' sons; but they are your boys. For every thousand soldiers killed in France there is one additional millionaire in America."[101]

By attacking the NPL's position on the war, the IVA was also attacking its economic philosophies. A state-owned bank, grain elevator, or mill sounded suspiciously like socialism to many conservative Dakotans. Even more treasonous was the NPL's suggestion that the wealth of the "rotten rich" be conscripted along with the sons of the poor. These were not subjects to joke about, not when entire nations were in revolution. By the election of 1920, voter confidence in NPL leadership noticeably dropped. A special election on October 28, 1921, marked the first successful recall of state officials in United States history. But action against the NPL took place outside the polling place as well. Many Dakotans recall the schoolyard, backyard, and corner-store brawls that began when an IVA man and an NPL man would mix it up. Tactics on both sides were so dirty that state officials urged all parties to tone down their campaigns of intimidation and violence.[102]

Whether they were toned down or not, charges of socialism, communism, and un-Americanism proved too powerful for the league to overcome. In November 1921 Arthur Townley began to serve a jail sentence for conspiring to discourage enlistment. In 1922 he resigned his membership in the NPL. By then, however, NPL coffers were nearly dry. For the next ten years NPL opponents ruled the North Dakota government and rolled back many of the NPL's innovations. Some leaders like William Langer and William Lemke would rise again when rural producer radicalism found a new voice amid devastations of the 1930s. Neither would ever stray far, however, from charges of socialism or communism. In the 1950s, when McCarthyism turned its attention to agricultural organizations, some men who had been active in the NPL, the American Society of Equity, the Farmers' Holiday Association, and other radical farm organizations in the early decades of the century would vigorously deny ever having had an association with the socialist or communist fellow travelers of their day.[103] By forgetting their ties to the full range of rural producer radicalism, these leaders helped to bring a rich heritage of the countryside to its knees.

When rural Americans attacked Germans, socialists, communists, anarchists, and other radicals in the 1920s, they did so in the name of patriotism. And in a strange sense they were being true to their country—if radically so. The Klan, the IVA, and other conservative organizations singled out members of their communities who in broad ways resembled official enemies of the United States government. As the Ku Klux Klan saw it, part of the acid test of 100-percent Americanism was 100-percent loyalty to the government and its policies. If members had to break the law to protect the country, they would do so without regret. In the 1930s, however, some Americans began to believe that the American government itself should be considered an enemy. For them the requirements of 100-percent Americanism thus became militant action against the government and outspoken support for the government's foreign opponents. Of course, even this pronounced antistatism was not entirely new. Throughout the history of the United States rural folks have felt that their government did not represent them, care about them, or protect them, and they have risen up together to make their feelings known. What was new, however, and what made the American fascist movements of the 1930s similar to some radical organizations today, was the targeting of individual members of the federal government—and Jews in particular—for murderous rage.

The vast majority of rural people voted for Franklin D. Roosevelt in 1932 and in some manner welcomed the programs of the New Deal. States where a Democratic candidate for president had not won in years boasted significant tallies for the man who told Americans that

that they had "nothing to fear but fear itself." Yet many rural people felt a deep ambivalence toward the changes the New Deal brought. Those who joined the Farmers' Holiday Association did not think much of the idea of reducing production on their farms; those who joined the Southern Tenant Farmers' Union did not think much of the Agricultural Adjustment Administration's programs at all. Those who listened to Huey Long wondered whether wealth could not be distributed more justly. Nevertheless, most rural Americans voted for Roosevelt again in 1936 and agreed to participate in the new programs, to see how they went, and to put down their arms for a time. Indeed, the new Democratic coalition owed much of its strength to those rural people who turned away from the party of Lincoln to join the party of Roosevelt.

Other rural people, however, were so firmly steeped in the traditions of radical intolerance, and particularly of anticommunism and anti-Semitism, that they simply could not begin to go along with the New Deal. Increased centralization of the government, a burgeoning federal budget and bureaucracy, the repeal of Prohibition, a planned economy, "charity programs" for all—even African Americans, Native Americans, and whites of the "lower sort"—all these things sounded more like communism to them than 100-percent Americanism. In fact, some Americans believed that the New Deal was part of an international conspiracy to take over the United States, a conspiracy that only a paramilitary counteroffensive could deflect. Finally, as the United States inched closer to another war in Europe, against a country whose leaders seemed to hate Jews and communists as much as some Americans did, those Americans wondered whose side to be on.

There were more than 120 fascist organizations in the United States in the 1930s and 1940s, some of which were based in urban America and appealed to urban men and women. Nevertheless, two of the best-known leaders of American fascism in the Great Depression had come to maturity in rural regions and appealed to men and women with rural roots, experiences, and values. William Dudley Pelley and Gerald B. Winrod associated their leadership, for example, with their commitment to evangelical Protestantism, which they had reconfirmed through visions, healing experiences, and conversions. Likewise, they feared the moral decay that had been brought about by urbanization and immigration. Finally, they found the New Deal intolerable because it constricted the independence of American farmers and small businessmen, heralded labor organizations, funded lewd art projects, repealed Prohibition, and recognized the Soviet Union. If they could have had their way, both men would have put most white Christian Americans back home on the farm.

Pelley and Winrod found much to hate in the New Deal, but what they hated most was the power the Roosevelt administration had given to Jews. Both read and were deeply influenced by the classic anti-Semitic text *The Protocols of the Learned Elders of Zion*, which purportedly revealed an ancient Jewish plot to destroy Christian civilization by fomenting war and corrupting governments. Moreover, it demonstrated the "Jewish connection" to the Bolshevik Revolution in Russia. Pelley and Winrod believed that they could see the "hidden hand" of the Jews at work in the New Deal. Bernard Baruch, James Warburg, Arthur Rothstein, and many others in the Roosevelt administration were either Jewish or, they were sure, supported the Jewish conspiracy. In fact, both men believed that Roosevelt himself had Jewish ancestors.[104] Certainly such a potential anti-Christ could not be permitted to guide America's future.

Pelley and Winrod's anti-Semitism and anticommunism made them sympathetic to some of the ideas and strategies of the Third Reich and extremely unsympathetic to the entry of United States into World War II. Many other rural Americans, of course, wanted to avoid war too. North Dakota senator Gerald Nye, for example, led a special congressional committee to investigate alleged profiteering by munitions manufacturers in World War I. Others agreed with Little Falls, Minnesota, aviation hero Charles Lindbergh that the problems of America should be solved before aiding Europeans be considered. Only Pelley and Winrod's followers, however, resisted the war—even after Pearl Harbor—because they genuinely admired the Nazis. After a vision, Pelley announced the formation of the Silver Legion (subsequently called the Silver Shirts), which would bring the "work of Christ militant into the open."[105] For his part, Winrod founded the Defenders of the Christian Faith—150,000 strong—through which he uncritically supported the Nazis' attacks on "fanatic" Jews.

Although neither Pelley nor Winrod was ever accused of a violent crime, both undoubtedly fomented acts of violence among their followers. Pelley's Silver Shirts dressed in military attire—including special-issue hats, shirts, and pants—followed elaborate rituals and command hierarchies, and marched in military-style musters. Pelley himself suggested sending Christmas cards to Jews that read: "Dear Shylock, in this season, / When we're all bereft of reason, / As upon my rent you gloat, /

I would like to cut your throat."[106] His followers threatened, harassed, and attacked Jews in several midwestern cities. When opponents organized and marched against them, Pelley dreamed of the day he could court-martial and punish every offender. Winrod warned his opponents that his followers held dear a tradition of frontier justice. If one of his enemies were to come to power in the United States, he predicted (or suggested?), a "rugged individualist would probably kill him."[107]

One other trait linked these leaders of American fascism to each other, to their followers, to Americans like them in the past, and to our contemporary political landscape: Pelley and Winrod revered the American countryside and its virtuous, productive citizenry. As children, both men had struggled with poverty and deprivation in the rural periphery; as adults they held high the moral and physical lessons such experiences had wrought. Moreover, they believed that rural America was the only real America and its inhabitants the only real Americans. When Winrod visited an eastern city, he felt that he was not even in his own country. The strange and alien people there neither spoke his language nor breathed the same air that men from Middle America did. Pelley also believed that "the finest Specimens of American manhood" came from and spoke for its "Little Towns." His plan was to raze all large cities, move white Christian Americans back to suburbs, single-family homes, and especially farms. Farmers, after all, were the "ultimate producers of wealth from Nature's Storehouse."[108]

Even William Dudley Pelley, one of the most radically "conservative" rural men of the twentieth century, a harbinger of today's neo-Nazi movement, shared the language of rural producer radicalism with colonial land rioters, Whisky Rebels, Grangers, and Populists who had gone before him. He believed in the righteousness of small production and the moral decay that accompanied big business, big cities, and big government. Beneath a thick layer of hatred, arrogance, and intolerance, he believed he was protecting rural men and women and their productive ways of life. Yet just like the South Carolina Regulators, the Paxton Boys, the Ku Klux Klan, and a host of other vigilantes, he never understood that he could have advocated decency and democracy instead of division and death. Such ignorance would have been merely a pity if it had not been so very dangerous besides.

3

RURAL RADICALISM IN OUR TIME

AT FIRST GLANCE, Randy and Vicki Weaver's childhoods in Iowa and their subsequent married life in Idaho could not have been more different. Although they had grown up amid the slowly undulating midwestern prairie, as adults they gazed over the roughest mountain terrain in the northwestern United States. Although they had once lived in tightly knit farm communities, cruised Main Street on Saturday nights, and attended churches and schools where folks had known one another for generations, they settled in an isolated place, built a cabin out of plywood boards, educated their three children at home, and sometimes did not see neighbors for weeks at a time.[1] Most different of all, however, were the two political environments the Weavers inhabited. Both Weavers, but Vicki in particular, had flourished in the traditional heartland of rural producer radicalism. Her family had owned a large hog farm for more than a century. Vicki had learned to bake, sew, and make home repairs even better than her mother. In the 1980s Vicki's brother likely had supported increased government spending to curb the farm crisis; her sister married a member of a rock-and-roll band. In the mountains, however, the Weavers lived among people who believed that conventional agrarian ways of life were doomed and conventional agrarian politics irrelevant because Zionists already controlled the federal government and were preparing to enslave all white Christian Americans. They converted to Identity Christianity, a belief system popular among right-wing extremists. And they definitely did not listen to rock and roll. In Iowa the Weavers had been described as an "all-American couple."[2] After their move to Idaho they seemed, to most people, as far out of the American mainstream as any family could be.

The distance between Iowa and Idaho, between the politics of producerism and the culture of vigilantism, between progressive and regressive ideologies, and between the American left and right may seem large to us. But for the Weavers, and many other Americans like them, it was short indeed. As a farm girl in Iowa, Vicki Weaver had first become suspicious of the power of the federal government when the Department of Transportation ordered a new highway to run right through their farmhouse. Likewise, as a summer farm hand, Randy had first learned to confront unjust authority when a local farmer had paid him less than his older brothers to weed some fields. As children and teenagers, both Weavers attended conservative Protestant churches where they heard admonitions about the coming of the end of the world. Finally, as young parents living in Cedar Falls, the Weavers encountered the organizations and ideologies of the far right. The more they heard and read the more ardently they believed that the United States had come under the control of the enemy: Jews, communists, atheists, homosexuals, perhaps even Satan himself. More than mainstream preachers knew, more than even evangelical radio preachers of the New Right would admit, the end of the world was near.[3]

In 1983 the Weavers loaded their three children—Sara, Samuel, and Rachel—into a car and set out in search of a mountaintop home where they could live simply and await Armageddon. Vicki's parents, David and Jeane Jordison, and her sister, Julie, hoped that getting "out in the woods" would help them "return to reality."[4] If anything, however, the Weavers' move served to strengthen and deepen their unconventional beliefs. After a long journey, they settled high on Ruby Ridge, seven miles outside Naples in Boundary County, Idaho, population 8,332. Boundary County was already the home of the Aryan Nations, of the Order, and of cells of several other "hate" organizations of our time. Soon the Weavers began discussing the possibility of creating a white separatist nation in the Pacific Northwest, a proposal backed by both the neo-Nazi and Klan groups. In 1988 Randy Weaver ran for county sheriff, promising that he would enforce only the laws that people endorsed; he won more than a quarter of the votes cast. Meanwhile he and his family continued to prepare for the coming of the end of the world or, barring that, the invasion by the Zionist Occupational Government (ZOG). They armed their children and made sure they could defend themselves when the day came.

It came faster than even they had anticipated. After attending the Aryan Nations World Congress in the summer of 1986, Randy Weaver landed on a federal list of dangerous white separatists and became the object of a sting operation. When he sold a shotgun that was one-quarter inch shorter than allowed by law to an undercover agent of the Bureau of Alcohol, Tobacco, and Firearms, he was arrested. Even though he told the agents, "You'll never fool me again," he was released without bond. Randy Weaver did not appear in court. "Whether we live or whether we die," he and Vicki announced, "we will not obey your lawless government."[5] Randy also purportedly warned that he would kill any official who tried to arrest him. Thus for nearly eighteen months United States marshals surrounded the cabin on Ruby Ridge while the Weavers lived on their food reserves, wild game, garden produce, and gifts from more than fifty local supporters. As time passed, neo-Nazis, survivalists, skinheads, and other militant extremists from around the country gathered along the road leading to their home.

On Friday, August 21, 1992, the tense stand-off was broken by gunfire. Thirteen-year-old Sam Weaver and Kevin Harris, a family friend who had been living with the Weavers off and on for many years, went outside with Sam's dog. The dog heard something in the bushes; the boy and man followed, hoping they could flush out some game and augment the family's dwindling supply of protein. Instead they came upon a group of five marshals who had been ordered to scout out the area for a possible hostage-rescue-type operation. Afraid that the dog would give him away, Marshal William Degan shot it. Then Sam Weaver shot and killed Degan. The other marshals opened fire, wounding Harris and killing Sam Weaver with a bullet to the back. His last words as he ran back up the mountain were "I'm coming, Dad."[6]

By this point, the government's patience was spent. The FBI's elite Hostage Rescue Team was brought in—with orders to shoot to kill. Altogether more than a hundred FBI agents as well as Idaho national guardsmen and a variety of other state and local officials, with cars, helicopters, and armored vehicles gathered at Ruby Ridge. The crowds behind the barricades grew larger as well. Some carried signs that read, "Your home could be next" and "Government Lies/Patriot Dies." Others yelled, "Baby killer, baby killer." Several were arrested for illegal possession of firearms. All the while no one knew that Vicki Weaver was also dead. The day after the initial shoot-out, Randy and Sara had gone to an outbuilding (known as the birthing shed because Vicki went there during menstruation and childbirth) to tend to his son's body. He was shot and wounded. As he and Sara had run in terror back to the cabin, Vicki had held the door open with one arm and cradled ten-month-old Elshiba in the other. Suddenly a bullet struck her in the back of the head, and blood and bone fragments flew through the air. For more than a week Vicki's corpse lay under the kitchen table, wrapped in a plastic sheet, while the baby cried for her mother to nurse her and the rest the family waited to be killed by the government.[7]

Finally, on August 30, 1992, Weaver and Harris gave themselves up to authorities and were indicted for the murder of William Degan. They had been convinced to come out by James "Bo" Gritz, a former Green Beret commander and paramilitary specialist who had known Weaver in the army during the Vietnam War. In the 1980s Gritz had purportedly served as the exemplar for Hollywood's Rambo character. By the 1990s he had become a celebrity in the survivalist right. "In the end it came down to Sara," Gritz said later. "She had this fear that the government would not keep its part of the bargain [of safety for the family]. She wept and wept. But we said the battle was in the courts now."[8] Gritz, like Weaver, believed that the initial sting had been illegal and that the stand-off was proof of ZOG's devotion to killing white Christians by whatever means necessary. When he left the compound, he gave his supporters in the crowd a Nazi salute. "The time is now," one of them said. "Let's take America back."[9]

The tragic story of Randy and Vicki Weaver will long be remembered as one of the most important events in the history of the contemporary far right. Like the FBI engagement with David Koresh and his followers in their compound in Waco, Texas, which ended in the deaths of more than seventy of them on April 19, 1993, the Ruby Ridge incident galvanized thousands of Americans who had distrusted the government but until then had not believed that FBI agents might actually invade their homes or kill their wives and children. Within two months of Vicki's death, Bo Gritz, Louis Beam, the leader of one of the latest reincarnations of the KKK, and John Trochmann, a Weaver friend, called a meeting at Estes Park, Colorado. There they announced plans to establish a "leaderless resistance" to the government, in particular, militia cells that would teach Americans how to prepare for the assault of ZOG. By early April

1995 there were militias on guard in thirty-six states across America. As many as fifteen thousand men trained, gathered arms, and distributed literature that explained the international conspiracy and the constitutional right to bear arms. Not all of these men lived as simply as the Weavers: by 1995 news about Ruby Ridge, Waco, the militia movement—even recipes for homemade bombs and other weapons—was available on the Internet.[10]

Information about militias reached two army buddies who also believed that the federal government was an enemy of the American people. Timothy McVeigh had grown up in Lockport, New York, a failing rust-belt town far removed from centers of political, economic, or cultural influence. From a young age he had been fascinated with guns, military paraphernalia, and warfare. At age eighteen he joined the army, excelled as a soldier, and rose quickly through the ranks. His interest in guns was extreme even among the other army men.[11] But his ultimate military aspirations were not to be fulfilled. Shortly after he completed his tour in the Gulf War, McVeigh failed to qualify for a highly selective Special Forces unit and then was relieved from duty altogether. Strangely, McVeigh did not seem to be as upset about these events as his buddies thought he would be. As it turned out, McVeigh was beginning to wonder whether the United States government should be fought for or fought against. He was particularly worried after the passage of the Brady bill, which required a ten-day waiting period for all gun purchases. He allegedly feared that the bill was just the beginning of the government's attempt to take all weapons from whites and restrict their ability to defend themselves.[12]

Terry Nichols was of a like mind. Nichols's brother, James, was a farmer from Sanilac County, Michigan, one of the most rural counties in the state. Terry, however, never succeeded at much that he attempted. He was in his mid-thirties when he joined the army, where he quickly became popular with the younger recruits. Meeting for the first time, McVeigh and Nichols developed an especially strong friendship. They both believed that the government had become part of a larger conspiracy to take away the freedoms of white Americans, in part by taking away their guns. After his discharge, Nichols allegedly began to stockpile arms and ammunition. He lived in Michigan for a time and reportedly looked into joining a local militia. Both he and McVeigh started to read books and watch films that depicted the armed resistance of white patriots. They were especially fond of *The Turner Diaries*, a novel that described in violent detail the recapture of the United States by white Christian patriots and the annihilation of all minorities—in one section of the novel by a huge truck-bomb blast.[13] By 1995 they were allegedly ready to take action: their reading, their own experiences, the militia movement, passage of the Brady bill, the assaults on Ruby Ridge and Waco told them that the government needed to be destroyed before it could destroy them.

The Weavers' story (and by extension McVeigh's and Nichols's) also reminds us that radicalism in rural America—however terrible it has become—is not easy to understand within the boundaries of conventional political definitions and conventional understandings of the past. Some of the Weavers' beliefs—that the government was corrupt, unresponsive, and controlled by a greedy elite who scorned the values of a simple freehold lifestyle—bound them to the rural producer radicalism expressed in words and deeds by colonial land rioters, Shaysites, Whisky Rebels, Populists, and members of the Nonpartisan League, Industrial Workers of the World, and the Farmers' Holiday Association. All of these groups have been associated with the American left. But the Weavers were more obviously linked to rural America's culture of vigilantism, in which any person or organization that threatened the hegemony of white Christian American manhood could be targeted for collective violence. These actions and ideologies are associated with the extreme right. Native Americans, African, Chinese, Mexican, Japanese, and German Americans, labor-union activists, socialists, and communists, Mormons, Catholics, and Jews all knew men like Randy Weaver—and some who made Weaver seem almost benign.

But most confusingly and uncomfortably, the Weaver story shows us that the roots of violence, racism, and hatred can be and have been nourished in the same soil and from the same experiences that generated rural movements for democracy and equality. In many places and at many times in the American past, the best and worst, the most forgiving and most vengeful, the most egalitarian and most authoritarian, the brightest and darkest visions of American life were alive in the same men's souls, nurtured at the same dinner tables, learned in the same schools, and preached from the same pulpits. Not two sets of beliefs, then, but two expressions of the same beliefs and circumstances bound left and right together in an unwavering, desperate, synthetic embrace. This interrelationship cannot and should not be ignored. Historians and politicians who perpetuate a false division between the left and right in the rural past and present, who marginalize the extremes of American politics, or who refuse to acknowledge the essential "Americanness" of groups they find unconscionable do so at their peril. For however much scholars and politicians may want to recover a usable Populist past by ignoring its sourer side, they must nonetheless recognize that the curdled populism of hatred, intolerance, and vigilante violence has—temporarily perhaps—seized the day in our United States.

After the shooting, the Weaver girls were sent back to live among Vicki's Iowa relatives and friends, whom they could barely remember. It was difficult, even sickening at times, for the Jordisons to have such hatred and bitterness in their house. They were disgusted by the racist and anti-Semitic literature that came in the mail and by the checks, large and small, that poured in for the girls' support and their father's legal defense from groups like the KKK. But the Jordisons could not cast the Weaver girls away by pretending that they bore no resemblance to themselves. The Jordisons and the Weavers were related by blood.

"Let's keep the grain and export the farmers":

THE FAILURE OF RURAL PRODUCER RADICALISM
IN POSTWAR AMERICA

But if Randy and Vicki Weaver had grown up in the traditional seedbed of rural producer radicalism, why did they choose hatred and violence over collective protest for democratic change? Instead of attending Family Day at the Aryan Nations compound why weren't they singing at a Farm Aid concert or trying to stop a local farm foreclosure? We cannot know the answer to this question completely, as it requires a psychological inquiry that falls outside the parameters of this book. But we can discover part of the answer by exploring the social and political context in which their choice was made. As Alan Brinkley has argued, the transformation of the reform liberalism of the early twentieth century (with ties to rural producer radicalism) into the compensatory liberalism of our time neglected the values and frustrated the ambitions of lower-middle-class and working-class whites in rural America. Moreover, it effectively limited whatever radical change they might otherwise have endorsed. Whereas North Carolina Regulators, Shaysites, Whisky

Rebels, Populists, Nonpartisan Leaguers, and members of the Farmers'
Holiday Association all demanded fundamental changes to the economic and political structure of the United States, few liberal politicians
or influential groups in the mid-twentieth century sought measures
nearly as transformative. Instead they sought a corporate-friendly liberalism that did not change capitalism but softened its edges and supposedly spread its opportunities to all Americans. By the 1970s a growing
number of white men in rural America had come to believe that this
kind of liberalism had little or nothing to offer them.

Although many farm radicals were deeply suspicious of New Deal
programs for agriculture that controlled production and empowered
"brainy" government experts, one thrust of the Agricultural Adjustment
Act suited them just fine—the tax on large processors to pay for farm
subsidies. As we have seen, corporate middlemen had long been targets
of rural producer radicals who believed that these "nonproducers"
siphoned off profits made by honest laborers. Now the profits of some
middlemen were, at least in a small way, being distributed back to small
producers who desperately needed them. Other early New Deal programs
had the same effect on corporations and monopolies: the National Re-
covery Act forced big businesses to control prices and wages. The Wagner
Act legalized collective bargaining and prevented owners from retaliating
against union organizers or strikers. According to the most ardent antimonopolists in the early New Deal, this assault on "bigness" was critical
to the ongoing social, cultural, and moral health of the nation. As New
Dealer Saul Nelson put it, for example, "The monster is a menace not because of the way he acts, but simply because he is too large. [We must
fight for] the maintenance of the freedom of individual opportunity and
the encouragement of small independent businesses."[14] To others, this
fight meant keeping a check on the size of the federal government too.
Simply regulating large corporations and monopolies was a bad idea,
they argued, not only because it would allow monopolies to persist, but
also because it would lead to a burgeoning bureaucratic state. Robert
Jackson, a prominent member of the Justice Department in 1937, feared
that someday super-powered bureaucrats might "operate the whole business life of the United States from a government office building."[15]

Despite the fervor of antimonopolism in the early New Deal, however, the era of reform liberalism had already passed. Most antimonopolists realized that it was impossible to re-create an economy based on
small production. Moreover, as the Supreme Court overturned key

pieces of antimonopolist legislation—including the first AAA—and the 1937 recession forced New Dealers to reassess their goals, the reform of corporate capitalism was nearly forgotten. A new breed of Roosevelt officials even argued against such a reform: "It is ridiculous to speak of breaking up 'big business,'" said Representative Maury Maverick of Texas in 1939. "We need big business. We need monopolies. . . . To talk of returning to arts and crafts is not only romantic, it is impossible."[16] Likewise, these officials believed that a powerful federal government was not an evil but a necessity. The state needed to become a strong and constant presence with powers separate from, even insulated from the representatives of the people in Congress.[17]

Thus by 1945 many if not all of the programs of the New Deal had lost their roots in reform liberalism. Rather than do away with large corporations, the government nurtured them. Likewise, government programs validated the ambitions of big farms, big industries, and big labor unions. Small producers were still important, of course, but not for what they produced as much as for what they—like all Americans, rich or poor, black or white, young or old—consumed. Thus federal programs and policies were designed to protect Americans' purchasing power more than their productive power. Social security and unemployment compensation, fiscal policy, and even farm subsidies were designed to spread the benefits of the marketplace across the spectrum of human experience without damaging the economy in any fundamental way. In a sense they redistributed income just as the first AAA had, but with one crucial difference. By 1940 this redistribution of wealth was being paid for by all taxpayers, not just by large corporations. As Brinkley puts it, "The liberal vision of political economy in the 1940s . . . rested on the belief that protecting consumers and encouraging mass consumption, more than protecting producers and promoting savings, were the principal responsibilities of the liberal state. . . . It would not reshape capitalist institutions. It would reshape the economic and social environment in which those institutions worked."[18] Barton Bernstein remarks that however radical they seemed to some, these were conservative achievements at best.[19]

Liberalism moved even further from its roots in the 1960s and 1970s. In those years, a commitment to social welfare and individual freedom led many whites—elites in particular—to join with leaders of minority groups to bring race, ethnicity, gender, and sexuality into sharp focus. Such issues and alliances troubled some rural whites. Not

only had they been raised in a landscape of traditional racial and gender divisions and taught to respect a hard-earned dollar, but they were
conservative about many other issues as well—abortion, homosexuality, divorce—anything that seemed to neglect the teachings of the
Bible. And they were especially wary of any suggestion that they might
voluntarily or involuntarily give up their guns, those long-time fixtures
of rural self-defense. Still, as long as rising standards of living and a
shared faith in American nationalism and internationalism prevailed,
many rural Americans, in the North especially, tried to accommodate
new government programs and the ideas behind them. When both
these trusts were perceived as betrayed in the late 1960s and early
1970s, however, the frailty of the Democratic alliance between eastern
liberals, poor African Americans and Hispanics, and rural and urban
lower-middle-class and working-class whites was made plain.

George Wallace understood these frustrations and he made the
most of them. Some Americans on farms and in small towns and working-class white neighborhoods were tired of sending their sons off to
fight the Vietnam War, a war the government did not seem to want to
win. They were tired of turning on the television every night and finding more footage devoted to the gyrations of anti-war demonstrators
than to the war itself. They were tired of the emerging women's libera-
tion movement, which seemed to discount the value of motherhood
and by extension the power of patriarchy. They were tired of being told
what to do and where to go by "pointy-headed bureaucrats with their
briefcases."[20] And they were tired of seeing their incomes stagnate and
their children's chances to succeed fade while the government set up
special programs so that African Americans and other "disadvantaged"
Americans could have a better chance. Since the early nineteenth century, rural Americans had struggled to establish and maintain their
place in the American middle class. By 1968, and increasingly in the
1970s and 1980s, they found no more room for themselves there, and
few politicians willing to listen to their point of view.

Wallace voters were angry. Many were also racist, sexist, and
antielitist; they were not necessarily political conservatives, as conven-
tionally understood. They were, more exactly, Americans for whom
New Deal and Great Society liberalism had not delivered on its
promise, if it had made a promise at all. This conviction was underscored by the results of a confounding election-year poll: the majority
of those who supported Wallace for president in 1968 (the year Richard

M. Nixon and Hubert H. Humphrey were the major contenders) had named Robert Kennedy as their second choice.[21] It would take time and even more stagnation of the economy, but by 1980 disaffection and frustration of working-class and middle-class whites would effect a profound realignment of the political parties and help to launch a major cultural shift away from "bigness" and toward the political and cultural right, with all its contradictions. By 1996 the Republican Party—despite its desire to provide tax cuts to the rich and to continue protection for large corporations—would have inherited the rhetorical mantle of Populism in American politics. In January 1996, Republicans and Democrats alike would cheer when they heard a small-town southern-born president tell them that "the age of big government is over."[22]

Despite the transformation of liberalism and the emergence of the New Right, several farm-based organizations—the National Farmers' Union (NFO) and the American Agriculture Movement (AAM) especially—continued to swim against the tide. Like rural producer radicals before them, they advocated small production and stressed the fundamental importance of agrarian life to democracy in the United States. They did so in the context of two economic crises in the countryside which threatened the future of family farming in the United States and made rural Americans question the commitment of the federal government to small production. Their small successes reveal how meaningful the old slogans of rural producer radicalism still were to many farmers. Their failures reveal how difficult it had become to effect significant change within the modern liberal state.

When World War II ended, the needs of hungry people in Europe and Asia forced crop prices higher and convinced GIs to return to their country homes to make a living. Within ten years, however, global overproduction translated into falling prices, even pockets of poverty, in the most prosperous and powerful nation on earth. Farmers had often been caught in a squeeze between the costs they paid for consumer goods and the prices they received for crops. In the 1950s, however, they were more dependent on consumer goods than they had been before and thus the squeeze was tighter as well. The conversion of nearly every farm from horsepower to diesel power which was completed in this decade simultaneously increased productivity and costs. In 1948 a farmer in Webster City, Iowa, for example, could buy a tractor for $2,000 and sell hogs for $20.00 per hundredweight and corn for $1.25

a bushel. By 1960 the tractor was going for $3,500, while hogs were fetching only $12.00 per hundredweight and corn a dollar per bushel.[23] Although farmers loved being their own boss, many realized that they could do better working in factories, where wages and benefits were rising, than running their own farms. Between 1960 and 1970 around one hundred thousand farmers sold their farms and abandoned whatever hope remained of independent proprietorship.[24]

Economic frustrations like these were bad. Learning that the government agency that was supposed to be helping farmers to succeed was actually trying to encourage them to quit was even worse. Some farmers had long suspected that the USDA was not really on their side: farm programs did, after all, provide incentives for expansion, not conservation, and historically a far greater proportion of the USDA's budget went to large landholders than to small. In July 1962, however, they discovered the whole truth. A study published for the USDA's Committee for Economic Development argued that profitability in farming could be guaranteed only by a significant reduction of the number of farms in operation. Thus it recommended that in the next five years nearly twenty million acres of cropland and one-third of all farmers be "retired." Afterward, the free market, not production controls or farm subsidies, would take over. The remaining farms would be bigger and better, more efficient, more powerful in negotiations with buyers and distributors, and more like the successful corporations of the international economy.[25]

Farmers across America were outraged, determined to stand up for themselves and their ways of life, and ready to take charge of their futures. In September 1955 hog producers had joined together to begin the National Farmers' Organization (NFO) in Corning, Iowa. Their goal, like that of the Farmers' Holiday Association of the Great Depression era, was to raise prices for crops to cost-of-production plus a small profit. But to do so, they needed to increase their bargaining power with purchasers who set crop prices. Since the late nineteenth century, farmers had used cooperatives for this purpose. Seven million farmers belonged to nearly ten thousand cooperatives in 1955. Still, prices for crops did not rise. The NFO concluded that only "holding actions" (like the FHA's strikes) would demonstrate the collective power and resolve of small farmers. By the late 1950s as many as 180,000 farmers had joined the NFO and promised to keep farm products off the market until prices increased and costs declined. Organizer Oren Staley told members in Des Moines in 1962 that they were "the most underpaid group in America." Again and again, he asked, "Are you with us?" Again and again the crowd roared its affirmation of the NFO's political agenda and of rural producer radicalism as a whole.[26]

The NFO staged a series of holding actions for various commodities between 1959 and 1969. The first important action was in 1962 and involved hogs and cattle. NFO leaders assigned "checkers" to establish roadblocks on major routes into market cities to see whether farmers were violating their agreement not to sell. Pressure tactics like these were effective. Hog receipts fell 20 percent and prices rose. Thus in August 1964 the hog-and-cattle holding action was repeated. In March 1967 the NFO turned its attention to dairy products. Members attracted national attention by pouring thousands of gallons of milk onto city streets. One Wisconsin dairyman, for example, spilled out the milk of 450 cows. As historian Gilbert Fife tells it, in the spring of 1968, NFO members "killed several hundred calves and mature cattle, and threatened to destroy 12 million pounds of meat if packers did not negotiate prices and sign contracts."[27] Finally, in 1969, farmers organized the "farmers' survival drive"—a parade of tractors which converged on Washington, D.C. "The time for complacency is past," announced one driver.[28]

Although they certainly attracted attention, the holding actions and tractorcades sponsored by the NFO did not halt the depopulation of the countryside. Nor did they change the federal government's commitment, through subsidies and tax policies, to large-scale production. They did not even raise prices for long. In many cases, as soon as holding actions had secured higher prices and were called off, members rushed their products to market and deflated prices once again. Moreover, the flagrant waste of food angered many urban Americans who by the 1960s could hardly remember the ties to agriculture they (or even their food) once had. "Now I wouldn't pay them two cents more for a tubful if I could help it," a city woman reportedly declared when she saw milk flowing down the street.[29] Violence also accented the class divisions that had divided farmers for most of the century. Unlike a labor union that could control labor by a closed shop, struggling farmers could not force their wealthier neighbors to participate in holding actions—except through intimidation and threats. During each holding action, farmers who did not participate complained that their tires had been slashed, windows broken, fences cut, and barns burned. In Bonduel, Wisconsin, in 1964, one truck on its way to market refused to stop for NFO pickets. Two picketers were killed under its wheels. Only the quick work of local policemen saved the life of the driver from the hands of the angry crowd that gathered at the scene of the accident.

A temporary solution to the problems faced by small producers in the United States came with a reversal of fortune: the agricultural boom of the mid-1970s. Burgeoning farm exports—the 1973 U.S./Soviet wheat deal led the way—and surging crop prices encouraged farmers to plant fence row to fence row on as much land as they could fence. Improved economic conditions made farmers happy. The ambitious, hi-tech management style many of them adopted made the officials at the USDA ecstatic. To encourage even more farmers to do what Secretary of Agriculture Earl Butz recommended—"get bigger, get better, or get out"—the Farmers' Home Administration provided low-cost loans for land and new equipment.[30] Soon many a farmer who had once owned a quiet half-section of corn or wheat or cotton became a "windshield farmer"—one whose landholding was so vast that he could supervise the entire operation only from behind the wheel of a pick-up truck.[31]

Rising land prices also dramatically changed farm life. In Iowa, for example, an acre of farm land rose from $419 in 1970 to $2,066 in 1980. Surging values like these turned many farmers into "paper millionaires" practically overnight. Moreover, increased collateral in land provided even more opportunities to take out loans. Soon some farm families began to enjoy the prosperity of the postwar era and to indulge in the consumer culture that had been out of reach. In the South, purchases of such domestic products as washing machines and passenger cars diminished the difference between southern and northern farmers in all but the poorest (often African American) enclaves. In the North, farmers began to do things their parents and grandparents would never have even imagined, such as taking family vacations in Florida.[32]

The vacations ended as quickly and as suddenly as they had begun. As the United States increased production of foodstuffs, so did other nations. Soon global markets were flooded and prices began to plummet. Lost income encouraged farmers to try to grow even more, but (as always) overproduction merely drove prices down further. Three years of killer drought destroyed many harvests in the Southeast. Meanwhile, inflation and the oil crisis created by an Arab embargo increased prices for essential consumer goods. In 1980 the Carter administration placed an embargo on exports to the Soviet Union after that nation invaded Afghanistan. The final blow, however—the blow that, as one official explains, "threw [farmers] into the[ir] windshield[s]"—was sharply rising interest rates.[33] Many farmers had taken out loans with adjustable rates, never thinking the rates could rise much above 12 or 14 percent. By the early 1980s they would have risen to nearly 22 percent. Inevitably, land values began to plummet—declining by more than 50 percent in some regions. Average family incomes followed suit. In Iowa, for example, the average net income fell more than 50 percent in 1981–82. By 1983 it was actually in negative numbers.[34]

What happened next was, in the words of one Georgia farmer, "a nightmare that [will] never go away."[35] From North Dakota to Texas and Alabama to Colorado, farmland that had been held by families for more than a century was lost to foreclosure in less than half a decade. Children whose families grew food endured the humiliation of being unable to buy it themselves.[36] Huge numbers of men struck out for the Sun Belt, in search of a job, any job, that might help them save their land. Farm women likewise sought off-farm employment in factories and offices. They learned to combine new sets of authorities and responsibilities with all the others they had juggled before. As farms failed, so did rural businesses; towns began to resemble ghettos with boarded-up stores and abandoned buildings in the midst of verdant pastures, fields, and orchards. Families neglected health care and waited for hours in lines for emergency food distributions. Not surprisingly, rates of rural suicides increased. So did domestic violence and murder. Jim Jenkins, the Minnesotan who murdered his banker and then committed suicide, was hardly the only rural American to kill and be killed by the overwhelming grief brought on by loss of land, community, and independence.[37]

Desperation was countered by activism. In 1977 four farmers sitting in a small restaurant in a hard-hit area of eastern Colorado concluded that times were bad and getting worse, and that they had to do something about it. Moreover, they said that the federal government was not only unresponsive to the needs of small producers but actually made life worse for them by encouraging indebtedness and dishonesty. Similarly, large farm organizations—even the once-radical Farmers' Union—had begun to represent their own interests with more fervor than their constituencies'. They had, for example, supported the Farm Bill of 1977, which clearly favored large-scale over small-scale production. Now the associated credit agencies of the American Farm Bureau Federation and the Farmers' Union were actually foreclosing on land. A new farmers' organization that could speak for all farmers and demand

the return to 100-percent parity (100 percent of the buying power of
the agricultural sector during the good years between 1909 and 1914)
was overdue. Dependent on the programs of government and the representation of lobbyists, neither of which had the best interests of
small producers in mind but merely paid lip service to them, family
farmers had become politically lethargic—a lethargy that had done
them no small amount of harm.[38]

These four farmers began the American Agriculture Movement,
which in the late 1970s spread like wildfire across the countryside. Organized in small cells with no dues, no rules, and no formal leadership,
the AAM boasted eleven hundred local offices in forty states by the
middle of 1978. Members agreed that a farm strike was the best way to
increase prices. But attracting national attention to the problems
farmers were facing and the importance of family farming to American
culture was even more important. To this end, AAM members held
loud and angry press conferences and gathered in large groups at local
farm foreclosures. Like so many rural groups before them, the AAM
made use of their collective strength (both literal and figurative) to
promote action and gain attention. As William Browne noted, "the
combined effect was one designed to demonstrate anger, activism, pur-
poseful resolve, and an implied threat of disruption and perhaps even
violence if cooperation was not forthcoming."[39]

AAM members proved their resolve and their ability to disrupt
when they staged two tractorcades on Washington in 1978 and 1979.
On January 18, 1978, three thousand farmers went to Washington in
tractors, campers, and pick-ups, determined to make an impression on
lawmakers and emphasize their uncompromising demand for 100-per-
cent parity. This they did. Forgotten for so many years, now farmers
basked in the media and congressional attention. "They poured out of
every corner to meet with us," one farmer recalled. "When I saw all
that, I knew we were damned important." Another remembered, "We
thought we owned the damned town, we knew it, by God." Legislators
did agree to some emergency changes to the farm bill. Nevertheless, an
offer of 100-percent parity, which would have increased food prices in
urban America, was not forthcoming. Now anger replaced the thrill of
power and influence. "We were sold out," said one member. "It was a
setup from day one."[40]

The second tractorcade took an even angrier and less compromis-
ing tone as the AAM tried to "shut down Washington." On February 5,

On February 5, 1979, the American Agriculture
Movement sponsored a second tractorcade in
Washington, D.C.
George Tames / NYT Pictures.

1979, a line of tractors twenty-five miles long snarled traffic coming into the city. Farmers rammed police cars with their tractors, delayed commuters for hours, and even contributed to the cancellation of an important presidential meeting. Eventually, police succeeded in corralling the farm vehicles on the Washington Mall, but incidents of property destruction and personal intimidation continued. A few farmers drove their tractors up the steps of the Capitol, released chickens and goats on the grass, threw tomatoes at Secretary of Agriculture Robert Bergland, and set three old tractors on fire. Not surprisingly, congressmen were much less impressed with the activists than they had been the year before. When one complained that "they didn't have any trouble [like this] last year," the farmers replied, "Yeah, and we didn't get anything last year either." Later, President Ronald Reagan would make a joke out of such altercations, saying "Let's keep the grain and export the farmers."[41]

Not surprisingly, the AAM never succeeded in achieving its goal of 100-percent parity. Moreover, it was broadly criticized for being unwilling to compromise, bargain, or even negotiate in the ways that lobbyists in the modern state were expected to. But that was just the point; the leaders of the AAM refused to act like lobbyists because they did not want to be lobbyists. They did not want to be entrenched members of the Washington bureaucracy but genuine representatives of rural people. Thus their radicalism became their undoing. Although the AAM remains a strong renegade voice challenging the agribusiness establishment in Washington, the economic and cultural positions of farmers are as tenuous as ever. While the Farm Bill of 1985 did provide debt relief and bankruptcy protection to small farmers who had managed to survive, its provisions still provided significant incentive for expansion and for the majority of payments to go to the minority of landholders. The total phase-out of farm subsidies passed by the 1996 Republican Congress may impair the viability of small producers more than any earlier farm bill did. Many farmers—including those in the Iowa Farm Bill Study Team who agreed that the federal bureaucracy had to go, but could not simply abandon farmers overnight—may soon see that neither compensatory liberalism nor Newt Gingrich conservatism will solve farmers' problems in the long run. That will require a different kind of imagining altogether.

Grass-roots organizations of the early 1980s were more successful in helping farm families than the AAM was in changing the federal government's business-as-usual. First in Iowa, and then in many other states, farm activists—including representatives of the AAM—joined with religious, educational, and philanthropic groups to help farmers survive the crisis. Beginning in 1982, the Iowa Farm Unity Coalition, for example, provided the model on which the National Save the Family Farm Coalition was based. It included Prairiefire Rural Action groups, the Farm Survival Hotline, ninety-nine county Farm Survival committees, the Iowa Inter-Church Agency for Peace and Justice, the Bank Closing Response Team, and the Farm Credit System Task Force. Together these agencies tried to help farmers find food, access social services and health care, renegotiate debt, hire a lawyer, avoid foreclosure, cope with an unavoidable foreclosure, and even test their water for contaminants.[42]

Like the Populists, Nonpartisan Leaguers, and socialists before them, the National Save the Family Farm Coalition moved quickly to form alliances outside the farm belt. For example, the AAM shipped wheat to the wildcat strikers of the United Mine Workers in West Virginia. The Iowa Coalition welcomed support from the state office of the United Automobile Workers. For the first time in half a century, farm activists saw clearly that the economic circumstances of farmers and workers were linked. They saw that as the farm crisis deepened so did the trend toward deindustrialization in much of the Northeast and Midwest. Large employers, like the Chrysler plant in Kenosha, Wisconsin, had traditionally provided jobs not just to men and women in town but also to farmers who left farming or needed extra cash.[43] When it closed in the 1980s, suddenly and permanently, a major economic influence in the countryside disappeared too. All across the landscape the same pattern emerged. Traditional factories closed up and many workers moved away. Then, sometimes, if a town was "lucky," a new employer moved in. These new employers, however, like the builders of the Saturn plant in Spring Hill, Tennessee, attached their own strings with predictable consequences: lower wages, fewer benefits, decreased controls over safety, surging land prices, and higher worker and community turnover. The fundamental changes of postindustrial capitalism forced political activists in the tradition of rural producer radicalism to consider links with people whose lives had once seemed altogether different from their own.[44]

Farm activists also made alliances with feminist groups. As we have seen, farm women had participated in many of the community-based farm organizations in the past, including the Grange, the People's Party, and the Farmers' Holiday Association. They had used their own skills as community organizers to help their families endure. In this kind of day-to-day way, farm women had looked to promote equality in their marriages, workplaces, and communities without upsetting traditional ways of life.[45] During the farm crisis of the 1980s, however, women's specific concerns crept closer to the forefront of farm politics than they had before. Groups of female farmers and farm wives gathered to support one another and demonstrate their solidarity as women. Likewise, women organized to address such specific feminist issues as passage of the Equal Rights Amendment and the rising rates of domestic violence in rural America. Some ran for public office. Those who still preferred more supportive than activist roles answered hot lines, met with farmers in trouble, and advised friends. On all levels, and in a variety of ways, individual women, women's skills, and even women's rights were central to the grass-roots activism of the 1980s. More than they ever had before, women defined the work and the network of rural producer radicalism.[46]

The farm coalitions also reached out to environmentalists. Like miners and loggers, farmers had at first been reluctant to join the contemporary environmental movement. They had considered the land part of "nature's capital" provided for them to use to feed the world and from which to profit. But in the late 1970s and early 1980s some farmers began to realize that the pesticides and other chemicals they used on the farm were not just killing bugs, they were endangering the lives of rural people. They thought back to the USDA's reaction to what one historian calls the "bombshell in Beltsville," the 1962 publication of Rachel Carson's *Silent Spring*.[47] So certain were government officials of the safety of chemicals used in farming that they had laughed off suggestions that DDT was ruining the environment and risking lives. For two more decades, federal programs made it as easy to buy chemicals as to buy children's shoes. Now some farm people looked to organic farming and sustainable agriculture as possible ways to survive the crisis and survive as a people.[48]

Finally, some farm activists also joined hands with the urban poor through Jesse Jackson's Rainbow Coalition. In his bid for the presidency in 1988, Jackson spent many hours with farmers and their families in Iowa and other states, seeking common cause among the diverse people who found themselves on the short end of the Reagan revolution. Even Jackson admitted that Iowa farmers were unlikely supporters of his mission. But they surprised him. In January 1987 Jackson arrived in Greenville, Iowa, to deliver a campaign address. He chose Greenville in part because he knew it had been the headquarters of the Ku Klux Klan in Iowa in the 1920s. Also he believed that many Iowans had never seen a black person before. Iowans filled the tiny church to overflowing, more excited than any group Jackson had ever seen. "There was an emerging sense of a deep and abiding reunion," he said later. "Lots of romance in it. People were trying to say so many things, like they wish they had done this a long time ago."[49]

The sight of Iowa farmers grasping hands with African Americans, Hispanic Americans, Native Americans, gay rights activists, and welfare mothers puzzled many Americans. What did clean-cut, Christian farmers have in common with people like them? But the Rainbow

Coalition enraged the leaders of far-right groups who had also tried to join the farm crisis activists in the heartland. Beginning in 1978, for example, the AAM looked toward the leaders and ideologies of the right. By 1979 its own rhetoric had hardened, moving away from extolling agrarian virtues to condemning a corporate conspiracy and international bankers for the farmers' troubles. Even the peace-and-justice activists of the Iowa Family Farm Coalition tried to work with right-wing groups. More and more often, throughout the farm crisis, recruiters for the Posse Comitatus, the Aryan Nations, Lyndon Larouche's many groups, and a host of smaller organizations traveled to farm auctions and solicited funds from, and disseminated literature to, angry farmers.[50] These groups were extremely varied in their beliefs. They shared a common conviction, however, that conventional political mobilization was pointless. The federal government was under the control of international Zionists, they said. It had no intention of helping farmers, not now or ever. It intended to take them captive.

Explanations for the farm crisis that put the blame on un-American conspirators, Jews, and corrupted elites made more sense (and sounded more familiar) to many rural Americans than the activists on the left wanted to admit. It certainly felt more comfortable than creating alliances with the urban poor. And to some farm men, it felt more comfortable than attending support-group meetings or domestic-violence awareness lectures. And anyway, many wondered, why would this nation's most honorable citizens suffer so terribly unless the government had been subverted by its enemies? Hadn't that all happened before, even in this century? Not a long road, then, but a very short one led some rural Americans from political activism on the left to intolerance, hatred, anti-Semitism, and in some cases vigilantism on the right. It was a well-traveled route.

"Get violent, whitey":

THE TRIUMPH OF VIGILANTISM IN POSTWAR AMERICA

It was confusing all right, the pundits agreed, when they thought about it later. Why did the good farm folks in Wisconsin, who had elected and supported Robert La Follette's Progressive Party for so many years, replace him—well, replace his son anyway—with the most rabid anti-communist of our time? Perhaps it was because Joseph McCarthy hadn't run for office as an anticommunist. Perhaps it was because he had actually been a Democrat at one time in his career. Or perhaps it was simply because he was a nice farm boy and a war veteran and the naive voters back home had not seen his sourer side. But, if so, why had the people of Wisconsin, the people of rural Wisconsin especially, voted for McCarthy even after his notorious speech in Wheeling, West Virginia, when he announced the discovery of twenty purported communists in the United States government, and even after the subsequent hunt for subversives in every branch of government? Why did some of them support him even after his death, when in many circles his name had become synonymous with fascism?

Anticommunism was nothing new in rural America—not in La Follette country or anywhere else. Neither were contradictory political views. Indeed, McCarthyism was merely the most recent (and in some respects the least viscous) expression of radical patriotism in rural America. In the early twentieth century the KKK, the IVA, and a host of anti-German groups had targeted anarchists, socialists, and communists for suppression. Likewise, the leaders of American fascism in the New Deal era had believed that a Jewish conspiracy in the highest echelons of government was trying to turn the United States toward communism. Given this history and the shocking events of the Cold War—when despite the Allied victory in Europe and Asia, procommunist forces seemed to have won more hearts and minds there than prodemocracy forces had—support in rural America for a new "red scare" was not illogical. To people with a traditional suspicion of the government and a traditional intolerance of diversity, McCarthyism was as natural as the fertilized soybeans growing in their fields. And it would be just as toxic in the long run, when taken in excessively large quantities.[51]

Rural Americans loved it when McCarthy went after communists, but they loved it even more when he went after rich, elite, eastern communists. Unlike earlier groups of radical patriots like the KKK which blamed immigrants for world communism, McCarthy focused on "silver spoon" gentry. From his speech in Wheeling until his death, McCarthy reminded listeners that the young communists in the State Department, the army, the film industry, and everywhere else "have had all the benefits that the wealthiest nation on earth has to offer—the finest homes, the finest college educations, the finest jobs . . . we can give."[52] "Ivy Leaguers" took a particularly large number of shots. The new president of Harvard University, McCarthy said, was a "rabid anti-anticommunist," shielding himself in "a cloak of phony, hypocritical liberalism."[53] Earlier, Alger Hiss had been taken to task for his Harvard connections; Dean Acheson for having attended Groton, Yale University, and Harvard Law School. McCarthy ridiculed Adlai Stevenson for "carrying a Ph.D. from Dean Acheson's Cowardly College of Communist Containment." Perhaps, some suggested, McCarthy was merely attacking the men who had refused to accept him in the Washington social circle. As historian David Bennett wrote, McCarthy's "rumpled, muscular, crude . . . but unafraid" persona did not fit in there. Even so he did not simply carry out a personal vendetta. He acted in the tradition of many other men who believed that the government had been created to serve such rumpled men as themselves.[54]

Because it expressed long-standing hatreds and resentments and reflected the larger mood of a nation under the constant shadow of war, militant anticommunism survived the death of McCarthy in many places in the United States. Between 1950 and 1990 hundreds of small and a few large groups have dedicated themselves to rooting out communists and preparing for the possible invasion of the North American continent. Rural people alone, of course, did not join these organizations any more than they alone had joined the Ku Klux Klan or many other antiradical groups of the early twentieth century. Nevertheless, many of the new militant anticommunist groups either were based in rural areas, had major support from rural areas, or had leaders who had grown up in rural areas. Likewise, some rural people continued to support militant anticommunist associations even after urban conservatives had backed away from them.[55] They brought with them a fondness for collective action and vigilante-style justice that survived all the attempts of modernity to make them obsolete.

Robert Welch—one of the most influential American anticommunists after McCarthy's time—grew up on a North Carolina farm, the son and grandson of farmers and Baptist preachers. He moved to Massachusetts to begin a candy factory but left neither his evangelism nor his intolerance behind. When the McCarthy hearings ended, he found his calling. In 1958 he started the John Birch Society (JBS), through which he helped to bring McCarthyism to the grass roots, through community-by-community organizing. Welch subscribed to the notion that a great global conspiracy sought to obliterate Christianity and the American

Constitution. He also believed that the JBS was the only hope to stop the Red Menace which, by Welch's own estimates, already controlled up to 80 percent of the United States government. JBS members also maintained that educating the public through the dissemination of literature and the sponsorship of youth programs was the key to salvaging civilization.[56]

During the peak of its popularity in the 1960s, the JBS boasted four thousand chapters and an annual budget of over five million dollars for the publication and distribution of literature and the staffing of JBS libraries. Members also became involved in domestic campaigns to weaken the image of the United Nations, which they maintained was merely a front for communism. For example, JBS members attempted to stop children from collecting money for UNICEF at Halloween and sent hundreds of protest letters to the Xerox Corporation when it produced television specials that seemed to paint a favorable image of the United Nations. These activities turned off many urban conservatives who had initially been interested in the JBS project. Many rural people, however, including large numbers of Mormons, sustained their interest and support. People in Idaho, Oregon, Utah, and Washington became, by the late 1960s, mainstays of the JBS operation.[57]

In the late 1950s Welch added racial integration to his list of un-American activities. Like many other southerners, Welch refused to believe that African Americans in the United States would protest for civil rights unless they had been compelled by communist agents to do so. Thus he told whites that they were experiencing "two revolutions at once." The JBS published a book by this name and distributed more than half a million copies. "Fully expose the 'Civil Rights' fraud," Welch argued in 1965, "and you will break the back of Communist conspiracy." Counter to the perceptions of most liberals and, increasingly, the national media, Welch believed that civil-rights activists were dangerous lawbreakers and that southern sheriffs like Bull Connor of Birmingham, Alabama, who opposed them were true patriots. Welch believed that Martin Luther King, Jr., was one of the most sinister communists ever to have lived in the United States.[58]

The John Birch Society also became a focal point and organizational vanguard of postwar anti-Semitism. Welch himself always denied that he hated Jews or held them responsible for communism. In fact, he proudly displayed lists of Jewish members of the JBS. His libraries, however, were full of the classic and soon-to-be classic works of anti-Semitism including the *Protocols of the Learned Elders of Zion* and Gary

Allen's *None Dare Call It Conspiracy,* which described the machinations of "international bankers and financiers" to topple democracy. Welch blamed Jews themselves for creating anti-Semitism, suggesting that they used it as a smoke screen for their bolshevism. Finally, Welch was no stranger to the hard-core anti-Semites of the Cold War era. Some of the most notorious anti-Semites of the past half-century, including Robert Jay Mathews, the founder of the violent neo-Nazi group called the Order, began their careers of hatred in the John Birch Society.[59]

But some rural Americans believed that the JBS did not go far enough in its racism, anti-Semitism, or anticommunism. Generally speaking, JBS members preferred reading and writing to killing and maiming. Other Americans had different priorities. In the American South, for example, where the Freedom Movement of the 1960s rocked traditional race relations to their core, partly because rural African Americans organized in resistance to oppression, racial radicalism made a third stand. Several different offshoots of the Ku Klux Klan as well as locally organized White Citizens' Councils set out to end the civil rights movement by force of vigilante violence.

Together, these militant white supremacist organizations were responsible for many of the most notorious acts of racial violence of our time, including the bombing of Birmingham's Sixteenth Street Baptist Church, the assassination of Medgar Evers, and the torture deaths of Michael Schwerner, Andrew Goodman, and James Chaney. Samuel Holloway Bowers, the Imperial Wizard of the White Knights of the KKK in Mississippi, was himself responsible for planning and carrying out nine murders, seventy-five bombings, and three hundred miscellaneous assaults.[60] Small wonder that the groups' violence was so intense and widespread. Organizers did not mince words about what members should do to African Americans associated with civil rights. Charles Conley ("Connie") Lynch of Clarksville, Texas, for example, celebrated the deaths of the four little girls who died in the Birmingham church bombing. "When I go out to kill rattlesnakes, I don't make no difference between little rattlesnakes and big rattlesnakes. . . . So I kill 'em all, and if there's four less niggers tonight, then I say, 'Good for whoever planted the bomb!' We're all better off. . . . I believe in violence, all the violence it takes either to scare the niggers out of the country or to have 'em all six feet under." At the scene of a near lynching, one of Lynch's followers asked a federal investigator, "Did you ever smell a nigger burn? It's a mighty sweet smell."[61]

George Lincoln Rockwell's American Nazi Party did not have the same widespread impact that the KKK did, but his beliefs have nevertheless endured into our own day. Rockwell unequivocally hated Welch and the "moderate" JBS. He accused them of being as bad for the country as communists were, because they were unwilling to take real action against communism. And unlike Welch, Rockwell did not beat around the bush when it came to his racial attitudes. He fervently believed that both integration and miscegenation were communist plots to weaken white men by taking away white women. "I don't hate niggers any more than I hate monkeys," he once said. "But they don't belong out here in the streets with our women."[62] He blamed Jews for fomenting the civil rights movement and believed that African Americans, Jews, "queers," and other obvious enemies of "decent white America" should be executed. To prove his point he drove a "hate bus" through the South during the Freedom Rides of the early 1960s. He dressed his followers in Nazi uniforms and marched in the streets of the nation's capital. When he died he requested burial in a national cemetery—in complete Nazi regalia.

Robert DePugh also didn't think that Welch and the JBS were taking the communist threat seriously enough. For one, they did not know a thing about survivalism or military-readiness techniques. His group, the Minutemen, however, were armed and ready for the communist invasion—whether it came from without or within—as well as for urban race riots and thermonuclear war. Begun in Norborne, Missouri, in 1965, the Minutemen claimed twenty-five thousand members before its demise at the hands of federal prosecutors in 1968. They were, DePugh explained, "principally concerned with training themselves for guerrilla warfare. After the Communist takeover, they will deploy over hill and dale, dig in, and repulse with small arms any effort to enslave them."[63] To protect themselves, they also adopted a leaderless organizational format whereby small cells of men would be scattered across the countryside and two dozen regional coordinators would arrange activities without any knowledge of the actual membership of individual cells. Activities included instruction and practice in marksmanship, military maneuvers, and wilderness survival. Members learned to eat caterpillars and lizards, ford streams, and track invaders.[64]

The Minutemen also distributed anticommunist, racist, and anti-Semitic literature, much of which suggested that the United States government was already under the control of Zionists and communists and that the urban poor were preparing to wage war on whites. As DePugh declared, "We must be willing to continue to fight for liberty even though we no longer have the legal support of established authority and prepare ourselves to take any action—no matter how brutal—that may be required to renew the protection of the United States Constitution for future generations."[65] DePugh also maintained connections with Rockwell's American Nazi Party, George Harwell's white separatist organization in Clay County, Illinois, Billy James Hargis's evangelical crusade in Tulsa, Oklahoma, and several leaders of what was becoming known as Identity Christianity. This belief system, which originated as British Israelism, suggested that Jews were not actually God's chosen people—white Christian Americans were. Jews and all people of color were either the offspring of Satan or members of a different subhuman species.[66] In either case they were undeserving of citizenship—or any rights at all—in the United States.

When DePugh was brought to trial on weapons and conspiracy charges, the extent of the violence he advocated became fully known. Most distasteful were the warnings he had sent to twenty legislators who had voted to abolish the House Un-American Activities Committee. "Traitors, Beware! Even now the crosshairs are on the backs of your necks."[67] This was bad. It got worse, though, when he republished the warning on posters just weeks after the assassination of President John F. Kennedy. Later, New Orleans prosecutor James Garrison suggested that Kennedy's presumed killer, Lee Harvey Oswald, may have once belonged to a Minutemen cell. While this proved untrue, some Minutemen did plan violent acts against American leaders. They tried to rob banks, plotted to put cyanide into the air-conditioning system at the United Nations, and considered assassinating President Lyndon B. Johnson and United Nations ambassador Arthur Goldberg. None of these crimes was committed, and DePugh himself was sent to prison in 1968.[68] In another generation, however, a similar unconscionable act would be carried out by men in a rented truck packed with fertilizer and diesel fuel.

Since the end of the Vietnam War, hate groups have increased in size, number, and diversity of beliefs. Some groups have also grown more similar in temperament to the mainstream political right. Most important, they have nearly all adopted the paramilitary and survivalist style that Robert DePugh's Minutemen originated. Indeed arms, survivalist training, and military-style maneuvers are the stock in trade of most right-wing groups today. Yet, to many Americans outside the new hate groups, paramilitarism is another of the aspects of rural radicalism which seem contradictory. If people associated with the far right are against American military intervention in world affairs, for example, why do they seem to love the military? If they believe themselves to be radical patriots, why do they hate the United States government? If Timothy McVeigh was such a "good soldier," why did he purportedly target a federal building that housed recruiters and support services for the armed services?

The answers to these questions are found in the same political and economic circumstances that brought about farm activism on the left. As James William Gibson explains it, the Vietnam War was a crushing blow to all Americans—but most of all to working- and middle-class white men who had believed in the righteousness of the military's anti-communist ideology. To them—Randy Weaver was one, Bo Gritz and Jim Jenkins two others—it was unimaginable that so many lives had been lost for nothing and that the most powerful government on the earth could have been defeated by a tiny, underdeveloped Asian nation. Weren't American men the strongest, bravest, and most deadly on earth? To them the Vietnam War was not just emotionally and psychologically debilitating. It was politically alienating. It suggested that the American government could no longer be trusted to fight the good fight and to honor the men who had done so. It suggested that the American government would rather pull out of a war than do what was necessary to win. It suggested that the American government was not man enough to get the job done and to do it right.[69]

But perhaps individual American men still were. Perhaps they could "bring the war back home" and, as Rambo put it so well, "win it this time." For many men in rural America—where farming and industry offered dead ends, incomes were stagnating at best, farm organizations had been either demasculinized or feminized, and the promise of a good life was practically a joke—paramilitarism and survivalism offered a chance to prove their masculinity and honor. Moreover, these activities provided opportunities for them to participate in vigilante organizations as so many of their forefathers had in the past. Beginning in the late 1960s and continuing throughout the 1980s and 1990s, rural men linked their quest for what Susan Jefford calls "the remasculinization of America" to their age-old heritage of hatred, intolerance, and violence.[70]

Henry Beach, a former member of William Dudley Pelley's Silver Shirts, began a new organization in 1969 for exactly these purposes. The Posse Comitatus, whose name means in Latin "power of the county," quickly spread through the West, Midwest, and parts of the upper South. Members believed that no authority higher than the county sheriff and no constitutional amendment beyond the first twelve were legally binding on any American. Moreover, they believed that the present government was fully overrun by Zionist conspirators. Thus if they were to comply with any federal regulation—from paying taxes to making social-security payments or honoring fish and wildlife regulations or even getting a driver's license—they would be complicit in an international conspiracy. Beach believed that direct, vigilante action was required to stop the conspiracy. "In some instances of record," he wrote, "the law provides for the following prosecution of officials of government who commit criminal acts or who violate their oath of office. . . . He shall be removed by the posse to the most populated intersection of streets in the township and, at high noon, be hung by the neck, the body remaining until sundown as an example to those who would subvert the law."[71]

The Posse found many willing listeners to their theories during the farm crisis. To desperate farmers, a government-conspiracy theory explained how they could have so suddenly come upon hard times. Moreover, the Posse's detailed legal clinics made it really seem possible that people could refuse to pay their taxes on constitutional grounds and that they could refuse to allow federal agents on their farms. Two farmers—at least—followed this line of reasoning to their graves. Gordon Kahl was a struggling farmer in Medina, North Dakota, who first refused to pay his taxes in 1970. When four carloads of agents came to arrest him in 1983, he and his son killed two agents, wounded four more, and escaped. Kahl spent months on the run, going from Posse safe-house to safe-house throughout the West and South. Scores of agents surrounded his final hideout in the Ozarks; when a hand-thrown grenade lit the thousands of rounds of ammunition stored there, the bunker exploded in flame. Later Kahl's body had to be identified by dental records.[72]

Nebraska farmer Arthur Kirk also listened when the Posse talked. He was in danger of losing the land his family had farmed for many years. Deeply in debt to a local bank in Grand Junction, Kirk sold cattle he had promised as collateral. He warned local officials not to try to serve him with legal papers of any kind. He believed, as members of the

Posse and a related organization had told him, that if he posted special notices on the property no state authority could trespass on it. He did this, but still the officials came. Kirk pointed a weapon at the first one. Soon a state SWAT team swarmed around the farmhouse. Kirk stayed inside surrounded by weapons including M-16s and an elephant gun loaded with armor-piercing ammunition. Finally he went outside to reach a fortified bunker by his windmill. "Fucking Jews!" he shouted as he ran. He shot more than fifty rounds at the police before he was killed by bullets to the shoulder and leg. Inside the house, investigators found Posse literature that read, "I don't think the CIA or the FBI is part of the U.S. government. I think it is part of the Mossad, the Jewish police. In fact, I think the Mossad is world-wide and that all police organizations like the CIA and FBI in all countries are under the Mossad."[73] Kirk's wife never forgave agents for denying her access to her husband and spent the next several years traveling around the Midwest telling her story and warning that the Mossad was preparing to come after other families too.

It was not only the economic crisis of the 1970s and 1980s that pushed people like Kahl and Kirk away from traditional agrarian protest to paramilitarism, anticommunism, and Identity Christianity. By that time much of the political mainstream was listening to similar, albeit subtler, messages from the New Right. While a survey found that an ordinary person's fear of the right in 1968 had ranked well down the list, by 1980 "the irrelevant right" had become very relevant indeed. In the 1950s and 1960s such anticommunist crusaders as Billy James Hargis of Tulsa, Oklahoma, traveled in converted buses to small-town revivals. In the late 1970s and 1980s such anticommunist evangelicals as Billy Graham, Jim Bakker, and Pat Robertson took limousines to Republican national conventions.[74] During their conversion to Identity Christianity, Vicki and Randy Weaver purportedly listened to evangelical radio shows daily. The sermons did not force the Weavers to become white separatists, but they did reinforce the Weavers' hatred of bigness in government and industry, fear of communism, their belief that Americans were a chosen people, and their desire to reinvent American patriotism. So must have the secular sermonizing of politicians of the New Right. As conservative commentator Kevin Phillips remarked—metaphorically, but nonetheless prophetically—"[these new conservatives] have more in common with Andrew Jackson than with Edmund Burke. Their hope is to build cultural siege-cannon out of the populist steel of Idaho, Mississippi, and working-class Milwaukee, and then blast the Eastern liberal establishment to ideo-institutional smithereens."[75]

The racism and anti-Semitism of rural hate groups was encouraged by the evangelism—secular and sacred—of the New Right as well. For all their protestations to the contrary, evangelicals continued to associate America's financial problems with international bankers. In Pat Robertson's 1995 book, *The New World Order*, the preacher defines the international conspiracy that threatens the collapse of freedom and liberty in the United States. And while he claims to have no animus toward Jews, those primarily responsible are European bankers, financiers, and industrialists—people whom more forthright Populists would have simply called Jews.[76] Likewise the New Christian Right's use of racial code words to describe the decay of American society has fooled few Americans on either side of the political aisle. In short, the most powerful and violent rural groups in recent years have combined anticommunism, paramilitarism, racism, and anti-Semitism and taken to extremes the intolerances of the mainstream culture of the New Right. Moreover, they have done so at a time when even the most ardent advocates of compensatory liberalism have backed away from that position and when the tradition of reform liberalism and rural producer radicalism is hard even to recall.

But what exactly are the new groups that have taken root in the countryside? The best known and most closely watched is the Aryan Nations. Begun by Richard Butler in 1979, the Aryan Nations is located on a fenced and guarded compound at Hayden Lake, Idaho. Butler chose Idaho for its rugged beauty, inexpensive land, low tax rate, and socially conservative population—some of whom he recruited as members.[77] The Aryan Nations believes that Jews are waging war to eliminate all white Christians of English, Germanic, and Scandinavian heritage. Homosexuality, popular culture, and immigration are all part of the larger plot to dilute and destroy the gene pool of white men. The Holocaust too was a hoax, perpetuated by Jewish bankers and intellectuals to justify the killing of millions of white Christians. The Nations anticipates and prepares for the coming race war. As Butler's ally William Potter Gale puts it, "God said you're gonna do it that way, and it's about time somebody is telling you to get violent, whitey."[78]

Get violent they did. By the mid-1980s an offspring of the Aryan Nations had proved even deadlier than the parent organization. Named for an elite guard in the German army, the Bruder Schweigen, the Silent Brotherhood, or Order, was the brainchild of Nations member Robert

Jay Mathews who had been inspired—like Timothy McVeigh—by the 1978 William Pierce novel *The Turner Diaries*. In the novel, ZOG begins to attack white Christian Americans. In response, small cells of militarily prepared men retaliate, eventually reclaiming the nation for their kind. In the process, African Americans, Jews, Asians, and Chicanos are summarily executed, murdered, bombed, and tortured.[79]

This reclamation sounded like a good idea to Mathews and his fellows in the Order, but it would cost money. To prepare for their own battle, the Order counterfeited money, robbed stores, and held up armored cars for heists of millions of dollars. Then they began to buy land, arms, and other provisions necessary to establish survival camps and hideouts. Finally they chose their targets for execution. First on the list was Alan Berg, a well-known radio talk-show host in Denver, who often asked neo-Nazis to phone him and then lambasted them on the air. Order members ambushed Berg at his car, pumping his body full of more than thirty bullets. When the murder weapon was found at the home of one of the members of the Order, a nationwide manhunt for Mathews began. It ended with a firestorm—not unlike the one that ended Gordon Kahl's life—when a magnesium illumination flare was fired from an FBI helicopter circling a house on Whidbey Island in Puget Sound, where Mathews was hiding. The flare burned through the roof of the house, ignited the stores of ammunition inside, and, as James Coates phrased it, "incinerat[ed] Mathews in the fire of his own engines of hatred."[80]

Other groups in our time have also taken up arms against intolerable elements in American society. The Covenant, the Sword, and the Arm of the Lord (CSA), for example, was founded in 1976 by Texas fundamentalist minister Jim Ellison, who moved to the Ozarks when he converted to Identity Christianity. Like Idaho, the Ozarks are rugged, inexpensive, and popular among fundamentalists, radical patriots, and back-to-the landers. But even there, the CSA stood out for its beliefs. Ellison practiced polygamy and was said to have kidnaped hitchhikers to become new members. On the CSA compound, believers stored sophisticated equipment that enabled them to produce hand grenades and cyanide compounds, and they built a weaponry-training facility modeled after the FBI facility in Quantico, Virginia. Targets held cardboard cutouts of Menachem Begin and Golda Meir. Ellison was proudest of the support—through funds and armaments—that he gave to other radical patriot groups. The CSA, for example, provided the MAC 10 gun that the Order used to murder Alan Berg.[81]

But CSA members also did some dirty work themselves, so much in fact that eventually the federal government shut the compound down. In 1983 Richard Wayne Snell killed an African American state trooper in Arkansas with a gun he had specially altered at the compound. Next Ellison and William Thomas torched the Beth Shalom synagogue in Indianapolis, Indiana. Finally, in April 1985, CSA recruit David Tate, who had ties to the Order and the California Klan, murdered a thirty-year-old Missouri state trooper named Jimmie Linegar. He escaped into the Missouri countryside, where for six days he lived out a real-life survivalist fantasy. When he finally gave himself up, the FBI authorized a full-scale raid on the CSA compound. SWAT teams stormed the gates while residents fled to hide in a center bunker. They agreed to surrender on the promise that their leaders would not be jailed with African Americans.[82]

Some violent acts were not sponsored or organized by specific groups, but were nevertheless expressions of the extremist ideology that had pervaded the countryside in the 1980s. In Wileyville, California, for example, two survivalists were suspected of killing as many as twenty-five people, especially young women they lured into their compound and then tortured to death, all the while explaining that they were searching for the perfect "warrior wives."[83] In Cokeville, Wyoming, a couple took an arsenal of weapons into an elementary school. This was so commonplace, however, that even a town council member who saw them was not alarmed. Then the couple announced that they were beginning "the Brave New World" and took all 167 teachers and children hostage. For six hours teachers sang and held terrified children who were packed into a single classroom. The ordeal ended when a gasoline bomb exploded in the woman's hands, killing her in front of the children, and her husband committed suicide. More than twenty children suffered severe burn injuries.[84]

In Seattle in 1985, a knock on the door on Christmas Eve began a nightmare that tied the extreme right of the post-Vietnam era with the anti-Semitism and anticommunism of the Cold War. David L. Rice, an unemployed loner who was a member of the militantly anticommunist organization called the Duck Club, forced his way into the home of Charles and Annie Goldmark. As a Christmas ham baked in the oven, he compelled the wealthy lawyer, his wife, and two children—twelve-year-old Derek and ten-year-old Colin—to lie on the floor. Then he handcuffed and tied their hands behind them. Next he chloroformed them. Finally, he took a steam iron and carving knife and stabbed and bludgeoned them. Eventually all would die of massive bleeding and head injuries. Their bodies were found by family friends who had been invited for Christmas dinner.[85]

At his trial, David Rice admitted to the slayings and insisted that he had been sane at the time. He had killed the Goldmark family, he claimed, because thirty thousand Communist Chinese and forty thousand North Korean troops were poised at the borders ready to attack the United States. He had to do something to stop the invasion, so he murdered the most prominent communist in Washington state. But, as it turned out, Charles Goldmark was not a communist. His mother had joined the Communist Party of America in the 1930s but quit soon afterward. When his father, John Goldmark, had been a state legislator from rural Washington—where the Goldmarks had moved to get away from "all the crazy people back east"—the local paper wrote a series of articles accusing him of having communist ties as well. Eventually John Goldmark sued the paper for libel and won the case. When a local judge ordered no damages paid, many local people understood this action as an affirmation of Goldmark's guilt. In any case, John Goldmark had died of cancer in 1979. His son David and his family had long since moved to Seattle. But when Rice learned that he had killed the wrong man, he was unrepentant. "Sometimes soldiers have to kill," he explained. As for the deaths of young Derek and Colin, he said, "It might have been necessary to sacrifice these lives for the greater good of mankind."[86]

More children's lives would be sacrificed at Ruby Ridge and in Waco and Oklahoma City. Many had already been sacrificed at Ludlow, Colorado, Conestoga, Pennsylvania, and the Mormon settlements on the Mississippi River. The history of bloodshed in rural America has been a long one. It has passed through every region and touched many a country town. Without a better understanding of its meanings, origins, and especially its ties to the politics of democracy and equality which have also been practiced in rural America, there will be no reason for the bloodshed to stop. Men who rape, kill, torture, and mutilate because they don't like how another person looks or behaves, what he or she believes, or for whom he or she works deserve no mercy from historians, politicians, or any other Americans. Yet we all must remember that these angry chants and threats have long been a part of the larger American chorus that, if it ever were to surrender the urge to hate and kill, might also break into song.

A Note on Method

EVERY AUTHOR makes choices about which materials to include and which approaches to follow in order to create clear meanings and parameters. I have made my share of these too. *Rural Radicals* explains the origins of the rural movements that have become an important part of American politics—again. In essence, it asks where all these angry white rural men have suddenly come from and why their views seem to defy easy political categorization. In doing so, it also defines aspects of the rural experience which have drawn rural people together over time and which have made their experiences stand apart from those of urban people from colonial times to the present day.

To write this sort of book, I had to decide first what I meant by the term "radical." Obviously, I did not choose to limit my definition of radical to those who took action on the left, who advocated the rights of the working-class or poor, or who joined socialist or communist causes. Some rural people have done all these things. But only a tiny fraction of white farmers ever wanted to forsake their dream (however unattainable) of independent production and land ownership. Moreover, for years, white farmers have been chronically ambivalent about linking their problems to those of wage workers. These aspirations and ambivalences identify most (though not all) rural whites as petit bourgeois rather than peasant or working-class. But just because white farmers were petit bourgeois did not mean that they could not be rad-

ical. Members of the rural "old middle class" have been radical because they have defied the trajectory of "bigness" in emerging liberal,
industrial, and postindustrial capitalism. Most have agreed with the
basic tenets of capitalist production, but they have disagreed with one
another, within families and communities, and over time, about how
best to negotiate a small but important place for themselves within it.
Finally, I also think that militant conservatives can act radically. Their
radicalism stems from both their willingness to use violence and their
willingness to defy state and federal authorities to carry out their acts
of hatred.

Even more important to the book than my definition of "radical"
is my definition of "rural." What do I mean by rural and how is rural
life a causative factor in the examples of radicalism I provide? Is there
even such a thing as *rural* radicalism at all? Perhaps rural America is
nothing but a setting where some radical acts take place. I disagree.
There is no doubt that until the 1910s particular aspects of the rural experience—being on the frontier, being on the social and cultural periphery of American life, being exploited in a particular way by
industrialization—caused particular hopes and particular fears. Likewise, a well-established gun culture and close but militantly self-defensive communities produced and sustained particular kinds of collective
acts of violence—what I have called vigilantism. During and after
World War I, however, outmigration and the spread of mass culture did
blur the lines between rural and urban America. Thus while some rural
people continued to follow their peculiarly rural political paths, they
were also joined by urban people who came to the countryside purposefully to partake of its rich heritage. Moreover, rural people took
their heritage with them when they moved to cities and became a little
bit more like urban people themselves. Even though the twentieth century complicates the picture of rural politics, I do not think it utterly
unravels it. After all, at the same time as rural and urban people were
becoming more alike in the ways they lived, rural Americans were also
growing even more peripheral to the mainstream culture—practically
becoming a curiosity. Rural radicalism might be a curiosity today too,
if it were not so lethal.

But what then is the "rural" foundation on which this somewhat
malleable and porous radicalism is constructed? In most of my examples, rural places belong to one of the last three classifications (of eight)
from the current United States census: communities of 2,500 or less not

adjoining a metropolitan area; communities of 2,500 or less adjoining a metropolitan area, or communities of between 2,500 and 50,000 not adjoining a metropolitan area. When my examples diverge from this standard they do so for one of two reasons. First, they diverge for historical reasons. In 1676 places with even 2,500 population would have been major metropolises, and thus neither I nor anyone else would consider them rural. In fact, throughout the colonial and early national periods, the radical people I refer to are actually men and women of the frontier or others living on the periphery of British North America. Examples from modern America diverge for a somewhat more subjective reason. Everett, Washington, and Ludlow, Colorado—even Lockport, New York—had well over 2,500 population, but because they were dependent on extractive industries, they were far removed from centers of economic and political power, and their citizens often felt just as marginal to urban society as did those of any isolated country town. Even with advanced technology and the information superhighway, this feeling is as true today as ever.

These definitions influenced my choice of movements or organizations or trends to include in the study. Again, the acid test was whether the movements were rurally based—that is, whether they were founded by, filled with, or led by rural people. For example, the first Ku Klux Klan was rural because it emerged from rural America. Although it became urbanized in the 1920s, it remained sufficiently rural to include because rural people were still very much involved and so were people in nearby southern and midwestern cities who were not very far removed from a rural experience themselves. Likewise, the John Birch Society of the 1950s and 1960s was not completely rural, but rural enough to include because Robert Welch had been a farm boy from North Carolina and because rural people remained the core of the organization long after its famous Orange County urban professionals disavowed their membership. Similarly both the KKK and the JBS are critical progenitors of today's groups. Somewhat more problematic are contemporary radical groups (like the Aryan Nations) who recruit new members from federal prisons and urban organizations—like the Los Angeles Police Department—and set up compounds in the countryside because laws are less strict and taxes and land values are low. But as noted in the text, I have taken my lead from sociologist James Aho, who maintains that leaders of hate groups also choose rural America because they feel support from the people there and indeed are successful recruiting members of the local communities for their groups. When the Freemen of Jordan, Montana, first attracted national attention in March 1996, some officials claimed that they were outsiders. Soon enough, we learned that many members were friends and relatives of townspeople.

I do not discuss any movements that were organized or fully supported by urban people, or thought up by eastern liberals, urban romantics, or college professors, even if they were located in rural areas or had rural people or rural life as the objects of their politics. Thus I do not include the environmental movement despite its concern for the wilderness and for agricultural environmental destruction and despite the fact that some rural people have been excited by it. Nor do I discuss the various back-to-the-land movements; they were designed for people who needed to go "back" to the land. I do not examine the Nashville Agrarians because they were not farmers or loggers or miners, but literary critics. I do, however, include some groups with important ties to urban organizations, especially the Industrial Workers of the World, the Southern Tenant Farmers' Union, and the various communist sharecropper organizations in the South and Southwest. Moreover, I include groups from the nonfarming areas of rural America. Not all rural people are farmers. For centuries, many have lived in towns, worked in industry or manufacturing, or provided services to others in their communities. Sometimes they have joined with farmers to protest; at other times they have turned against them.

But owing to the limits of time and length, I have left out some groups that probably belong here, including the Know-Nothing Party, the anti-Masonic movement, the Foxfire movement, members of the various Sagebrush Rebellions, and the Women's Christian Temperance Union. Moreover, I do not discuss many of the important and autonomous radical movements begun by people of color in the rural United States. I have left out, for example, explorations of Pontiac's Uprising, the Ghost Dance movement, slave uprisings, rural components of the civil rights movement, and the Mexican migrant workers' movements. It would be fascinating to learn more about the ways these movements reflected the experiences of rural people of color in the United States and to explore ways in which political and cultural syntheses between and among multicultural radical traditions might have taken place. But the purpose of this book is to locate the origins of a self-defined white-male radicalism. Thus although race and gender are critical tools for analysis, extensive discussions of autonomous experiences of women and people of color do not appear within it.

On April 19, 1995, I was one of the millions of Americans shocked and horrified by the bombing of the Alfred P. Murrah Federal Building in Oklahoma City. I was also confused. Why would two former members of the military who still sported their boot-camp haircuts and loved to collect weapons allegedly target the government for destruction? Today I understand that for centuries rural people have struggled to maintain a dignified, "small" way of life in the midst of overwhelming forces of wealth, bureaucracy, and power. To do so, they have sometimes turned to the politics of hope, sometimes to the politics of hate, and sometimes to both at once. Unfortunately, tragically, in our time it has become easier to imagine "taking America back" by force than by democratic change. Studying rural radicalism reminds us again and again of the amazing flexibility and power of the idea of America. From the far left and the far right and all the points of confluence in between, men and women believe that they are upholding the traditions of their nation. And, as hard as it is to admit, they are. Today I understand better the origins of the hatreds that have led people to organize militias, to plan for invasions, and to hoard fertilizer and diesel fuel. But I am still shocked and horrified. I will never forget the price we have paid to understand ourselves better.

A Note on Sources

THE LITERATURE on radicalism in the United States is vast and has grown in both quantity and quality in the past generation. The numerous studies of labor radicalism in the eighteenth and nineteenth centuries have increased our understanding of the many different conceptions of republicanism which were maintained in the nation's early years. See, for example, Herbert G. Gutman, *Work, Culture, and Society in Industrializing America: Essays in American Working-Class and Social History* (New York: Random House, 1976); Stephanie McCurry, "The Two Faces of Republicanism: Gender and Proslavery Politics in Antebellum South Carolina," *Journal of American History* 78 (1992): 245–64; David Montgomery, *Beyond Equality: Labor and the Radical Republicans, 1862–1872* (Urbana: University of Illinois Press, 1981); Daniel T. Rodgers, "Republicanism: The Career of a Concept," *Journal of American History* 79 (1992): 11–38; and Sean Wilentz, *Chants Democratic: New York City and the Rise of the American Working Class, 1788–1850* (New York: Oxford University Press, 1984). We also know much more than we did about why urban women in voluntary associations sometimes did and sometimes did not become radicalized by those experiences and ties. See Nancy F. Cott, *Bonds of Womanhood: "Woman's Sphere" in New England, 1780–1835* (New Haven: Yale University Press, 1976); Karen Halttunen, *Confidence Men and Painted Women: A Study of Middle-Class Culture in America, 1830–1870* (New

Haven: Yale University Press, 1982); Regina Kunzel, *Fallen Women and Problem Girls: Unmarried Mothers and the Professionalization of Social Work, 1890–1945* (New Haven: Yale University Press, 1994); Teresa Anne Murphy, *Ten Hours' Labor: Religion, Reform, and Gender in Early New England* (Ithaca: Cornell University Press, 1992); and Mary P. Ryan, *Cradle of the Middle Class: The Family in Oneida County, New York, 1790–1865* (Cambridge: Cambridge University Press, 1981). And scholars of the revolutionary era continue to insist that the colonial and early national eras were the most radical of all. See, especially, John Keane, *Thomas Paine: A Political Life* (Boston: Little, Brown, 1995); Gary B. Nash, *The Urban Crucible: Social Change, Political Consciousness, and the Origins of the American Revolution* (Cambridge, Mass.: Harvard University Press, 1979); Gordon S. Wood, *The Radicalism of the American Revolution* (New York: Knopf, 1992); and Alfred F. Young, ed., *The American Revolution: Explorations in the History of American Radicalism* (De Kalb: University of Northern Illinois Press, 1976).

It is surprising then to discover how small the literature is that explores rural radicalism and how tiny the literature is that explores rural radicalism over time. Much of the work that does exist is outdated, including Theodore Saloutos, *Farmer Movements in the South, 1865–1933* (Berkeley: University of California Press, 1960); Theodore Saloutos and John D. Hicks, *Agricultural Discontent in the Middle West, 1900–1939* (Madison: University of Wisconsin Press, 1951); and Carl Taylor, *The Farmers' Movement, 1620–1920* (New York: American Book Co., 1953). More recently, Patrick H. Mooney and Theo J. Majka published *Farmers' and Farmworkers' Movements: Social Protest in American Agriculture* (New York: Twayne, 1995). One reason for this shortage of scholarly work is the tendency by intellectuals on the left to identify radicalism as also being substantially on the left, and particularly concerned with the working class. Because they also tend to associate rural people with the middle class, they naturally conclude that most rural people cannot be radical. Thus the new compilation of forty-six biographies by Mari Jo Buhle, Paul Buhle, and Harvey J. Kaye titled *The American Radical* (New York: Routledge, 1994) includes Paul Robeson and Mother Jones but not Nathaniel Bacon, Daniel Shays, or a single leader of the People's Party. In fact, only a handful of the radicals included were men or women who addressed rural issues at all.

A similar problem finds its genesis in the "new rural history." Since the publication of Steven Hahn and Jonathan Prude's seminal collection, *The Countryside in the Age of Capitalist Transformation: Essays in the Social History of Rural America* (Chapel Hill: University of North Carolina Press, 1985), an outpouring of work in "new rural history" has hit the library shelves. Much of this excellent work, summarized in David B. Danbom's *Born in the Country: A History of Rural America* (Baltimore: Johns Hopkins University Press, 1995), examines the private worlds, customs, and habits of mind of rural people in the United States. A sampling of these include John Mack Faragher, *Sugar Creek: Life on the Illinois Prairie* (New Haven: Yale University Press, 1986); Jane Marie Pederson, *Between Memory and Reality: Family and Community in Rural Wisconsin, 1870–1970* (Madison: University of Wisconsin Press, 1992); and Sonya Salamon, *Prairie Patrimony: Family, Farming, and Community in the Midwest* (Chapel Hill: University of North Carolina Press, 1992). Substantially less has been devoted to public politics. And, from my vantage point, much of the work that calls itself rural in fact examines rural life through the lens of urban experience. Hahn and Prude's overriding concern with proletarianization, for example, suggests that rural life is interesting to them only when it can address larger trends in capitalist development and class formation. That no essays in the volume discuss rural life after 1896 suggests that the authors believe that the "dreaming was over" after the defeat of Populism.

Individual rural uprisings and social movements have, of course, been studied—some of them to a greater extent than they probably ever deserved. An important debate that seems to have no end in sight has emerged around the rise of capitalism in British North America. In essence what such scholars as Christopher Clark, James Henretta, Allan Kulikoff, Michael Merrill, and Winifred Rosenberg have been wondering is whether and when colonial farmers interacted with and became part of the market, and in what way this interaction changed their ideas about personal liberty and political-economic liberalism. The seminal works include Christopher Clark, *The Roots of Rural Capitalism: Western Massachusetts, 1780–1860* (Ithaca: Cornell University Press, 1990); Sue Headlee, *The Political Economy of the Family Farm: The Agrarian Roots of American Capitalism* (New York: Praeger, 1991); James A. Henretta, "Families and Farms: Mentalité in Pre-industrial America," *William and Mary Quarterly* 35 (1978): 3–32; Allan Kulikoff, "The Transition to Capitalism in Rural America," *William and Mary Quarterly* 46 (January 1989): 120–44; Michael Merrill, "Cash Is Good to Eat: Self-Sufficiency and Exchange in the Rural Ec nomy of the United States,"

Radical History Review, no. 4 (1977): 42–71. The most judicious measurement of these accounts to date appears in Gordon S. Wood's *The Radicalism of the American Revolution* (New York: Norton, 1992), where he writes, "Many northern farmers—how many is a matter of controversy—were not as yet deeply involved in the larger market economy of the Atlantic world. . . . They were acquisitive, to be sure, and few were truly self-sufficient" (p. 67).

Likewise, the People's Party has generated three generations of interpretation and debate. The first generation wrote at the time of the New Deal and infused their work with the heady spirit of reform and renewal which liberals felt at that time. John D. Hicks, *The Populist Revolt: A History of the Farmers' Alliance and the People's Party* (Minneapolis: University of Minnesota Press, 1931), looks back in a friendly and familiar way on those rural reformers who seemed to him to have anticipated the inauguration of the welfare state. A review of the importance of this work is found in Martin Ridge, "Populism Redux: John D. Hicks and *The Populist Revolt*," *Reviews in American History* 13 (1985): 142–54. Hicks's rose-colored glasses were quickly smashed of course under the shoes of Richard Hofstadter and other revisionists who saw something sinister in the Populists' defense of provincialism, nativism, nationalism, and anti-Semitism. Hofstadter's *Age of Reform: From Bryan to FDR* (New York: Vintage, 1955) has provided grist for the historiographic mill ever since it was published. But Hofstadter was mild compared with others, sociologists in particular, who overtly linked Populism with American fascism. See Victor C. Ferkiss, "Populist Influences on American Fascism," in Theodore Saloutos, ed., *Populism: Reaction or Reform?* (New York: Holt, Rinehart, and Winston, 1968).

The third wave of interpretation of Populism came with the publication of Lawrence Goodwyn's *Democratic Promise: The Populist Moment in America* (New York: Oxford University Press, 1976). In this well-known account, Populist intolerance fades away in the face of grassroots collectivism, interracial harmony, and gender inclusiveness. Since then work has continued to look at regional variations of Populism, its legacy in different states, and its overall importance to the nation. See, for example, Peter H. Argersinger, *The Limits of Agrarian Radicalism: Western Populism and American Politics* (Lawrence: University Press of Kansas, 1995); Robert C. McMath, Jr., *American Populism: A Social History, 1877–1898* (New York: Hill and Wang, 1993); McMath, *Populist Vanguard: A History of the Southern Farmers' Alliance* (Chapel Hill: University of North Carolina Press, 1975); Jeffrey Ostler, *Prairie Populism: The Fate of Agrarian Radicalism in Kansas, Nebraska, and Iowa, 1880–1892* (Lawrence: University Press of Kansas, 1993); and Marilyn P. Watkins, *Rural Democracy: Family Farmers and Politics in Western Washington, 1890–1925* (Ithaca: Cornell University Press, 1995).

The recent claim to the heritage of Populism by the American right has also provided opportunities of scholarship. See especially Michael Kazin, *The Populist Persuasion: An American History* (New York: Basic Books, 1995). Kazin diminishes Populism somewhat by reducing it to a form of rhetoric rather than a political movement. Nevertheless, he makes important leaps over conventional boundaries that, more often than not, have only blocked our view of the past. See also Lawrence Goodwyn, "The New Populism," *Progressive* 48 (June 1984): 18–20; Allen D. Hertzke, *Echoes of Discontent: Jesse Jackson, Pat Robertson, and the Resurgence of Populism* (Washington, D.C.: CQ Press, 1993); and William Schneider, "The New Shape of American Politics," *Atlantic Monthly*, January 1987: 50–54.

Chapter 1: The Politics of Producerism

A large number of works on crowd behavior came out of British Marxism in the 1960s and 1970s. Best known are Robert C. Allen, *Enclosure and the Yeoman: The Agricultural Development of South Midlands, 1450–1850* (Oxford: Clarendon Press, 1992); Peter Burke, *Popular Culture in Early Modern Europe* (New York: Harper & Row, 1978); Eric Hobsbawm, *Primitive Rebels: Studies in Archaic Forms of Social Movements in the Nineteenth and Twentieth Centuries* (New York: Norton, 1959); and George Rudé, *The Crowd in History: A Study of Popular Disturbances in France and England, 1730–1848* (New York: Wiley, 1964). It did not take long for American scholars of the revolutionary period to find crowd behaviors influencing the war. See Richard Maxwell Brown, "Violence and the American Revolution," in Stephen G. Kurtz and James H. Hutson, eds., *Essays on the American Revolution* (Chapel Hill: University of North Carolina Press, 1973), 81–120; Edward Countryman, "'Out of the Bounds of the Law': Northern Land Rioters in the Eighteenth Century," in Alfred F. Young, ed., *The American Revolution: Explorations in the History of American Radicalism* (De Kalb: Northern Illinois University Press, 1976), 39–61; Dirk Hoerder, *Crowd Action in Revolutionary Massachusetts, 1765–1780* (New York: Academic Press, 1971); and Pauline Maier, *From Resistance to Revolution: Colonial Radicals and the Develop-*

ment of American Opposition to Britain, 1765–1776 (New York: Knopf, 1972).

The New Jersey, New York, and Vermont stories are told together in Countryman, "'Out of the Bounds of Law,'" as well as in Richard M. Jellison, ed., *Society, Freedom, and Conscience: The American Revolution in Virginia, Massachusetts, and New York* (New York: Norton, 1976). See also Rowland Berthoff and John M. Murrin, "Feudalism, Communalism, and the Yeoman Freeholder: The American Revolution Considered as a Social Accident," in Steven G. Kurtz and James H. Hutson, eds., *Essays on the American Revolution* (Chapel Hill: University of North Carolina Press, 1973); Edward Countryman, *The American Revolution* (New York: Hill and Wang, 1985); Larry R. Gerlach, *Prologue to Independence: New Jersey in the Coming of the American Revolution* (New Brunswick, N.J.: Rutgers University Press, 1976); Richard P. McCormick, *New Jersey from Colony to State, 1609–1789* (New Brunswick, N.J.: Rutgers University Press, 1964); Thomas L. Purvis, "Origins and Patterns of Agrarian Unrest in New Jersey, 1735–1754," *William and Mary Quarterly,* 3d ser., 39 (1982), 600–27; and Gordon S. Wood, *The Radicalism of the American Revolution* (New York: Knopf, 1992).

Of the three states, New York has been the site of the most study and debate. See Patricia U. Bonami, *A Factious People: Politics and Society in Colonial New York* (New York: Columbia University Press, 1971); Edward Countryman, *A People in Revolution: The American Revolution and Political Society in New York, 1760–1790* (Baltimore: Johns Hopkins University Press, 1981); and Sung Bok Kim, *Landlord and Tenant in Colonial New York: Manorial Society, 1664–1775* (Chapel Hill: University of North Carolina Press, 1978). Three earlier works that still cause considerable commotion are Carl Becker, *History of Political Parties in the Province of New York, 1760–1776* (Madison: University of Wisconsin Press, 1909); Staughton Lynd, *Anti-Federalism in Dutchess County, New York: A Study of Democracy and Class Conflict in the Revolutionary Era* (Chicago: Loyola University Press, 1962); and Irving Mark, *Agrarian Conflicts in Colonial New York, 1711–1775* (New York: Columbia University Press, 1940). On Vermont's unique heritage, see Michael A. Bellesiles, *Revolutionary Outlaws: Ethan Allen and the Struggle for Independence on the Early American Frontier* (Charlottesville: University Press of Virginia, 1993); and Peter S. Onuf, "State Making in Revolutionary America: Independent Vermont as a Case Study," *Journal of American History* 67 (1980–81): 797–815.

The best discussions of the North Carolina Regulation can be found in A. Roger Ekirch, *"Poor Carolina": Politics and Society in Colonial North Carolina, 1729–1776* (Chapel Hill: University of North Carolina Press, 1981); Marvin L. Michael Kay, "The North Carolina Regulation, 1766–1776: A Class Conflict," in Young, ed., *The American Revolution*, 73–106; and James P. Whittenburg, "Planters, Merchants, and Lawyers: Social Change and the Origins of the North Carolina Regulation," *William and Mary Quarterly*, 3d ser., 34 (1977): 215–38. On the revolutionary South in general, see Richard R. Beeman, *The Evolution of the Southern Backcountry: A Case Study at Lunenburg County, Virginia, 1746–1832* (Philadelphia: University of Pennsylvania Press, 1984); Jeffrey J. Crowe and Larry E. Tise, eds., *The Southern Experience in the American Revolution* (Chapel Hill: University of North Carolina Press, 1978); Ronald Hoffman, "The 'Disaffected' in the Revolutionary South," in Young, ed., *The American Revolution*, 273–318; Hoffman et al., eds., *An Uncivil War: The Southern Backcountry during the American Revolution* (Charlottesville: University Press of Virginia, 1985); Rhys Isaac, *The Transformation of Virginia, 1740–1790* (Chapel Hill: University of North Carolina Press, 1982); Robert D. Mitchell, *Commercialism and Frontier: Perspectives on the Early Shenandoah Valley* (Charlottesville: University Press of Virginia, 1977); and Jerome J. Nadelhaft, *The Disorders of War: The Revolution in South Carolina* (Orono: University of Maine Press, 1981).

Of course, the postrevolutionary uprisings have a literature of their own, however closely tied they were to the collective actions of the prerevolutionary period. For overviews, see Richard Maxwell Brown, "Back Country Rebellions and the Homestead Ethic in America, 1740–1799," in Brown and Don E. Fehrenbacker, eds., *Tradition, Conflict, and Modernization: Perspectives on the American Revolution* (New York: Academic Press, 1977): 79–92; and Barbara Karsky, "Agrarian Radicalism in the Late Revolutionary Period, 1780–1795," in Erich Angermann et al., *New Wine in Old Skins: A Comparative View of Socio-Political Structures and Values Affecting the American Revolution* (Stuttgart: Klett, 1976), 87–114.

On Shays's Rebellion and early New England in general, see Van Beck Hall, *Politics without Parties: Massachusetts, 1780–1791* (Pittsburgh: University of Pittsburgh Press, 1972); Robert E. Moody, "Samuel Ely: Forerunner of Shays," *New England Quarterly* 5 (1932), 105–34; Marion Lena Starkey, *A Little Rebellion* (New York: Knopf, 1955); David Szatmary, *Shays' Rebellion: The Making of an Agrarian Insurrection* (Amherst:

University of Massachusetts Press, 1980); and Alan Taylor, *Liberty Men and Great Proprietors: The Revolutionary Settlement on the Maine Frontier, 1760–1820* (Chapel Hill: University of North Carolina Press, 1990). The best source on the Whisky Rebellion remains Thomas P. Slaughter, *The Whiskey Rebellion: Frontier Epilogue to the American Revolution* (New York: Oxford University Press, 1986).

On the political and social changes in the Jeffersonian and Jacksonian eras, see Joyce Appleby, *Capitalism and a New Social Order: The Republican Vision of the 1790s* (New York: New York University Press, 1984); Richard L. Bushman, "Opening the American Countryside," in James A. Henretta et al., eds., *The Transformation of Early American History* (New York: Knopf, 1991), 239–56; James A. Henretta, "The Transition to Capitalism in America," in ibid., 218–38; Pauline Maier, "The Transforming Impact of Independence, Reaffirmed: 1776 and the Definition of American Social Structure," in ibid., 194–217; Elizabeth Perkins, "The Consumption Frontier: Household Consumption in Early Kentucky," *Journal of American History* 78 (September 1991): 486–510; Arthur M. Schlesinger, *The Age of Jackson* (Boston: Little, Brown, 1946); and Steven Watts, *The Republic Reborn: War and the Making of Liberal America, 1790–1820* (Baltimore: Johns Hopkins University Press, 1987).

Unlike the rich and highly contentious literature on Populism, the literature on post-Populist producer radicalism is scattered and badly in need of new interpretive study. Classic studies include Garin Burbank, *When Farmers Voted Red: The Gospel of Socialism in the Oklahoma Countryside, 1910–1924* (Westport, Conn.: Greenwood Press, 1976); David Danbom, *The Resisted Revolution: Urban America and the Industrialization of Agriculture* (Ames: Iowa State University Press, 1979); Gilbert Fite, *George N. Peck and the Fight for Farm Parity* (Norman: University of Oklahoma Press, 1954); Robert L. Morlan, *Political Prairie Fire: The Nonpartisan League, 1915–1922* (Minneapolis: University of Minnesota Press, 1955); and Saloutos and Hicks, *Agrarian Discontent in the Middle West.*

Radicalism in the Great Depression, however, has been of great interest for many years. See Alan Brinkley, *Voices of Protest: Huey Long, Father Coughlin, and the Great Depression* (New York: Vintage, 1983); Lowell K. Dyson, *Red Harvest: The Communist Party and American Farmers* (Lincoln: University of Nebraska Press, 1982); Richard Lowitt, *The New Deal and the West* (Bloomington: Indiana University Press, 1984); Arthur M. Schlesinger, *The Politics of Upheaval* (Boston: Houghton Mifflin, 1960); John Shover, *Cornbelt Rebellion: The Farmers' Holiday Associ-*

ation (Urbana: University of Illinois Press, 1965); and Catherine Mc-
Nicol Stock, *Main Street in Crisis: The Great Depression and the Old Middle
Class on the Northern Plains* (Chapel Hill: University of North Carolina
Press, 1992).

On women in farm movements, see Mark Friedberger, "Women
Advocates in the Farm Crisis of the 1980s," *Agricultural History* 67
(Spring 1993): 224–34; Donald Marti, "Sisters of the Grange: Rural
Feminism in the Late Nineteenth Century," *Agricultural History* 58 (July
1984): 247–61; Mary Neth, "Building the Base: Farm Women, the Rural
Community, and Farm Organizations in the Midwest, 1900–1940," in
Wava G. Haney and Jane B. Knowles, eds., *Women and Farming: Chang-
ing Roles, Changing Structures* (Boulder, Colo.: Westview Press, 1988),
339–55; Nancy Grey Osterud, *Bonds of Community: The Lives of Farm
Women in Nineteenth-Century New York* (Ithaca: Cornell University Press,
1991); Osterud, "Gender and the Transition to Capitalism in Rural
America," *Agricultural History* 67 (Spring 1993): 14–29; William C. Pratt,
"Women and the Farm Revolt of the 1930s," *Agricultural History* 67
(Spring 1993): 214–23; Leslie A. Taylor, "Femininity as Strategy: A Gendered Perspective on the Farmers' Holiday," *Annals of Iowa* 51 (Winter
1992): 252–77; and Marilyn P. Watkins, "Political Activism and Com-
munity-Building among Alliance and Grange Women in Western
Washington, 1892–1925," *Agricultural History* 67 (Spring 1993):
197–213. On men and associationalism, see Mark C. Carnes, *Secret Ritual and Manhood in Victorian America* (New Haven: Yale University
Press, 1989); Mary Ann Clawson, *Constructing Brotherhood: Class, Gender, and Fraternalism* (Princeton: Princeton University Press, 1989).

Chapter 2: The Culture of Vigilantism

In the late 1960s and 1970s urban race riots and rising crime rates propelled many historians and sociologists to examine the history of violence in the United States. Naturally most of them went looking to
urban areas for their analyses. But some researchers believed that the
violent temperament of many Americans and their ardent attachment
to guns traced back to the frontier experience as well. On frontier vigilantism, see Richard Maxwell Brown, *The South Carolina Regulators*
(Cambridge: Belknap Press, 1963); Brown, *Strain of Violence: Historical
Studies of American Violence and Vigilantism* (New York: Oxford University Press, 1975), 67–90; Brown, ed., *American Violence* (Englewood
Cliffs, N.J.: Prentice-Hall, 1970); William E. Burrows, *Vigilante!* (New

York: Harcourt Brace Jovanovich, 1976); and Richard Slotkin, *Regeneration through Violence: The Mythology of the American Frontier, 1600–1860* (Middletown, Conn.: Wesleyan University Press, 1973).

On the persecution of the Mormons, see James B. Allen and Glen M. Leonard, *The Story of the Latter-Day Saints* (Salt Lake City, Utah: Desert Book Company, 1976); Leonard J. Arrington, *Brigham Young: American Moses* (New York: Knopf, 1985), and Arrington, *New Views of Mormon History* (Salt Lake City, Utah: University of Utah Press, 1987); Ivan J. Barrett, *Joseph Smith and the Restoration* (Provo, Utah: Brigham Young University Press, 1967); Fawn M. Brodie, *No Man Knows My History: The Life of Joseph Smith, the Mormon Prophet* (New York: Knopf, 1945); Richard L. Bushman, *Joseph Smith and the Beginnings of Mormonism* (Urbana: University of Illinois Press, 1984); Klaus J. Hansen, *Mormonism and the American Experience* (Chicago: University of Chicago Press, 1981); and Marvin S. Hill, *Quest for Refuge: The Mormon Flight from American Pluralism* (Salt Lake City, Utah: Signature Books, 1989).

On racial and industrial conflict, particularly in California and the Rocky Mountain West, see Tomas Almaguer, *Racial Fault Lines: The Historical Origins of White Supremacy in California* (Berkeley: University of California Press, 1994); Sucheng Chan, *This Bittersweet Soil: The Chinese in California Agriculture, 1860–1910* (Berkeley: University of California Press, 1986); Cletus E. Daniel, *Bitter Harvest: A History of California Farmworkers, 1870–1941* (Ithaca: Cornell University Press, 1981); Alan Derickson, *Workers' Health, Workers' Democracy: The Western Miners' Struggle, 1891–1925* (Ithaca: Cornell University Press, 1988); David R. Roediger, *The Wages of Whiteness: Race and the Making of the American Working Class* (London: Verso, 1991); Alexander Saxton, *The Indispensable Enemy: Labor and the Anti-Chinese Movement in California* (Berkeley: University of California Press, 1971); and Saxton, *The Rise and Fall of the White Republic: Class Politics and Mass Culture in Nineteenth-Century America* (London: Verso, 1990).

On Euro-American ideas about Native Americans and Africans see James Axtell, *After Columbus: Essays in the Ethnohistory of Colonial North America* (New York: Oxford University Press, 1988); Robert Berkhofer, *The White Man's Indian: Images of the American Indian from Columbus to the Present* (New York: Knopf, 1978); John Demos, *The Unredeemed Captive: A Family Story from Early America* (New York: Knopf, 1994); George M. Frederickson, "The Social Origins of Racism in the United States," in Frederickson, *The Arrogance of Race: Historical*

Perspectives on Slavery, Racism, and Social Inequality (Middletown, Conn.: Wesleyan University Press, 1988), 189–205; Stephen Greenblatt, *Marvelous Possessions: The Wonder of the New World* (Chicago: University of Chicago Press, 1991); Winthrop Jordan, *The White Man's Burden: Historical Origins of Racism in the United States* (New York: Oxford University Press, 1974); Edmund Morgan, *American Slavery, American Freedom: The Ordeal of Colonial Virginia* (New York: Norton, 1976); Richard C. Trexler, *Sex and Conquest: Gendered Violence, Political Order, and the European Conquest of the Americas* (Ithaca: Cornell University Press, 1995); and Stephen Saunders Webb, *1676: The End of American Independence* (New York: Knopf, 1984).

On the history of racial radicalism in the New South, see Edward L. Ayers, *The Promise of the New South: Life after Reconstruction* (New York: Oxford University Press, 1992); Ayers, *Southern Crossing: A History of the American South, 1877–1906* (New York: Oxford University Press, 1995); Ayers, *Vengeance and Justice: Crime and Punishment in the Nineteenth-Century American South* (New York: Oxford University Press, 1984); Kathleen M. Blee, *Woman of the Klan: Racism and Gender in the 1920s* (Berkeley: University of California Press, 1991); W. Fitzhugh Brundage, *Lynching in the New South: Georgia and Virginia, 1880–1930* (Urbana: University of Illinois Press, 1993); David M. Chalmers, *Hooded Americanism: The History of the Ku Klux Klan, 1865–1965* (Durham, N.C.: Duke University Press, 1987); Kenneth T. Jackson, *The Ku Klux Klan in the City, 1915–1930* (New York: Oxford University Press, 1967); Shawn Lay, *The Invisible Empire in the West: Toward a New Historical Appraisal of the Ku Klux Klan of the 1920s* (Urbana: University of Illinois Press, 1992); William Pierce Randel, *The Ku Klux Klan: A Century of Infamy* (Philadelphia: Chilton, 1965); Allen W. Trelease, *White Terror: The Ku Klux Klan Conspiracy and Southern Reconstruction* (New York: Harper & Row, 1971); Wyn Craig Wade, *The Fiery Cross: The Ku Klux Klan in America* (New York: Simon and Schuster, 1987); and C. Vann Woodward, *The Strange Career of Jim Crow*, 3d rev. ed. (1955; rpt., New York: Oxford University Press, 1974).

Early twentieth-century radical patriotism is covered in useful books that also discuss postwar events. See especially David H. Bennett, *The Party of Fear: From Nativist Movements to the New Right in American History* (Chapel Hill: University of North Carolina Press, 1988); Leonard Dinnerstein, *Antisemitism in America* (New York: Oxford University Press, 1994); Frederick C. Luebke, *Bonds of Loyalty: German-Americans*

and World War I (De Kalb: Northern Illinois Press, 1974); Richard Gid
Powers, *Not without Honor: The History of American Anticommunism*
(New York: Free Press, 1995); Leo Ribuffo, *The Old Christian Right: The
Protestant Far Right from the Great Depression to Cold War* (Philadelphia:
Temple University Press, 1983); and Michael S. Sherry, *In the Shadow of
War: The United States since the 1930s* (New Haven: Yale University
Press, 1995).

Chapter 3: Rural Radicalism in Our Time

Contemporary rural radicalism has received abundant attention in
periodicals and newspapers since the late 1980s and particularly since
the Ruby Ridge incident in 1992, the deaths of the Branch Davidians
in Waco, Texas, and the April 19, 1995, bombing of the Murrah Federal Building in Oklahoma City. Extensive coverage of the bombing,
militia movement, and related far-right groups appeared in all major
national newspapers between April 20 and the indictment of
McVeigh and Nichols on August 1, 1995. Many excellent interpreta-
tive pieces have also appeared. This essay has drawn especially from
the *New York Times*, the *Washington Post*, the *New Republic*, *Harper's*,
Dissent, the *Nation*, and *Commentary*. See especially Sidney Blumen-
thal, "Her Own Private Idaho," *New Yorker*, July 10, 1995: 27–33;
James Coates, *Armed and Dangerous: The Rise of the Survivalist Right*
(New York: Hill and Wang, 1987); Kenneth S. Stern, *A Force upon the
Plain: The American Militia Movement and the Politics of Hate* (New
York: Simon & Schuster, 1996); and Jess Walter, *Every Knee Shall Bow:
The Truth and Tragedy of Ruby Ridge and the Randy Weaver Family* (New
York: ReganBooks, 1995).

An excellent group of sources in social and cultural history, soci-
ology, and anthropology on the farm crisis of the 1970s and 1980s is
emerging. See, for example, Jane Adams, *The Transformation of Rural
Life: Southern Illinois, 1890–1990* (Chapel Hill: University of North
Carolina Press, 1994); Peggy F. Barlett, *American Dreams, Rural Reali-
ties: Family Farms in Crisis* (Chapel Hill: University of North Carolina
Press, 1993); William P. Browne, *Private Interests, Public Policy, and
American Agriculture* (Lawrence: University of Kansas Press, 1988);
Osha Gray Davidson, *Broken Heartland: The Rise of America's Rural
Ghetto* (New York: Free Press, 1990); Mark Friedberger, *Shake-Out: Iowa
Farm Families in the 1980s* (Lexington: University Press of Kentucky,
1989); Neil Harl, *The Farm Debt Crisis of the 1980s* (Ames: Iowa State

University Press, 1990); Jack Temple Kirby, *Rural Worlds Lost: The American South, 1920–1960* (Baton Rouge: Louisiana State University Press, 1987); Howard Kohn, *The Last Farmer: An American Memoir* (New York: Summit Books, 1988); Andrew Malcolm, *Final Harvest: An American Tragedy* (New York: Times Books, 1986); Patrick H. Mooney, *My Own Boss? Class Rationality and the Family Farm* (Boulder, Colo.: Westview Press, 1988). On modern farm women, see Deborah Fink, *Open Country, Iowa: Rural Women, Tradition, and Change* (Albany: State University of New York Press, 1986); Rachel Ann Rosenfeld, *Farm Women: Work, Farm, and Family in the United States* (Chapel Hill: University of North Carolina Press, 1985); Carolyn Sachs, *The Invisible Farmers: Women in Agricultural Production* (Totowa, N.J.: Rowman & Allanheld, 1983).

On postwar agricultural policy in general, see William P. Browne et al., *Sacred Cows and Hot Potatoes: Agrarian Myths in Agricultural Policy* (Boulder, Colo.: Westview Press, 1992); Peter Daniel, "A Rogue Bureaucracy: The USDA Fire Ant Campaign of the 1950s," *Agricultural History* 64 (Spring 1989): 99–114; Gilbert Fite, *American Farmers: The New Minority* (Bloomington: Indiana University Press, 1981); Michael W. Flamm, "The National Farmers Union and the Evolution of Agrarian Liberalism, 1937–1946," *Agricultural History* 68 (Summer 1994): 54–80; Linda J. Lear, "Bombshell in Beltsville: The USDA and the Challenge of Silent Spring," *Agricultural History* 66 (Spring 1992): 151–70; William Mueller, "How We're Gonna Keep 'Em Off of the Farm," *American Scholar* 56 (Winter 1987): 57–67; John L. Shover, *First Majority—Last Minority* (De Kalb: Northern Illinois University Press, 1976); Ingolf Vogeler, *The Myth of the Family Farm: Agribusiness Dominance of U.S. Agriculture* (Boulder, Colo.: Westview Press, 1981).

The far right garnered a great deal of scholarly attention in the early Cold War era and again in the 1980s and 1990s as the Cold War came to an end. On the earlier period, see David Harry Bennett, *Party of Fear: From Nativist Movements to the New Right in American History* (Chapel Hill: University of North Carolina Press, 1988); Richard Gid Powers, *Not without Honor: The History of American Anti-Communism* (New York: Free Press, 1995); and Michael S. Sherry, *In the Shadow of War: The United States since the 1930s* (New Haven: Yale University Press, 1995). See also Daniel Bell, ed., *The New American Right* (New York: Criterion Books, 1955); Phillip Finch, *God, Guts, and Guns* (New York: Seaview/Putnam, 1983); Arnold Forster and Benjamin

Epstein, *Danger on the Right* (New York: McGraw-Hill, 1963); Donald Janson and Bernard Eismann, *The Far Right* (New York: McGraw-Hill, 1963); J. Harry Jones, Jr., *The Minutemen* (Garden City, N.Y.: Doubleday, 1968); Jonathan Martin Kolkey, *The New Right, 1960–1968* (Washington, D.C.: University Press of America, 1983); Scott G. McNall, *Career of a Radical Rightist* (Port Washington, N.Y.: Kennefort Press, 1975); and Robert A. Schoenberger, ed., *The American Right Wing: Readings in Political Behavior* (New York: Holt, Rinehart, and Winston, 1969).

On the New Right, hard right, and New Christian Right since 1968, see Dan T. Carter, *The Politics of Rage: George Wallace, the Origins of the New Conservatism, and the Transformation of American Politics* (New York: Simon and Schuster, 1995); Alan Crawford, *Thunder on the Right: The "New Right" and the Politics of Resentment* (New York: Pantheon, 1980); Frances Fitzgerald, "A Disciplined, Charging Army: The Reverend Jerry Falwell," *New Yorker*, May 18, 1981: 54–60; Dean M. Kelly, *Why Conservative Churches Are Growing: A Study in Sociology of Religion* (New York: Harper & Row, 1977); Daniel Maguire, *The New Subversives: Anti-Americanism of the Religious Right* (New York: Continuum, 1982); Kevin Phillips, *Boiling Point: Republicans, Democrats, and the Decline of Middle-Class Prosperity* (New York: Random House, 1993); and Richard A. Viguerie, *The Establishment vs. the People: Is a New Populist Revolt on the Way?* (Chicago: Regnery Gateway, 1983). On some of the reasons why liberalism failed to live up to its promise, see Alan Brinkley, *The End of Reform: New Deal Liberalism in Depression and War* (New York: Knopf, 1995).

On the militant far right today, see James Coates, *Armed and Dangerous: The Rise of the Survivalist Right* (New York: Hill and Wang, 1987); Stern, *A Force upon the Plain;* and Walter, *Every Knee Shall Bow.* See also James A. Aho, *This Thing of Darkness: A Sociology of the Enemy* (Seattle: University of Washington Press, 1995), and Aho, *The Politics of Righteousness: Idaho Christian Patriotism* (Seattle: University of Washington Press, 1990); Marc Cooper, "A Visit With MOM: Montana's Mother of All Militias," *Nation*, May 22, 1995: 714–21; Phillip Finch, "Renegade Justice," *New Republic*, April 25, 1983: 9–11; James William Gibson, *Warrior Dreams: Paramilitary Culture in Post-Vietnam America* (New York: Hill and Wang, 1994); Alex Heard, "The Road to Oklahoma City," *New Republic*, May 15, 1995: 15–20; Susan Jefford, *The Remasculinization of America: Gender and the Vietnam War* (Bloomington: Indiana University Press, 1989); Michael Kelly, "The Road to Paranoia," *New Yorker*, June 19, 1995: 60–75; Lewis H. Lapham, "Seen but Not Heard: The Message of the Oklahoma Bombing," *Harper's*, July 1995: 29–36; Calvin Trillin, "I've Got Problems," *New Yorker*, July 26, 1986; Daniel Voll, "At Home with M.O.M.," *Esquire*, July 1995: 46–52, and Voll, "The Right to Bear Sorrow," *Esquire*, March 1995: 75–82.

NOTES

INTRODUCTION: AMERICAN RADICALISM—LEFT, RIGHT, AND RURAL

1. *Minneapolis Star Tribune*, July 9, 1995: 24a.

2. *New York Times*, August 13, 1995: 24.

3. *New Republic*, May 15, 1995: 15.

4. *Harper's Magazine*, July 1995: 30. See also James Coates, *Armed and Dangerous: The Rise of the Survivalist Right* (New York: Hill and Wang, 1987).

5. David Danbom, *Born in the Country: A History of Rural America* (Baltimore: Johns Hopkins University Press, 1995), 266. See also Danbom, "Romantic Agrarianism in Twentieth-Century America," *Agricultural History* 65 (Fall 1991): 1–12.

6. Sidney Blumenthal, "Her Own Private Idaho," *New Yorker*, July 10, 1995: 27–33.

7. *New York Times,* May 30, 1995: 17A.

8. Edmund S. Morgan, *American Slavery, American Freedom: The Ordeal of Colonial Virginia* (New York: Norton, 1975). See also Gordon S. Wood, *The Radicalism of the American Revolution* (New York: Knopf, 1992).

9. Richard Hofstadter, *The Age of Reform: From Bryan to FDR* (New York: Knopf, 1955), 20.

10. Hofstadter, *The Age of Reform* and *The Paranoid Style in American Politics and Other Essays* (Chicago: University of Chicago Press, 1964); Victor C. Ferkiss, "Populist Influences on American Fascism," in Theodore Saloutos, ed., *Populism: Reaction or Reform?* (New York: Holt, Rinehart, and Winston, 1968). The best-known description of the Populists as radical democrats is found in Lawrence Goodwyn, *The Populist Moment: A Short History of the Agrarian Revolt in America* (New York: Oxford University Press, 1978).

11. See, for example, Richard White, *"It's Your Misfortune and None of My Own": A New History of the American West* (Norman: University of Oklahoma Press, 1991), passim.

12. John Mack Faragher, *Sugar Creek: Life on the Illinois Prairie* (New Haven: Yale University Press, 1986).

13. Robert Hine, *Community on the Frontier: Separate but not Alone* (Norman: University of Oklahoma Press, 1980).

14. Richard Maxwell Brown, *Strain of Violence: Historical Studies of American Violence and Vigilantism* (New York: Oxford University Press, 1975); Richard Slotkin, *Regeneration through Violence: The Mythology of the American Frontier, 1600–1860* (Middletown, Conn.: Wesleyan University Press, 1973).

15. Catherine McNicol Stock, *Main Street in Crisis: The Great Depression and the Old Middle Class on the Northern Plains* (Chapel Hill: University of North Carolina Press, 1992), 10–11. See also Erik Olin Wright, "Varieties of Marxist Conceptions of Class Structure," *Politics and Society* 9, no. 3 (1980): 323–70; C. Wright Mills, *White Collar: The American Middle Classes* (New York: Columbia University Press, 1951).

16. Among the myriad works on the development of the capitalist economy in early America is Christopher Clark, *The Roots of Rural Capitalism: Western Massachusetts, 1780–1860* (Ithaca: Cornell University Press, 1990).

17. Richard C. Trexler, *Sex and Conquest: Gendered Violence, Political Order, and the European Conquest of the Americas* (Ithaca: Cornell University Press, 1995).

18. Deborah Fink, *Agrarian Women: Wives and Mothers in Rural Nebraska, 1880–1940* (Chapel Hill: University of North Carolina Press, 1992); Carolyn Sachs, *The Invisible Farmers: Women in Agricultural Production* (Totowa, N.J.: Rowman and Allanheld, 1983).

19. Mark Friedberger, "Women Advocates in the Farm Crisis of the 1980s," *Agricultural History* 67 (Spring 1993): 224–34.

20. James Coates, *Armed and Dangerous: The Rise of the Survivalist Right* (New York: Hill and Wang, 1987), 185–92.

21. Clyde Wilcox, *God's Warriors: The Christian Right in the Twentieth Century* (Baltimore: Johns Hopkins University Press, 1992), 46.

22. On the involvement of Mormons in the John Birch Society and contemporary radical patriotism, for example, see James A. Aho, *The Politics of Righteousness: Idaho Christian Patriotism* (Seattle: University of Washington Press, 1990), 114–32.

23. Michael Kazin, *The Populist Persuasion: An American History* (New York: Basic Books, 1995), 222. One has to think here of Ross Perot hugging Jesse Jackson at the 1995 United We Stand convention in Dallas, just days before Pat Buchanan was also received with open arms.

1: THE POLITICS OF PRODUCERISM

1. *New York Times*, July 25, 1994, B7. My account below is drawn from this source.

2. Thomas Jefferson, *Notes on the State of Virginia* (Chapel Hill: University of North Carolina Press, 1955), 164–65.

3. As quoted in Carl Taylor, *The Farmers' Movement, 1620–1920* (New York: American Book Co., 1953), 59.

4. Alan Taylor, *Liberty Men and Great Proprietors: The Revolutionary Settlement on the Maine Frontier, 1760–1820* (Chapel Hill: University of North Carolina Press, 1990), 4–5.

5. The best compilation of colonial riots can be found in Richard Maxwell Brown, "Violence and the American Revolution," in Stephen G. Kurtz and James H. Hutson, eds., *Essays on the American Revolution* (Chapel Hill: University of North Carolina Press, 1973), 81–120.

6. Ronald Hoffman, "The 'Disaffected' in the Revolutionary South," in Alfred F. Young, ed., *The American Revolution: Explorations in the History of American Radicalism* (De Kalb: University of Northern Illinois Press, 1976), 273–318.

7. Carl Becker, *The History of Political Parties in the Province of New York, 1760–1776* (Madison: University of Wisconsin Press, 1909), 22. See also Edward Country-

man, *A People in Revolution: The American Revolution and Political Society in New York, 1760–1790* (Baltimore: Johns Hopkins University Press, 1981), 71.

8. As quoted in Peter Burke, *Popular Culture in Early Modern Europe* (New York: Harper and Row, 1978), 179.

9. Burke, *Popular Culture in Early Modern Europe*, 178.

10. Peter Linebaugh, "The Tyburn Riot against the Surgeons," in Douglas Hay, ed., *Albion's Fatal Tree: Crime and Society in Eighteenth-Century England* (New York: Oxford University Press, 1975), 65–117.

11. Ibid., 204.

12. George Rudé, *The Crowd in History: A Study of Popular Disturbances in France and England, 1730–1848* (New York: Wiley, 1964), 6. See also John Stevenson, "Bread or Blood," in G. E. Mingay, ed., *The Unquiet Countryside* (London: Routledge, 1989), 23–35.

13. Robert C. Allen, *Enclosure and the Yeoman: The Agricultural Development of South Midlands, 1450–1850* (Oxford: Clarendon, 1992), 21.

14. Rudé, *The Crowd in History*, 34.

15. Brown, "Violence in the American Revolution," 85. See also Pauline Maier, *From Resistance to Revolution: Colonial Radicals and the Development of American Opposition to Britain, 1765–1776* (New York: Knopf, 1972), 4–5.

16. As quoted in Maier, *From Resistance to Revolution*, 4. See also Dirk Hoerder, *Crowd Action in Revolutionary Massachusetts, 1765–1780* (New York: Academic Press, 1971).

17. Edward Countryman, "'Out of the Bounds of the Law'": Northern Land Rioters in the Eighteenth Century," in Young, ed., *The American Revolution*, 41.

18. Alan Taylor, *Liberty Men and Great Proprietors*, 4.

19. David Danbom, *Born in the Country: A History of Rural America* (Baltimore: Johns Hopkins University Press, 1995), 54.

20. Edward Countryman, *The American Revolution* (New York: Hill and Wang, 1985), 85.

21. Rowland Berthoff and John M. Murrin, "Feudalism, Communalism, and the Yeoman Freeholder: The American Revolution Considered as a Social Accident," in Kurtz and Hutson, eds., *Essays on the American Revolution*, 264.

22. Berthoff and Murrin, "Feudalism," 267, 268n.

23. Gordon S. Wood, *The Radicalism of the American Revolution* (New York: Knopf, 1992), 6.

24. Ibid., 95.

25. Ibid., 115.

26. Countryman, *The American Revolution*, 84–85.

27. Berthoff and Murrin, "Feudalism," 270.

28. As quoted in Patricia Bonami, *A Factious People: Politics and Society in Colonial New York* (New York: Columbia University Press, 1971), 186.

29. The term "clinkers" is explained in Thomas Fleming, *New Jersey: A Bi-Centennial History* (New York: Norton, 1976), 34.

30. Countryman, *A People in Revolution*, 22.

31. Bonami, *A Factious People*, 212.

32. Ibid., 218.

33. As quoted in Countryman, "'Out of the Bounds of Law,'" 46.

34. As quoted in Marvin L. Michael Kay, "The North Carolina Regulation, 1766–1776: A Class Conflict," in Alfred F. Young, ed., *The American Revolution*, 84.

35. Marvin L. Michael Kay, "The North Carolina Regulation," 85.

36. Ibid., 75.

37. Countryman, "'Out of the Bounds of the Law'," 42.

38. As quoted in ibid., 47.

39. Ibid., passim. See also Countryman; *The American Revolution*, 135–36, 159, 239.

40. Ronald Hoffman, "The 'Disaffected' in the Revolutionary South," 291.

41. Richard Bushman, "Massachusetts Farmers in the American Revolution," in Richard M. Jellison, ed., *Society, Freedom, and Conscience: The American Revolution in Virginia, Massachusetts, and New York* (New York: Norton, 1976), 119.

42. Bushman, "Massachusetts Farmers in the American Revolution," 77–87.

43. Hoffman, "The 'Disaffected' in the Revolutionary South," 312.

44. As quoted in ibid., 307.

45. Pauline Maier, "The Transforming Impact of Independence, Reaffirmed: 1776 and the Definition of American Social Structure," in James A. Henretta et al., eds., *The Transformation of Early American History: Society, Authority, Ideology* (New York: Norton, 1991), 209.

46. Danbom, *Born in the Country*, 65.

47. James A. Henretta, "The Transition to Capitalism in America," in Henretta et al., eds., *The Transformation of Early American History*, 238.

48. As quoted in Jackson Turner Main, *The Antifederalists: Critics of the Constitution, 1781–1788* (Chapel Hill: University of North Carolina Press, 1961), 53.

49. David P. Szatmary, *Shays' Rebellion: The Making of an Agrarian Insurrection* (Amherst: University of Massachusetts Press, 1980), 59.

50. As quoted in Szatmary, *Shays' Rebellion*, 34.

51. Szatmary, *Shays' Rebellion*, 29, 34–35.

52. As quoted in Gordon S. Wood, *The Creation of the American Republic, 1776–1787* (New York: Norton, 1969), 285.

53. As quoted in Taylor, *The Farmers' Movement*, 41.

54. As quoted in James A. Henretta, "The Transition to Capitalism in America," 223.

55. As quoted in Szatmary, *Shays' Rebellion*, 43.

56. As quoted in Taylor, *The Farmers' Movement*, 3–4.

57. As quoted in Slaughter, *The Whiskey Rebellion*, 48.

58. As quoted in Szatmary, *Shays' Rebellion*, 97.

59. Ibid., 98.

60. As quoted in Marion L. Starkey, *A Little Rebellion* (New York: Knopf, 1955), 133.

61. Richard D. Brown, *Massachusetts: A Bicentennial History* (New York: Norton, 1978), 122.

62. James Roger Sharp, "The Whiskey Rebellion and the Question of Representation," in Steven R. Boyd, ed., *The Whiskey Rebellion: Past and Present Perspectives* (Westport, Conn.: Greenwood Press, 1985), 119.

63. Robert D. Mitchell, *Commercialism and Frontier: Perspectives on the Early Shenandoah Valley* (Charlottesville: University Press of Virginia, 1977).

64. Slaughter, *The Whiskey Rebellion*, 36.

65. As quoted in ibid., 140.

66. As quoted in ibid.

67. Ibid.

68. Ibid., 187.

69. As quoted in Taylor, *The Farmers' Movement*, 52.

70. As quoted in Sharp, "The Whiskey Rebellion and the Question of Representation," 124.

71. As quoted in Wood, *The Radicalism of the American Revolution*, 298.

72. Sharp, "The Whiskey Rebellion and the Question of Representation," 129.

73. As quoted in Wood, *The Radicalism of the American Revolution*, 298.

74. Taylor, *Liberty Men and Great Proprietors*, 213.

75. Ibid., passim.

76. Ibid., 216.

77. Maier, "The Transforming Impact of Independence, Reaffirmed," 205.

78. Steven Watts, *The Republic Reborn: War and the Making of Liberal America, 1790–1820* (Baltimore: Johns Hopkins University Press, 1987), 14.

79. As quoted in Alexander Saxton, *The Rise and Fall of the White Republic: Class Politics and Mass Culture in Nineteenth-Century America* (London: Verso, 1990), 144.

80. Saxton, *The Rise and Fall of the White Republic,* 133.

81. David E. Schob, *Hired Hands and Plow Boys: Farm Labor in the Midwest, 1815–60* (Urbana: University of Illinois Press, 1975).

82. Ray Allen Billington and Martin Ridge, *Westward Expansion: A History of the American Frontier,* 5th ed. (New York: Macmillan, 1982), 664.

83. Danbom, *Born in the Country*, 132.

84. Henretta, "The Transition to Capitalism in America," 220.

85. Patricia Nelson Limerick, *The Legacy of Conquest: The Unbroken Past of the American West* (New York: Norton, 1987), 124.

86. As quoted in Robert C. McMath, Jr., *American Populism: A Social History, 1877–1898* (New York: Hill and Wang, 1993), 28.

87. Michael McGerr, *The Decline of Popular Politics: The American North, 1865–1928* (New York: Oxford University Press, 1986), 5.

88. Lawrence Goodwyn, *The Populist Moment: A Short History of the Agrarian Revolt in America* (New York: Oxford University Press, 1978), 4. Only northern artisans, many of whom were immigrants, did not "vote as they shot."

89. As quoted in McMath, *American Populism*, 165.

90. As quoted in Taylor, *The Farmers' Movement*, 10–11.

91. Richard White, *"It's Your Misfortune and None of My Own": A New History of the American West* (Norman: University of Oklahoma Press, 1991), 58.

92. Michael Zuckerman, "A Different Thermidor: The Revolution beyond the Revolution," in Henretta et al., *The Transformation of Early American History*, 176.

93. Richard L. Bushman, "Opening the American Countryside," in Henretta et al., *The Transformation of Early American History*, 239–56.

94. McMath, *American Populism*, 8.

95. Danbom, *Born in the Country*, 134.

96. As quoted in Limerick, *The Legacy of Conquest*, 128–29.

97. Ibid., 127.

98. As quoted in McMath, *American Populism*, 135.

99. Lawrence Goodwyn, *Democratic Promise: The Populist Moment in America* (New York: Oxford University Press, 1976), 542.

100. Catherine McNicol Stock, *Main Street in Crisis: The Great Depression and the Old Middle Class on the Northern Plains* (Chapel Hill: University of North Carolina Press, 1992), 58.

101. Nancy F. Cott, *The Bonds of Womanhood: "Women's Sphere" in New England, 1780–1835* (New Haven: Yale University Press, 1977).

102. Nancy Grey Osterud, *Bonds of Community: The Lives of Farm Women in Nineteenth-Century New York* (Ithaca: Cornell University Press, 1991), 1–15 passim.

103. As quoted in ibid., 256.

104. Danbom, *Born in the Country*, 123.

105. As quoted in McMath, *American Populism*, 70.

106. As quoted in ibid., 72.

107. As quoted in White, *"It's Your Misfortune and None of My Own,"* 373.

108. McGerr, *The Decline of Popular Politics*, 215.

109. As quoted in Billington and Ridge, *Westward Expansion*, 680.

110. Goodwyn, *Democratic Promise*, passim.

111. Stock, *Main Street in Crisis*, 200–203.

112. As quoted in Theodore Saloutos and John D. Hicks, *Agricultural Discontent in the Middle West, 1900–1939* (Madison: University of Wisconsin Press, 1951), 34.

113. Saloutos and Hicks, *Agricultural Discontent in the Middle West*, 36.

114. Ibid., 54.

115. Danbom, *Born in the Country*, 166–75. See also Danbom, *The Resisted Revolution: Urban America and the Industrialization of Agriculture, 1900–1930* (Ames: Iowa State University Press, 1979).

116. Danbom, *Born in the Country*, 175.

117. As quoted in Theodore Saloutos, *Farmer Movements in the South, 1865–1933* (Berkeley: University of California Press, 1960), 194.

118. Theodore Saloutos, *Farmer Movements in the South*, 211.

119. Elwyn B. Robinson, *History of North Dakota* (Lincoln: University of Nebraska Press, 1966), 331.

120. Lowell K. Dyson, *Red Harvest: The Communist Party and American Farmers* (Lincoln: University of Nebraska Press, 1982), 6–7.

121. Stock, *Main Street in Crisis*, 17.

122. Saloutos and Hicks, *Agricultural Discontent in the Middle West*, 412. See also Stock, *Main Street in Crisis,* 25.

123. See, for example, Richard Lowitt, *The New Deal and the West* (Bloomington: Indiana University Press, 1984).

124. Stock, *Main Street in Crisis,* 134–36.

125. As quoted in Stock, *Main Street in Crisis*, 128.

126. As quoted in Saloutos and Hicks, *Agricultural Discontent in the Middle West*, 440.

127. As quoted in ibid., 439.

128. As quoted in ibid., 443.

129. Leslie A. Taylor, "Femininity as Strategy: A Gendered Perspective on the Farmers' Holiday," *Annals of Iowa* 51 (Winter 1992): 252–77.

130. As quoted in Stock, *Main Street in Crisis,* 140.

131. Dyson, *Red Harvest*, 150.

132. As quoted in David H. Bennett, *The Party of Fear: From Nativist Movements to the New Right in American History* (Chapel Hill: University of North Carolina Press, 1988), 251.

133. Alan Brinkley, *Voices of Protest: Huey Long, Father Coughlin, and the Great Depression* (New York: Vintage, 1983).

2. THE CULTURE OF VIGILANTISM

1. Jenkins's story is told with care in Andrew Malcolm's *Bitter Harvest* (New York: Times Books, 1986).

2. William E. Burrows, *Vigilante!* (New York: Harcourt Brace Jovanovich, 1976), 20–21.

3. Richard Maxwell Brown, *The South Carolina Regulators* (Cambridge, Mass.: Belknap Press, 1963), 25.

4. Ibid., 5.

5. Ray Allen Billington and Martin Ridge, *Westward Expansion: A History of the American Frontier,* 5th ed. (New York: Macmillan, 1982), 112.

6. As quoted in Brown, *The South Carolina Regulators,* 30.

7. Ibid.

8. As quoted in ibid., 38.

9. As quoted in ibid., 47.

10. As quoted in ibid.

11. As quoted in ibid., 52.

12. As quoted in ibid., 94.

13. Richard Maxwell Brown, *Strain of Violence: Historical Studies of American Violence and Vigilantism* (New York: Oxford University Press, 1975), 67–90.

14. Ibid., 96. There have been episodes of vigilantism in many other countries, including modern El Salvador, Philippines, South Africa, and Vietnam.

15. Thomas Dimsdale, *The Vigilantes of Montana; or, Popular Justice in the Rocky Mountains* (Norman: University of Oklahoma Press, 1953), 158, 205.

16. Kenneth S. Stern, *A Force upon the Plain: The American Militia Movement and the Politics of Hate* (New York: Simon and Schuster, 1996) 108–32.

17. As quoted in James B. Allen and Glen M. Leonard, *The Story of the Latter-Day Saints* (Salt Lake City, Utah: Desert Book Co., 1976), 28.

18. Fawn M. Brodie, *No Man Knows My History: The Life of Joseph Smith* (New York: Knopf, 1945), 87.

19. Richard White, *"It's Your Misfortune and None of my Own": A New History of the American West* (Norman: University of Oklahoma Press, 1991), 164–69.

20. Brodie, *No Man Knows My History,* 119.

21. As quoted in Ivan J. Barrett, *Joseph Smith and the Restoration* (Salt Lake City, Utah: Young House, 1967), 255.

22. Klaus J. Hansen, *Mormonism and the American Experience* (Chicago: University of Chicago Press, 1981), 82–83.

23. My account and quotations are from Richard Maxwell Brown, ed., *American Violence* (Englewood Cliffs, N.J.: Prentice Hall, 1970), 93–94.

24. Cletus E. Daniel, *Bitter Harvest: A History of California Farmworkers, 1870–1941* (Ithaca: Cornell University Press, 1981), 29.

25. As quoted in Sucheng Chan, *This Bittersweet Soil: The Chinese in California Agriculture, 1860–1910* (Berkeley: University of California Press, 1986), 375. My account draws from his work.

26. As quoted in ibid.

27. As quoted in ibid., 373.

28. As quoted in White, *"It's Your Misfortune and None of My Own,"* 334–35.

29. Ibid., 335.

30. Tomas Almaguer, *Racial Fault Lines: The Historical Origins of White Supremacy in California* (Berkeley: University of California Press, 1994), 72.

31. White, *"It's Your Misfortune and None of My Own,"* 335.

32. Ibid., 347.

33. Ibid., 293–96.

34. Joel Williamson, *The Crucible of Race: Black/White Relations in the American South since Emancipation* (New York: Oxford University Press, 1984).

35. As quoted in Edward L. Ayers, *Vengeance and Justice: Crime and Punishment in the Nineteenth-Century American South* (New York: Oxford University Press, 1984), 123.

36. Robert F. Berkhofer, Jr., *The White Man's Indian: Images of the American Indian from Columbus to the Present* (New York: Vintage, 1979), 71–85.

37. George M. Frederickson, "The Social Origins of Racism in the United States," in Frederickson, *The Arrogance of Race: Historical Perspectives on Slavery, Racism, and Social Inequality* (Middletown, Conn.: Wesleyan University Press, 1988), 189–205.

38. Stephen Greenblatt, *Marvelous Possessions: The Wonder of the New World* (Chicago: University of Chicago Press, 1991), 9.

39. Ibid.

40. James Axtell, *After Columbus: Essays in the Ethnohistory of Colonial North America* (New York: Oxford University Press, 1988), 241.

41. As quoted in ibid., 142.

42. Ian K. Steele, *Warpaths: Invasions of North America* (New York: Oxford University Press, 1994), passim.

43. John Demos, *The Unredeemed Captive: A Family Story from Early America* (New York: Vintage, 1994), 4.

44. Ibid., passim.

45. Axtell, *After Columbus*, 241.

46. As quoted in Edmund Morgan, *American Slavery, American Freedom: The Ordeal of Virginia* (New York: Norton, 1976), 252. See also Steele, *Warpaths*, 53–55.

47. As quoted in Morgan, *American Slavery, American Freedom*, 252.

48. Morgan, *American Slavery, American Freedom*, passim.

49. As quoted in Alvin M. Josephy, Jr., *Five Hundred Nations: An Illustrated History of North American Indians* (New York: Knopf, 1994), 254. See also Steele, *Warpaths*, 227–34.

50. Steele, *Warpaths*, 241.

51. As quoted in Josephy, *Five Hundred Nations,* 257–58.

52. As quoted in John Dunbar, ed., *The Paxton Papers* (The Hague: Martinus Nijhoff, 1957), 57–58.

53. As quoted in Josephy, *Five Hundred Nations*, 256.

54. As quoted in Thomas P. Slaughter, *The Whiskey Rebellion: Frontier Epilogue to the American Revolution* (New York: Oxford University Press, 1986), 28–29.

55. Slaughter, *The Whiskey Rebellion*, 77.

56. As quoted in White, *"It's Your Misfortune and None of My Own,"* 338.

57. White, *"It's Your Misfortune and None of My Own,"* 337–40.

58. As quoted in Josephy, *Five Hundred Nations*, 366.

59. Duane Schultz, *Over the Earth I Come: The Great Sioux Uprising of 1862* (New York: St. Martin's Press, 1992), 208–12.

60. Winthrop D. Jordan, *The White Man's Burden: Historical Origins of Racism in the United States* (New York: Oxford University Press, 1974), 3–26.

61. Frederickson, *The Arrogance of Race*, 202–3.

62. As quoted in Nancy MacLean, *Behind the Mask of Chivalry: The Making of the Second Ku Klux Klan* (New York: Oxford University Press, 1994), 126.

63. As quoted in William Pierce Randel, *The Ku Klux Klan: A Century of Infamy* (Philadelphia: Chilton, 1965), 8.

64. David M. Chalmers, *Hooded Americanism: The History of the Ku Klux Klan* (Durham, N.C.: Duke University Press, 1987), 13.

65. Ayers, *Vengeance and Justice*, 237.

66. MacLean, *Behind the Mask of Chivalry*, xii.

67. Ayers, *Vengeance and Justice*, 238.

68. Ibid., 255.

69. Ibid., 240.

70. As quoted in ibid.

71. Kenneth T. Jackson, *The Ku Klux Klan in the City, 1915–1930* (New York: Oxford University Press, 1967).

72. As quoted in Nancy MacLean, "The Lynching of Leo Frank Reconsidered," *Journal of American History* 78 (1991), 923.

73. As quoted in ibid., 938.

74. As quoted in ibid., 917.

75. As quoted in David H. Bennett, *The Party of Fear: From Nativist Movements to the New Right in American History* (Chapel Hill: University of North Carolina Press, 1988), 178.

76. C. Vann Woodward, *Tom Watson: Agrarian Rebel* (New York: MacMillan, 1938), 216–43.

77. As quoted in MacLean, "The Lynching of Leo Frank Reconsidered," 940–42; Bennett, *The Party of Fear*, 181; Wyn Craig Wade, *The Fiery Cross: The Ku Klux Klan in America* (New York: Simon and Schuster, 1987), 144.

78. As quoted in MacLean, "The Lynching of Leo Frank Reconsidered," 944.

79. As quoted in ibid., 920.

80. As quoted in Wade, *The Fiery Cross*, 145.

81. MacLean, *Behind the Mask of Chivalry*, 149.

82. Ibid., 212.

83. Wade, *The Fiery Cross*, 178–79.

84. As quoted in MacLean, *Behind the Mask of Chivalry*, 89.

85. As quoted in Chalmers, *Hooded Americanism*, 165.

86. Bennett, *Party of Fear*, 224.

87. As quoted in Richard K. Tucker, *The Dragon and the Cross: The Rise and Fall of the Ku Klux Klan in Middle America* (New York: Archon, 1991), 54.

88. Ibid., 102.

89. Bennett, *Party of Fear*, 233.

90. See, for example, Kathleen Neils Conzen, "Peasant Pioneers: Generational Succession among German Farmers in Frontier Minnesota," in Steven Hahn and Jonathan Prude, eds., *The Countryside in the Age of Capitalist Transformation: Essays in the Social History of Rural America* (Chapel Hill: University of North Carolina Press, 1985), 259–92.

91. Bennett, *The Party of Fear*, 184.

92. Ibid.

93. As quoted in Frederick C. Luebke, *Bonds of Loyalty: German Americans and World War I* (De Kalb: Northern Illinois University Press, 1974), 6.

94. Ibid.

95. As quoted in MacLean, *Behind the Mask of Chivalry*, 94.

96. As quoted in ibid., 82n.,226.

97. Chalmers, *Hooded Americans*, 312.

98. Robin D. G. Kelley, *Hammer and Hoe: Alabama Communists and the Great Depression* (Chapel Hill: University of North Carolina Press, 1990), 74.

99. As quoted in Garin Burbank, *When Farmers Voted Red: The Gospel of Socialism in the Oklahoma Countryside, 1910–1924* (Westport, Conn.: Greenwood Press, 1976), 170.

100. Elwyn Robinson, *History of North Dakota* (Lincoln: University of Nebraska Press, 1982), 356.

101. As quoted in ibid., 366.

102. Stock, *Main Street in Crisis,* 71–73.

103. Ibid., 214–15.

104. Leo Ribuffo, *The Old Christian Right: The Protestant Far Right from the Great Depression to Cold War* (Philadelphia: Temple University Press, 1983), 60.

105. As quoted in Ribuffo, *The Old Christian Right*, 57; Bennett, *The Party of Fear*, 244–48.

106. As quoted in Ribuffo, *The Old Christian Right*, 60.

107. As quoted in ibid., 106.

108. As quoted in ibid., 121, 64, 69.

3. RURAL RADICALISM IN OUR TIME

1. Philip Weiss, "Off-the-Grid," *New York Times Magazine*, January 8, 1995, 24.

2. Jess Walter, *Every Knee Shall Bow: The Truth and Tragedy of Ruby Ridge and the Randy Weaver Family* (New York: ReganBooks, 1995), 22.

3. Ibid., 40–45.

4. As quoted in ibid., 46.

5. As quoted in Kenneth S. Stern, *A Force upon the Plain: The American Militia Movement and the Politics of Hate* (New York: Simon and Schuster, 1995), 22.

6. As quoted in ibid., 31.

7. Walter, *Every Knee Shall Bow*, 196–98.

8. As quoted in Stern, *A Force upon the Plain*, 33.

9. As quoted in ibid.

10. Stern, *A Force upon the Plain*, 222–30.

11. John Kifner, "Oklahoma Bombing Suspect: Unraveling of a Frayed Life," *New York Times*, December 31, 1995: 1A.

12. Ibid.

13. *New York Times,* July 5, 1995: A1. See also Stern, *A Force upon the Plain*, 53–54.

14. As quoted in Alan Brinkley, *The End of Reform: New Deal Liberalism in Recession and War* (New York: Knopf, 1995), 61.

15. As quoted in ibid.

16. As quoted in ibid., 62.

17. Brinkley, *The End of Reform*, 63.

18. Ibid., 268.

19. Barton Bernstein, "The New Deal: Conservative Achievements of Liberal Reform," in Bernstein, *Toward a New Past: Dissenting Essays in American History* (New York: Pantheon, 1968).

20. Dan T. Carter, *The Politics of Rage: George Wallace, the Origins of the New Conservatism, and the Transformation of American Politics* (New York: Simon and Schuster, 1995); David H. Bennett, *Party of Fear: From Nativist Movements to the New Right in American History* (Chapel Hill: University of North Carolina Press, 1988), 336.

21. Bennett, *Party of Fear,* 337.

22. President Bill Clinton, quoted in *New York Times,* January 24, 1996: A14.

23. Gilbert Fite, *American Farmers: The New Minority* (Bloomington: Indiana University Press, 1981), 165.

24. Ibid., 166.

25. Ibid., 166–67.

26. As quoted in ibid., 160.

27. Fite, *American Farmers,* 162.

28. As quoted in ibid., 163.

29. As quoted in ibid., 161.

30. Fite, *American Farmers,* 202–6.

31. Peggy F. Barlett, *American Dreams, Rural Realities: Family Farms in Crisis* (Chapel Hill: University of North Carolina Press, 1993), 11.

32. David Danbom, *Born in the Country: A History of Rural America* (Baltimore: Johns Hopkins University Press, 1995), 256.

33. As quoted in Osha Gray Davidson, *Broken Heartland: The Rise of the Rural Ghetto* (New York: Free Press, 1990), 17.

34. Davidson, *Broken Heartland,* 17.

35. As quoted in Barlett, *American Dreams, Rural Realities,* 3.

36. Barlett, *American Dreams, Rural Realities,* 229.

37. Davidson, *Broken Heartland,* 94–100.

38. Fite, *American Farmers,* 160–202.

39. William P. Browne and John Dinse, "The Emergence of the American Agricultural Movement, 1977–79," *Great Plains Quarterly* 5 (Fall 1985): 224.

40. As quoted in ibid., 225–26.

41. As quoted in Howard Kohl, *The Last Farmer: An American Memoir* (New York: Summit Books, 1988), 180.

42. Davidson, *Broken Heartland,* 35, 122, 135.

43. Kathryn Marie Dudley, *The End of the Line: Lost Jobs, New Lives in Postindustrial America* (Chicago: University of Chicago Press, 1994).

44. Calvin Beale, *A Taste of the Country: A Collection of Calvin Beale's Writings* (University Park: Pennsylvania State University Press, 1990), 76–91.

45. Nancy Grey Osterud, *Bonds of Community: The Lives of Farm Women in Nineteenth-Century New York* (Ithaca: Cornell University Press, 1991), 288.

46. Deborah Fink, *Open Country, Iowa: Rural Women, Tradition and Change* (Albany: State University of New York Press, 1986), 218–21; Mark Friedberger, "Women Advocates in the Farm Crisis of the 1980s," *Agricultural History* 67 (Spring 1993): 224–34, passim.

47. Linda J. Lear, "Bombshell in Beltsville: The USDA and the Challenge of *Silent Spring,*" *Agricultural History* 66 (Spring 1992): 151–70.

48. Danbom, *Born in the Country,* 268–69.

49. As quoted in Elizabeth O. Colton, *The Jackson Phenomenon: The Man, the Power, the Message* (New York: Doubleday, 1989), 42.

50. Coates, *Armed and Dangerous,* 104–22. See also Browne and Dinse, "The Emergence of the American Agriculture Movement."

51. A somewhat different view can be found in Michael Paul Rogin, *The Intellectuals and McCarthy: The Radical Specter* (Cambridge: MIT Press, 1967), 59–103.

52. As quoted in Bennett, *Party of Fear,* 293.

53. As quoted in ibid., 305.

54. Bennett, *Party of Fear,* 295.

55. See, for example, the discussion of rural anticommunism in James A. Aho, *The Politics of Righteousness: Idaho Christian Patriotism* (Seattle: University of Washington Press, 1990), 114–32.

56. Bennett, *Party of Fear,* 315–18.

57. Aho, *Politics of Righteousness,* 114–32; see also Coates, *Armed and Dangerous,* 15.

58. Bennett, *Party of Fear,* 322–33.

59. Ibid., 323.

60. Wyn Craig Wade, *The Fiery Cross: The Ku Klux Klan in America* (New York: Simon and Schuster, 1987), 334.

61. As quoted in Wade, *The Fiery Cross,* 326–27.

62. As quoted in Bennett, *Party of Fear,* 324–25.

63. As quoted in Donald Janson and Bernard Eismann, *The Far Right* (New York: McGraw-Hill, 1963), 117.

64. Janson and Eismann, *The Far Right,* 119.

65. As quoted in ibid., 120.

66. For a complete discussion of Identity Christianity see Aho, *Politics of Righteousness,* 105–14; Coates, *Armed and Dangerous,* 77–102.

67. Bennett, *Party of Fear,* 325–26.

68. Ibid.

69. James William Gibson, *Warrior Dreams: Paramilitary Culture in Post-Vietnam America* (New York: Hill and Wang, 1994), passim.

70. Susan Jefford, *The Remasculinization of America: Gender and the Vietnam War* (Bloomington: Indiana University Press, 1989), passim.

71. As quoted in James Coates, *Armed and Dangerous: The Rise of the Survivalist Right* (New York: Hill and Wang, 1987), 105.

72. Coates, *Armed and Dangerous,* 104–13.

73. As quoted in ibid., 121.

74. Bennett, *Party of Fear,* 282–92.

75. As quoted in Alan Crawford, *Thunder on the Right: The New Right and the Politics of Resentment* (New York: Pantheon, 1980), 290.

76. Pat Robertson, *The New World Order* (New York: World, 1994). See also Michael Lind's review of Robertson's work in *New York Review of Books,* February 2, 1995: 21–25.

77. Aho, *Politics of Righteousness,* 185–211.

78. As quoted in Coates, *Armed and Dangerous,* 96.

79. Coates, *Armed and Dangerous,* 57–59.

80. Ibid., 76.

81. Ibid., 136–48.

82. Ibid.

83. Ibid., 187–88.

84. Ibid., 172.

85. Ibid., 158–59.

86. As quoted and reported in James A. Aho, *This Thing of Darkness: A Sociology of the Enemy* (Seattle: University of Washington Press, 1995), 47.

Index